BANGED UP

D0524915

BANGED UP

DOING TIME IN BRITAIN'S TOUGHEST JAILS

DAVID LESLIE

BLACK & WHITE PUBLISHING

First published 2014
by Black & White Publishing Ltd
29 Ocean Drive, Edinburgh EH6 6JL

1 3 5 7 9 10 8 6 4 2   14 15 16 17

ISBN: 978 1 84502 848 0

Copyright © David Leslie 2014

The right of David Leslie to be identified as the author
of this work has been asserted by him in accordance with the
Copyright, Designs and Patents Act 1988.

All rights reserved. No part of this publication may be reproduced,
stored in a retrieval system, or transmitted in any form, or by any means,
electronic, mechanical, photocopying, recording or otherwise, without
permission in writing from the publisher.

A CIP catalogue record for this book is available from the British Library.

ALBA | CHRUTHACHAIL

Typeset by Iolaire Typesetting, Newtonmore
Printed and bound by Gutenberg Press, Malta

ACKNOWLEDGEMENTS

I am most grateful to my friend John Boyce for the countless stories and invaluable help he so kindly gave while I was researching *Banged Up*. I am also grateful to staff at the National Archives for giving permission to quote from the previously confidential file on Snow.

CONTENTS

PREFACE   xi

1   INTO THE UNKNOWN   1

2   CUCKING AND DUCKING   12

3   THE THREE SISTERS   27

4   MASSACRE   37

5   PORRIDGE RIOT   49

6   FLIGHT TO FREEDOM   59

7   MOTHERS IN SHACKLES   66

8   DEATH ON THE MOOR   74

9   A DAY AT THE RACES   85

10 THE SPY   93

11 ESCAPE TO A LIFE SENTENCE   101

12 JOHN MCVICAR   105

13 LETTER FROM A RUNAWAY   114

14 ESCAPE WITH A BIBLE   122

15 HANGING CHAIR   128

16 MONEY FOR OLD ROPE   137

17 CLEAN SLATE   144

18 THE HAUNTED HANGMAN   155

19 ACID-BATH VAMPIRE   166

20	THE FATAL DAB	175
21	WOMEN ON THE SCAFFOLD	181
22	DEATH AT THE TOWER	190
23	TRAPPED BY SAUSAGES	198
24	A MAN CALLED SNOW	209
25	SUFFRAGETTES	220
26	INTERNEES	228
27	THE FENIANS	235
28	DEAD AND ROTTEN	245
29	CELEBRITY CON	254
30	THE NAUGHTY VICAR	263
31	A THIEVING QUEEN	272
32	RED-BLOODED BLUE BLOOD	281
33	DEADLY DRINK	290
34	LUM UP	293
EPILOGUE		307

PREFACE

THERE ARE MORE THAN 120 prisons in England holding over 80,000 men, women and young people whose crimes range from horrific to minor, terrible to trivial. Yet prisoners past, present and yet to come face one common quandary: how to endure the mind-numbing boredom that is life in gaol. For some, their time behind bars is short; for others, only death will end their incarceration. For all, the seconds and minutes pass at the same snail's pace.

Banged Up is the story of how and why six of the best-known prisons came into being, presenting stories of just a sample of the lives led by those held within them, the people who suffered the standard prison fare of anonymity and frustration. Dartmoor, Durham, Wandsworth, Pentonville, Wormwood Scrubs and Holloway – the world's best-known prison for women – have been and remain temporary lodging places for those whom society has deemed unworthy of freedom.

Four of these establishments have been the final stopping place throughout life's journey for men, women and teenagers before their last walk to the scaffold. However, all are witness to the determination of the human spirit to persevere and above all, preserve the last bastion of those locked into the darkness – humour.

1

INTO THE UNKNOWN

FOR THE ONE HUNDREDTH time that morning, Thomas Pitman wished he was back in the black hole that had been Dartmoor Prison. Its cold, damp walls had been hell, but now he felt he had been consigned to eternal damnation in the foulest pit of the underworld. Pitman had been forced to exchange his freezing, stone-walled cell in the terrible edifice that dominated the bleak moors around Princetown, in Devon, for a low-ceilinged, iron-barred, stinking, rat-infested corner below decks in the wooden barque *William Hammond*.

Thomas Pitman was on a voyage into the unknown, having been ordered to be transported to Western Australia and to stay there for the next fifteen years because he had stolen a lamb. The judge at the Quarter Sessions in Wells, Somerset, had told Pitman that if he behaved himself, and worked hard over the next decade and a half, he could ask permission to return to England. But the hapless convict knew he had been handed the equivalent of a life sentence. If he wanted to see his home again he would have to raise the price of his own ticket – and with a pittance for wages, that was a hopeless prospect.

It was January 1856. Thomas Pitman, already suffering from depression, would never again see the fields and farms of the West Country, or even the grim moors and quarries around Dartmoor. Nor did tens of thousands of others.

Transportation was first used as a form of government punishment in about 1610. Because there were so many crimes for which men, women and even children could be locked up or executed, British prisons became overcrowded. There were more than 200 offences for which the penalty was death, some so petty that it is hard to imagine an offender ending up on the scaffold. The list of these was known as the 'Bloody Code' and capital crimes included stealing a pocket handkerchief, stealing a horse, threatening violence to civilians 'when on the duty of the King', impersonating a Chelsea pensioner, shoplifting items worth more than five shillings, stealing from a rabbit warren, cutting down a young tree, stealing from a shipwreck or a naval dockyard, forging a will, setting fire to a church or church property, any robbery that left a victim in fear, damaging London's Westminster Bridge, stealing a letter, damaging a public building, extortion, maiming cattle or even spending a month with gypsies. A thief might get away with a few years in prison if he was arrested, but if he had blackened his face to try to avoid being seen in the dark, he was liable to be hanged in public.

Maybe it was no surprise that many judges felt they could not justify condemning somebody to death for these relative misdemeanours. Not all, though. In 1785 ten men found guilty of crimes that included stealing linen from an outhouse all paid the ultimate penalty when they were hanged together, while a few years later a boy aged thirteen was executed for stealing a spoon.

In showing mercy and not sentencing offenders to death, judges unwittingly condemned those before them to a punishment that many felt was even worse than taking a few steps to a scaffold and having a noose placed around their necks before the floor gave way beneath their feet, thus ending a miserable existence of hunger, cold and poverty. Sending prisoners to jail rather than having them hanged meant prison populations rapidly got out of control. Overcrowding became rife. There were fears that swelling numbers might cause jails to burst at the seams, allowing inmates to avoid old and often dishonest guards and simply run off. The answer, it was decided, was to introduce a new punishment – transportation.

Transportation would not just ease prison overcrowding but would also provide the London-based government with a plentiful supply of cheap, even free, labour for developing and working overseas plantations and populating colonies such as the West Indies, America and Australia. Helping these colonies grow would additionally provide benefits such as taxes for the King's ministers to spend. So from the early 1600s, prisoners from Perth to Plymouth, Aberdeen to Aberdare, began hearing the words 'transported to His Majesty's colonies' from the bench where a judge wasted little time in helping to ease the overcrowding problem.

In the early days of transportation, convicts went to the West Indies and America. Among them were thousands of Scots, but the government was determined there would be no repeat of the fiasco following the Jacobite Rising of 1715 when captured rebels were offered pardons on condition they agreed to be shipped off for life to the West Indies and America. In many cases they had simply turned seamen to re-cross the Atlantic and sneak back to Scotland. Now scores of Highlanders captured after the massacre at Culloden in 1746 and dragged to London in chains were told King George II was giving them an alternative to being hanged, drawn and quartered. They would be pardoned and spared, provided they agreed to be transported for life. Remembering what had transpired three decades earlier, some of the King's advisers recommended branding the Highlanders on their faces so that if they ever returned they would be instantly spotted. The idea was not put into practice, but the rebels were warned they would be put to death if they did come back. Many were joined by their families and most settled in the West Indies or America, although a handful risked death by creeping back to their beloved Highlands.

When the thirteen American colonies challenged the British over their supremacy over their affairs and eventually went to war in 1775, transportation to America was put to an end. By that time, more than 63,000 convicts had been dumped there. Now, as prisons once more began filling up, the government looked around for an alternative destination to which it could send miscreants. The solution was provided by then Lieutenant James Cook when he landed at Botany Bay, New South Wales, in April 1770. Once back in England, Cook reported the area would be highly suitable as a settlement. His findings were accepted, but it was not until May 1787 that the first fleet of eleven vessels, including six convict ships, left England for Australia. Seeking fresh water and extra supplies, the fleet called first at Rio de Janeiro and then Cape Town, finally berthing in Botany Bay on 18 January 1788. The trip had taken 250 days, and soon a penal colony was established at nearby Port Jackson. Over the next eighty years, upwards of 136,000 men and 25,000 women would be transported to Australia.

The nightmare for those sentenced to transportation began the moment they were hauled into court. Very often they never even saw their judges. At the Guildhall on Newcastle-upon-Tyne Quayside, the well of the dock, surrounded by spiked bars, was so deep that prisoners could not be seen once they were inside. They simply waited to be sentenced and were then dragged out and bundled a few yards into a waiting ship. Elsewhere, once their sentences had been pronounced, prisoners were kept in local jails before batches of them were herded to main prisons or onto convict hulks to await the arrival of a transport vessel. Usually they were held in solitary confinement and often spent most of the time in chains on a bread-and-water diet. Conditions were barbaric. Cells were generally damp, the walls covered in moss and fungus. There were no toilets, and anyone unable to wait until he or she was allowed out briefly for a toilet break simply had to live and eat among their own mess. They might have to wait months for transport to become available. Thomas Pitman had been held in these conditions at Dartmoor, where men from as far afield as the north of Scotland trickled in to join the wait to be shipped to the far side of the world.

If he felt himself hard done by, he was lucky when compared with others remanded to the hulks. These were even worse. They were mostly redundant Navy vessels, berthed in the Thames or in naval ports along the south coast, and usually built as men-of-war or slave ships but now rotting and unfit for voyaging. Prisoners fought with vermin for their food; there was no heating; typhoid, cholera, severe depression and tuberculosis were rife and brutality commonplace. Fruit was a rarity, bread was often mouldy and riddled with worms and meat frequently rotten. The only respite would be up to ten hours a day of hard labour on shore or watching someone, having been caught thieving or slacking, being whipped until their backs and backsides bled. There was the further release from this ordeal through death, and that was frequent. On average, one in four of those held on hulks died. It was not unusual for a condemned man, having been told he was being offered a pardon on condition he would be transported but held on board a hulk, to reject the chance to live and opt to be hanged.

At night inmates were chained to bare wooden bunks. Yet there was worse to come. The vast majority of those sentenced to transportation had never set foot on board a sailing ship; they had no idea of just how awful conditions could be on a long sea voyage through storms or under baking-hot skies. Convicts were normally accompanied by retired military men known as pensioners, who acted as their guards for the duration of the voyage. These pensioners usually took their families with them, hoping to become settlers once they reached Australia.

Just how bad it could be on board a transport ship is shown in the log of surgeon John Bower, who had the job of caring for 296 prisoners, made up of sixty-six from Dartmoor, eighty-eight from Portland prison, ninety from Portsmouth Jail and fifty-two unfortunates from hulks, who sailed on the convict ship *Pyrenees* with their thirty pensioner guards from Torbay, Devon, in January 1853 on a voyage to Freemantle, Western Australia, that would last eighty-seven nightmare days. Among the convicts were Alfred Andrews from Sussex, sentenced to seven years for sheep stealing; James Cooper, Kingston-on-Hull, given ten years for killing a cow; William Gingel, Marlborough, also awarded ten years for maiming a gelding; Joseph Keen from London, handed seven years for 'malicious destruction of trees' and Robert Mewburn of Northallerton, shipped off for seven years for stealing a pair of boots. According to Bower's log, which is held in the National Archives at Kew, Surrey, the surgeon noticed how much worse mentally the men brought from the hulks were compared with the others. The pensioner guards were accompanied by their families, made up of twenty-four wives, twenty-two sons and eighteen daughters.

Not everyone would complete the trip, however. Five children, three convicts and a Pensioner died. This is how Bower recorded the fates of the children:

Patrick Archer, aged 10 Months; diarrhoea, the mother stated that he was ill with looseness for the last two months, put on sick list 9 January 1853, died 10 January 1853; Ann Booth's child, aged 20 months, meningitis; put on sick list 2 March 1853, died 7 March 1853; Margaret Falassy, aged 2, meningitis, put on sick list 3 March 1853, died 14 March 1853; William Baldwin, aged 3, ileus, pain in the abdomen but had no fever or any alarming symptoms, the abdomen was tensed and tumid with some vomiting but no feculent matter could be detected; put on sick list 26 March 1853, died 26 March 1853; John Robinson, aged 14 months, sick or hurt, hydrocephalus; put on sick list 2 April 1853, died 15 April 1853.

The convicts who perished were John Rowland, eighteen, who died of a fever in March, while both James Hounslow, thirty-two, and William Austin, forty-one, succumbed to dysentery the following month. Fever also accounted for fifty-year-old Pensioner Patrick Hannon in March. Bower said most of the children taken on board were just not strong enough for such a long voyage, while he blamed the outbreak of fever that affected many of those on board – although most survived – on a sudden change of temperature and the 'moist close atmosphere in the ship coupled with the disagreeable smell from the airholds'.

Bower sticks to the facts in his log, something not all surgeons did. But maybe he had taken note of the comments by another surgeon, Robert Espie, who found himself looking after an all-female convict ship, the *Elizabeth*, which had sailed for New South Wales just under twenty years earlier. Espie was still regretting having asked the Admiralty if he could join an all-female convict cargo when he compiled his log, part of which reads:

What I have got to say must be brief, unless I do as some others are in the habit of doing who think to force their way to great notice at the Admiralty by writing a mass of silly trash. I, like a fine dotthead, asked to get appointed to a woman ship. I had very nearly suffered stabbing by one of the females before the ship left Woolwich. I had vainly imagined I knew how to manage convict women, having had two ships of that sort before, but from some cause or other I most decidedly did not succeed to my own satisfaction in this last ship, named the *Elizabeth*. I had imbibed (and have still a strong prejudice) against corporal punishment and I tried all I could by other means, such as solitary confinement, cutting their hair. These trifles only incited them to go to greater lengths to bid me utter defiance, with a thousand threatening of what they would do when they got to Sydney. Here now, let any man show me what is to be done, from the master of the ship down to the lowest boy are all opposed to the Doctor if he has done his duty by preventing prostitution. I saw clearly I had committed an error by being too lenient. I therefore prepared myself with a good stout piece of rope and when I thought they deserved it, I whipped them most soundly over the arms legs and back and this was continued (whatever the saints may think) till I had conquered every refactory spirit among them, and my certificates will testify that the government of New South Wales was perfectly satisfied with my conduct in every particular. So much for the discipline of a female convict ship. The whole of the persons under my charge on board the *Elizabeth* female convict ship landed at Sydney in a much better state of health than when they embarked.

By the time the *Elizabeth* reached Australia, the average voyage lasted around 100 days, long enough when convicts were alternating between freezing and sweltering in cramped lower decks. Some of the earliest voyages lasted up to nine months, yet remarkably women prisoners as old as eighty-two and children as young as eight somehow survived.

Thomas Pitman, convict number 3924, had suffered from depression when he laboured on a West Country farm before his arrest. Poor, ignorant men such as he knew they could expect no mercy when they appeared before magistrates and justices, but even he must have been appalled by the harshness of his sentence. For sneaking off with a lamb, Pitman was first sentenced to death and then told he would be pardoned but shipped off for the next fifteen years to a land he had never heard of. No one expected him to return, and he didn't. Instead, he ended up in a lunatic asylum, where he died in 1875, aged fifty-five. On the *William Hammond* he probably would have been miserable and afraid.

Ships doctors, called surgeons, were largely sympathetic to the plight of the convicts, but mindful that offending their Admiralty employers could mean the sack. Still, they were prone to painting a kinder picture than was the actual case. In *Two Years in New South Wales*, published in 1828, Scottish-born superintendent-surgeon Peter Miller Cunningham described what conditions on board his convict ships were like, and almost gave the impression that his charges were enjoying a luxury cruise. According to him:

[A]nd in fact every thing that can be thought of provided to secure health and proper comfort to the convicts during their voyage. Each is allowed a pair of shoes, three shirts, two pair of trowsers, and other warm clothing on his embarkation, besides a bed, pillow, and blanket – while Bibles, Testaments, prayer-books, and psalters, are distributed among the messes. The rations are both good and abundant, three quarters of a pound of biscuit being the daily allowance of bread, while each day the convict sits down to dinner off either beef, pork, or plum-pudding, having pea-soup four times a week, and a pot of *gruel* every morning, with sugar or butter in it. Vinegar is issued to the messes weekly; and as soon as the ship has been three weeks at sea, each man is served with one ounce of lime-juice and the same of sugar daily, to guard against *scurvy*.

Cunningham divided the convicts into groups under a leader who he terms the 'Captain of the Deck'. It was a much sought-after position – probably the equivalent to the modern-day prison passman – primarily because each holder was entitled to wine and rum:

The upper and lower decks are daily cleaned under the superintendence of the captains of the deck; being scrubbed, swabbed, scraped, or dry holystoned, according to the state of the weather; the whole of the prisoners being constantly kept on deck till the prison is thoroughly dry. Dancing is encouraged also every afternoon, and they may sing all day long, if they please. As they have but little to amuse themselves with, endeavours must be made to find amusement for them, and this can be no ways better accomplished than by giving them something to work at. Gambling is a prevailing vice, and requires great exertion to keep

9

it under; dice, cards, *pitch and toss*, and various other speculations, soon becoming general, unless checked; and to such a height of infatuation will this vice be carried, that I have known a country simpleton 'go' three whole days without food, having gambled away all his rations for that period. Until gambling is stopped, thieving will be carried on; because the fellow who loses his own dinner will always insure one out of some other person's mess.

Cunningham ordered the convicts to parade daily barefoot and with their trousers pulled up to their knees so he could check that they had washed – as many of them would not clean themselves during the voyage if not compelled:

The English convicts divide themselves into the two great classes of townies and yokels; while the Irish divide themselves into three, namely, the 'Cork boys,' the 'Dublin boys,' and the 'North boys'. The women are more quarrelsome and more difficult to control than the men, their tempers being more excitable, and a good deal being calculated on by them in respect to the usual leniency shown to their sex. They are certainly more abandoned in their expressions, too, when excited; but this probably arises not so much from greater profligacy of disposition, as from their having less control over their passions and their tongues. Formerly they lived promiscuously with the seamen on the passage out, and the voyage was certainly then brought to a close much more harmoniously than now. And as regards the crew themselves, really poor Jack is planted in a perfect garden of temptation, when among probably a hundred of such fair seducers, and is more an object of pity than wrath. To see twenty wicked fingers beckoning to him, and twenty wicked eyes winking at him, at one and the same time, no wonder his virtue should sometimes experience a fall.

Cunningham's account skirted over the lice, rats, fever and fear, but the fact was that the vast majority of convicts would have suffered anything just to get out of the dreaded hulks.

Before being led in chains onto the *William Hammond*, Thomas Pitman had been held in the relative luxury of Dartmoor, where guards were pleased to see the back of him. They were used to trouble, but Pitman, uncouth and stocky, had been caught fighting and records for the voyage reveal that when he went on board he was seen to have cuts on his nose and mouth. But for a man with mental problems who had spent his life in the open air working on the land, the prospect of being entombed for months on a rolling sea with not a blade of grass or a hill in sight must have been terrifying. What made the thought of what lay ahead even worse was that many, like Pitman, regarded this particular voyage of the *William Hammond* jinxed because the trip had a dramatic start.

As she sailed west to Plymouth, where the Dartmoor prisoners were to board, seaman John Gollately fell overboard and one of his colleagues, John Deady, assaulted the Chief Mate, David Kid, blaming him for the tragedy. Once the Dartmoor convicts were below decks locked in their stinking cells, they had to wait while a magistrate sentenced Deady to twenty-one days in jail. Then six of the crew became ill and had to leave.

During the voyage, Pensioner Henry Fraser died of tuberculosis, while some of the convicts suffered dysentery, diarrhoea and nyctalopia – night blindness, of which one of the causes is poor diet. All recovered. Kid meantime was discovered drunk on duty, having sneaked into the vessel's rum store.

The *William Hammond* sailed into Freemantle on 29 March 1856 and the following day Pitman was led down the gangplank and onto dry land in chains; the convicts were then loaded into carts that headed inland. Pitman was in a prison with no walls or roof, and no bars. As the days, weeks and months passed, his longing to be back in Dartmoor never left him, but became stronger, his misery worsened by knowing that whatever its horrors, Dartmoor had at least offered the possibility of escape.

2

CUCKING AND DUCKING

SINCE THE DAY WHEN Cain murdered his brother Abel, men and women have been committing crimes. But prisons only emerged relatively recently in the history of crime and punishment. During the latter half of the first millennium, when Vikings and Anglo Saxons dominated England, ordinary folk had no access to justice. Anyone caught stealing or killing expected savage retribution with the loss of a hand, ear, nose, tongue, or just to be put to death. Punishment became more inventive and even reasonable after the Magna Carta guaranteed – in theory if not always in practice – the right of anyone to a jury trial. Offenders might find themselves locked in an old barn without light, food or water, or literally thrown into a castle dungeon.

Typical of what they faced was the dungeon at Dunstanburgh Castle in Northumberland, where a tiny underground stream barely trickled over a stone in one corner, and in another was the open drain from the guardroom toilet above. Thirsty prisoners had to lick the stone – hence its name: 'the licking stone'. The Tudor era and the Middle Ages saw wrongdoers locked into stocks or the local pillory, where they faced being pelted with sticks, stones, rotten fruit or worse. Women generally found themselves strapped into a simple wooden chair known as a cucking stool and left either outside their home or at the spot where they were said to have offended long enough to suffer the further humiliation

12

of soiling themselves. Later on the punishment developed into the seat and victim being roughly lowered and raised in and out of a local pond. This led to the chair becoming known as the ducking stool. It was rare for anyone to actually be sentenced to a stretch in jail, but as the population increased, so did the number of criminals. Whereas felons had once either been executed if found guilty or set free, now magistrates were ordering men and women to be locked up.

As a result, small private jails sprang up, often in old, crumbling buildings run by gaolers who were open to bribery. The poorest inmates were kept in tiny, damp basements and fed bread and water, but anyone with the means to pay could buy a private room and have meals brought in by friends. Gaolers even allowed reading materials. A gaoler would hammer off the prisoner's manacles for a few pence, and for a few shillings a prisoner could have his family stay with him.

It mattered not whether inmates were mad or bad, they were all lumped together, and disease became widespread. Before releasing their charges after they had served their sentences, some gaolers even demanded money. The rich wanted thieves and murderers off their streets; very often criminals were given the choice of being executed or joining the Army or Navy.

Even the earliest cave dwellers had banished the sick or wicked from their colonies, and as the idea of exile as a form of punishment resurfaced in the 1600s with transportation, Australian townships formed – largely populated by convicts and their families – and so did a bizarre kind of snobbery; Australians declared they wanted no more criminals. So transportation Down Under slowed to a trickle. It would eventually die out altogether, the last convicts being shipped to Australia in 1868. That created the problem of what to do with those criminals left in Britain. Furthermore, then Home Secretary Sir Robert Peel's decision to replace the amateurish Bow Street Runners with the formation of a formal police service in London in 1829 meant more offenders being caught, even though the antics of those in charge – known as 'Peelers' or 'Bobbies' – was often worse than that of the men and women they arrested. Hulks were one solution, but the disgusting conditions meant that reformers such as Elizabeth Fry and John Howard loudly demanded improvements.

The result was a major expansion of prison-building to ease the pressure on existing jails such as Millbank, Coldbath Fields, and Brixton (all in London), and Durham and Dartmoor. These last two would play leading roles in the prisons story, along with the younger and newer Pentonville, Wandsworth, Holloway and Wormwood Scrubs.

Of these, Dartmoor was and is the granddaddy. It survives to this day, yet was originally intended to be a temporary prison. Save for a crafty move by an ambitious businessman who had everything to gain by having it erected on the moor, it might have been sited somewhere else. The prison was certainly needed. At the start of the 1800s, the success of the Army and Navy meant Britain was capturing tens of thousands of prisoners in wars across Europe and America and bringing them back. With her already overcrowded jails now bursting with foreigners, Britain crammed her own captives into hulks, many in south-west coast ports, where prisoners rotted while the government sweated over the drain on the revenue. It cost around £8 10s a year to hold a man in a hulk. This amount was many times more than the bill for a shore-based inmate. The modern equivalent of the bill for each hulk inmate was £35,000, less than the £47,000 a year each prisoner currently costs. But 1800s prisoners were held in filthy, primitive conditions and given only basic foodstuffs. Not for them the centrally heated cells with en-suite toilets, satellite television, recreation facilities, gymnasiums and a choice of hot daily meals now available to offenders. Prisoners of war were locked into castles and Army barracks and even naval dockyards, including one at Devonport. This created a huge security risk. Something needed to be done, and it wasn't long before the problem reached the ears of the Prince of Wales, who discussed it with his friend Thomas Tyrwhitt.

Tyrwhitt had begun farming on the Devon moor around Princetown, but the venture was a disaster. Now he saw a chance to cash in and save himself. Most of remote Dartmoor was in royal hands, as part of the Duchy of Cornwall. There was ample land on which to build a prison, and Princetown would be far enough away from the vital dockyards. Granite quarries on the moor would provide enough stone to build a dozen jails. Moreover, finding a free and constant supply of fresh water would never be a problem in an area constantly shrouded in mist and deluged by rain. The Duke would lease the necessary land while Tyrwhitt's farm could supply food, at least while the new prison was being built.

There remained the problem of the appalling weather, however. Government inspectors would be unlikely to approve the location if fog or snow prevented them from seeing more than a few feet in front of them. Tyrwhitt got around that by arranging for them to visit the area on a clear summer day. It was a clever move and enough to get the proposed site approved. In fairness, though, any climate was going to be better than the stifling conditions inside the hulks.

The job of creating a prison on Dartmoor was given to the brilliant designer and surveyor Daniel Alexander. The initial plan was to build a twenty-three-acre development with five three-storey blocks in a fan shape spreading out from offices and administration buildings. This prison would hold 5,200 prisoners and cost £86,000, with provision for another two blocks costing another £18,000, taking the total capacity to 8,400. However, the government saw Dartmoor as a temporary facility because it reasoned, naturally, that the wars would not last forever, adding to the argument that everything should be done on the cheap. As a result, Alexander was told to come up with something less expensive, and his revised plan was for a fifteen-acre jail to house

5,000 men, but that plan would not have room for more blocks. The cost was estimated at £70,000, and he was told to go ahead. A local company won the contract to build Dartmoor with a tender bid of £66,000, and on 20 March 1806, Tyrwhitt laid the foundation stone for the new jail.

There were problems from the start, and not surprisingly, most of them were caused by the weather. It was too hot in summer and too cold in winter for men to sweat or freeze in the quarries or dig out the course of a stream that would stretch nearly five miles and bring water from the River Walkham. The result was that, while the first inmates should have been in place by the end of that first year, rows over workmanship and pay, along with changes to the plans to make more room, led to delay after delay. So it was 1809 before the first batch of French prisoners marched barefoot seventeen miles over the moor from Plymouth. By then the cost had reached £128,000, which would have been even higher had the contractor not used timber salvaged from the hulks.

After that first group, wave after wave of men arrived and were marched through the mist and snow to Princetown. At its peak, Dartmoor held almost 10,000 men, giving it a population equivalent to a medium-sized town of the day. One side effect of the huge number was that there were so many men milling about that nobody was ever able to make an accurate count.

The huge number also made it difficult for guards to maintain total control, and inmates were allowed to set up their own systems of discipline and justice, holding their own courts where thieves, cheats and tell-tales were beaten or made to go without food. The prisoners established their own theatre and organised gambling. But all was not well, and before long, mounting resentment over their treatment would result in a terrible confrontation.

In London it wasn't only the deterioration of conditions in the hulks that led to increasing calls for more prisons to offer more humane treatment. The population of the capital was undergoing a spectacular rise. In 1800 it had been home to 1 million people; by 1840 that figure had almost trebled to 2.6 million; by 1860 it reached 3.2 million; and come the turn of the century, there would be a mind-boggling 6.7 million Londoners. Along with the population, crime rates also rose.

Almost from the day it had been opened in 1779, it had been obvious that London's main penitentiary, Millbank Jail in Pimlico, was a disaster. Prisons were not meant to reform or help inmates; it was accepted that most criminals would probably return to crime immediately after their sentences were over and they were freed. So the aim was to make sure they felt punished in the hope that this might deter at least some from reoffending. Prison regimes therefore operated on a 'separate' system, meaning inmates did most of their time in conditions as close to solitary confinement as possible. They were meant to be kept in separate cells, to walk along corridors with their faces turned to the walls so that they couldn't recognise other inmates or talk to them, and not to speak to anyone else. The men had to wear masks and the women veils, and even in chapel they were squeezed into individual cubicles. At Millbank it was soon discovered that the 860 men and women prisoners, most of them awaiting transportation, were communicating with one another through the ventilation system, something the guards often found difficult to prevent.

The prison was plagued with faults. It had been so badly planned that warders often got lost. Worst of all, though, was that the drains couldn't cope and regularly spewed human waste back into the jail. It was therefore no surprise that in 1822 rampant disease blighted Millbank, forcing the authorities to evacuate the inmates – among them 167 women – back to the hated hulks where the foul environment did nothing to improve their chances of recovery. Putting them back into the prison population would merely spread germs, and so in 1824 the victims were simply given pardons and released.

Pressure on cell space worsened, especially now that more

and more petty criminals were being caught and increasing numbers of debtors – someone sent to prison for being unable to pay their debts – locked up. The clamour for more new London jails became louder, and the first of these would be Pentonville. The foundation stone was laid in April 1840, and it opened its gates to its first prisoners in 1842. The total cost was £85,000. One proposal had been for it to be designed on what was known as the panopticon system, which consisted of a circular building with tiers of cells all facing the central hub where the administration and hospital units were housed. The thinking behind this was that a single guard based in the hub could see all the cells. But not everyone was in favour of this design, some arguing it restricted the size, and so the final layout for Pentonville was only a version of the panopticon, with five three-storey wings fanning out from the central hub. The authorities were so pleased with the final result that Pentonville became the model for most new jails and as a result was nicknamed the 'Model Prison'.

On a site measuring just less than seven acres, Pentonville was planned to house 430 inmates awaiting transportation in cells measuring thirteen feet long by seven feet wide and nine feet high. It would be heated by warm air funnelled through grilles in the floor. Each cell had a sink and a toilet. Workmen were told to create eighteen-inch-thick walls between cells so if inmates wanted to talk to one another they would have to shout and thus be heard by guards. Home Secretary Sir James Graham was determined Pentonville would only take convicts waiting to be shipped to Australia. In a letter to the Prison Commissioners, he declared:

Considering the excessive supply of labour in this country, its consequent depreciation, and the fastidious rejection of all those whose character is tainted, I wish to admit no prisoner into Pentonville who is not sentenced to transportation, and who is not doomed to be transported; for the convict on whom such discipline might produce the most salutary effect would, when liberated and thrown back on society in this country, be still branded as a criminal, and have but an indifferent chance of a livelihood from the profitable exercise of honest industry. I propose, therefore, that no prisoner shall be admitted into Pentonville without the knowledge that it is the portal to the penal colony, and without the certainty that he bids adieu to his connections in England, and that he must henceforth look forward to a life of labour in another hemisphere.

But from the day of his entrance into prison, while I extinguish the hope of return to his family and friends, I would open to him, fully and distinctly, the fate which awaits him, and the degree of influence which his own conduct will infallibly have over his future fortunes. He should be made to feel that from that day he enters on a new career. He should be told that his imprisonment is a period of probation; that it will not be prolonged above eighteen months; that an opportunity of learning those arts which will enable him to earn his bread will be afforded under the best instructors; that moral and religious knowledge will be imparted to him as a guide to his future life; that at the end of eighteen months, when a just estimate can be formed of the effect produced by the discipline on his character, he will be sent to Van Diemen's Land [Tasmania]; there, if he behave well, at once to receive a ticket-of-leave, which is equivalent to freedom, with a certainty of abundant maintenance – the fruit of industry.

If, however, he behave indifferently, he will, on being transported to Van Diemen's Land, receive a probationary pass, which will secure to him only a limited portion of his earnings, and impose certain galling restraints on his personal liberty. If, on the other hand, he behave ill, and the discipline of the prison be ineffectual, he will be transported to Tasman's Peninsula, there to work in a probationary gang, without wages, and deprived of liberty – an abject convict. Eighteen months of the discipline appear to me to be ample for its full application. In that time the real character will be developed, instruction will be imparted, new habits will be formed, a better frame of mind will have been moulded, or else the heart will have been hardened, and the case be desperate. The period of imprisonment at Pentonville, therefore, will be strictly limited to eighteen months.

Because convicts had to be examined by doctors to make sure they were fit enough to undertake the gruelling voyage to Australia, Graham's ruling meant the first Pentonville prisoners were generally fit and mentally stable. But standards dropped as pressure increased on the prison to take in greater numbers and ease overcrowding elsewhere. Poorer physical and mental health, combined with boredom, meant a dramatic increase in madness, something Henry Mayhew and John Binny, who conducted a series of investigations into prisons, noted when they were allowed to inspect Pentonville in 1862:

We perceive that the Model Prison was intended to be a place of instruction and probation, rather than one of oppressive discipline, and was originally limited to adults only, between the ages of eighteen and thirty-five. From the year 1843 to 1848, with a slight exception on the opening of the establishment, the prisoners admitted into Pentonville were most carefully selected from the whole body of convicts. A change, however, in the class of prisoners was the cause of some adverse results in the year 1848, and in their Report for that year the Commissioners say – 'We are sorry that, as to the health and mental condition of the prisoners, we have to make a much less satisfactory report than in any of the former years since the prison was established. It may be difficult to offer a certain explanation of the great number of cases of death and of insanity that have occurred within the last year. We have, however, reason to believe that in the earlier years of this institution, the convicts sent here were selected from a large number, and the selection was made with a more exclusive regard to their physical capacity for undergoing this species of punishment.'

Mayhew and Binny pointed out that by 1849 Pentonville had been forced to abandon the transportees-only policy: 'Accordingly, the period of confinement in Pentonville Prison was first reduced from eighteen to twelve months, and subsequently to nine months. Nevertheless, at the commencement of 1852, says an official document, there occurred an unusually large number of cases of mental affection among the prisoners, and it was therefore deemed necessary to increase the amount of exercise in the open air, and to introduce the plan of brisk walking. The change, we are told, produced a most marked and beneficial effect upon the general health of the inmates. Indeed, so much so, that in the course of the year following, there was not one removal to Bedlam.'

The two revealed: 'The cells distributed throughout this magnificent building are about the size of the interior of a large and roomy omnibus.' They went on to describe a typical cell:

At the extreme end of the cell is the small closet, well supplied with water-pipes; and in another part you see the shaded gas-jet, whilst in one of the corners by the door are some two or three triangular shelves, where the prisoner's spoon, platter, mug, and soap-box, &c., are stowed. On the upper of these shelves, the rolled-up hammock, with its bedding, stands on end, like a huge muff, and let into the wall on either side, some three feet from the ground, are two large bright eyelet holes, to which the hammock is slung at night. Then there is a little table and stool, and occasionally on the former may be found some brown paper-covered book or periodical, with which the prisoner has been supplied from the prison library. Further, there is, in the corner near the cupboard, a button, which, on being turned, causes a small gong to be struck in the corridor without, and at the same moment makes a plate or index outside the door, start out at right angles to the wall, so that the warder, when summoned by the bell, may know which prisoner has rung.

Pleasant though they thought the conditions were, the problem of overcrowding worsened. Things were so bad in London's Brixton Prison that it became normal for three or four men to be forced to share a cell meant for one; sometimes up to twenty men had to sleep on straw in the schoolroom with just a single blanket each for warmth. In 1847 the authorities ran out of room, and gave thirty-five inmates pardons and sent them home. More new jails were needed, and soon work started on the construction of Wandsworth and Holloway. Typically, though, yet again when it came to spending public money, prisons were at or near the bottom of the list of priorities. At Wandsworth – officially known as the Surrey House of Correction – the original proposal for a building in the panopticon style covering twenty-six acres and housing 1,000 inmates was eventually cut back to one for 788 inmates. It was modelled on Pentonville, but when it came to the chapel, the necessity to continue to operate the separate system came up against the cost.

At Pentonville the individual cubicles were causing problems relieved only by bringing in more guards, thereby increasing running costs. Some prisoners were caught passing notes to one another under the doors of their stalls while other convicts caused chaos by pretending to be ill. Extricating them meant having to first move scores of others. Male inmates had to be watched especially closely to stop them from craning their necks to see women convicts as they filed in.

Chaplains objected to worshippers being unable to pray together. Simply building a high screen between men and women was one suggested solution to keep them separated in the same space, but to remove the individual chapel stalls would have been to breach the principle of the separate system. The stalls continued, but the original building estimate of £100,000 had risen to £140,319 11s 5d by the time the first male convicts entered Wandsworth in November 1851, women following them a few months later.

Women worked almost exclusively in the prison washhouse and laundry. Later, another 250 cells were opened on the site. Room for them had been created by ripping out the toilets and sinks originally installed, committing inmates to the daily and humiliating practice of slopping out, one that would last in prisons all over Britain for many decades.

As the first inmates settled into Wandsworth, workmen were putting the finishing touches to the City of London House of Correction at Holloway. It opened in October 1852 and was built on a ten-acre site originally intended as a cemetery for victims of a cholera outbreak. Close by was Hampstead Heath, where more than a century earlier the notorious Dick Turpin, mounted on Black Bess, held up coachmen before moving on to Yorkshire, where he was caught and executed. It had taken nine years to actually open the prison, much of that time spent working out how to reduce the cost. Ten plans originally examined had been estimated to cost between £142,000 to £214,000. However, all were thrown out as being too expensive, their costs inflated due to their locations inside the city. Eventually, these suggested places were also eventually dismissed as being too unhealthy. The chosen design was estimated to cost £80,000 and would see the erection of four three-storey male wings each with seventy-two cells and two more wings each with fifty-six cells for women and juveniles on eight acres.

Mayhew and Binny inspected Holloway, and in a lengthy report they described what they saw in one of the cells: 'On the right hand corner by the door, were three small triangular shelves. The bedding was firmly rolled up, two blankets, a rug, pair of sheets, horsehair mattress and pillow which at night were put into a hammock suspended from two iron hooks. On the second shelf is a tin dish for gruel, a wooden salt cellar and wooden spoon. On the lower shelf a Bible, prayer book and hymnbook, combs and brush and a rubber brush for polishing the cell floor. And in a drawer materials for cleaning the cell windows.' On the right-hand side of the door was a small handle with which the prisoners could summon help from guards. It rang a bell outside, and a warder hearing it could open a small wooden trap in the cell door. After six in the evening guards put on soft shoes so inmates couldn't hear them approaching or patrolling. The investigators noted how they also spotted a 'wooden machine to which boys are fastened when they are whipped on the order of a magistrate'. Women prisoners wore blue gowns marked with a red stripe, petticoats of coarse twill, shifts of red striped calico, blue check neckerchiefs, woollen caps and dark-blue worsted stockings.

The abandonment of the panopticon and the adoption of a different layout designed by Major-General Edmund Du Cane, chairman of the Directors of Convict Prisons, was not the only new innovation when it came to building Wormwood Scrubs close to a spot in West London where young men had once fought duels. The bulk of the jail was actually built by convicts themselves. The DIY idea was new to England, although it had proved successful with the construction of a prison in New Hampshire, America, and then that of Sing Sing in New York State in 1826.

The 'Scrubs' began with a local contractor erecting the shell of a small corrugated-iron building to be used as accommodation for the unusual workforce that would follow. With snow falling in the winter of 1874, nine hand-picked convicts, all of them trustees close to release, moved in to finish off the work, allowing a further fifty convicts to move in. They constructed a brick wing into which another 100 men were moved, most of them convicts who had learned skills in the building industry before turning to crime. Like the initial team, they had been specially picked as unlikely to want to escape, but in case they did, they wore uniforms with large arrow symbols to make them instantly identifiable.

Gradually the workforce increased, and as it did, the prison slowly took shape. Prisoners even made their own bricks. However, the last of the initial four wings was not completed until 1891, seventeen years after the arrival of that first handful of inmates. While the government was happy that the self-build had saved many tens of thousands of pounds, the appearance of the Scrubs – or indeed its very existence – did not go down well with everyone. Some said it looked too much like a university or college, while others complained of having a prison dumped in their community. The *Kensington News* asked: 'Are we prepared for the infusion of convict element in our population? We object to Wormwood Scrubs being made a country residence for the Claimant and his friends.' Like it or not, though, it was there to stay.

Two hundred and fifty miles to the north, in Durham, conditions for prisoners had been almost unimaginably terrible in the city's two jails, the 400-year-old County Gaol, owned by the Bishop of Durham, and the House of Correction. The County Gaol was by far the worst. Prisoners lay on straw infested with vermin, and the building was overrun with rats. Weak inmates were bullied and forced to hand over their miserable ration of a pound of bread a day. Unless friends bribed the gaolers to allow them to visit and bring the inmate food, the weak simply starved.

Seeing two cells at the gaol, where both men and women were held while they awaited execution, a reformer described them as, 'totally dark and fitter for the reception of coals than any human being'. And reformer James Neild said in a magazine article, written after an inspection of the County Gaol in 1805, that it had 'the worst cells in the country'. His view of Durham was probably jaundiced by his visit there almost ending in tragedy when he slipped and was about to plunge down a deep shaft only for his coat to snag on a nail and save him from falling.

As Durham City expanded and the population grew, the narrow streets became more and more unsuitable. Often arguments broke out between coachmen, drovers, carters, horsemen and farmers over who had right of way, which in turn led to physical fights. The lanes around the County Gaol were also particularly narrow, so the Bishop, Barrington Shute, agreed a new prison was needed. Soon after, a site at Old Elvet was chosen. Bishop Shute even coughed up £2,000 to get the project started.

The foundation stone was laid by City of Durham Member of Parliament Sir Henry Vane-Tempest, a well-known racehorse owner, amid pageantry and celebrations on 31 July 1809. The occasion included a squad of soldiers firing a volley to mark the beginning of building a jail that stands to this day.

It all began in hope, but soon Durham Prison developed a reputation for being jinxed, as it was rocked by a series of problems. Irish-born architect Francis Sandys was experienced and highly respected. He was given the commission on the strength of his having designed the county prison at Worcester, but his ideas for Durham soon ran into trouble. The development seemed to leak money, mostly because contractors were either not up to the job or used cheap, substandard materials. As architect in charge of overseeing the new prison, Sandys was deemed responsible. He was sued by the local magistrates for £20,000, lost the action and disappeared, his career in tatters. The work was taken over and completed by two other leading architects, George Moneypenny, regarded as the expert when it came to prison design, and Ignatius Bonomi, best known for his work on the construction of railways. However, the hold-ups meant the first prisoners did not move into the 600 cells until 1819.

3

THE THREE SISTERS

THE MEN AND WOMEN who guard convicts like to be known as prison officers, but to most inmates they are warders or, more popularly, screws, a term that did not appear by accident. For decades, judges, when dealing with criminals, would sentence them to so many years of 'penal servitude with hard labour'. Penal servitude the criminals expected – it was really just a different way of telling them they were being punished; however, hard labour they dreaded.

Prisoners sent to Dartmoor were luckier than others, relatively speaking. They would perform their hard labour in the prison quarry, which at least meant being outdoors, although for the majority it at first guaranteed aching muscles and severely blistered hands as they swung 14 lb hammers at huge boulders. For most, though, hard labour would see them condemned to hundreds or thousands of pointless, mindless, soul-destroying hours on tread wheels or crank machines.

At Pentonville, the prison regime introduced the tread wheel, where teams of prisoners in individual stalls turned giant paddle wheels by walking on them for up to six hours a day. Sometimes the tread wheels pumped water or air into the prison, or they might even be used to grind flour. Tread wheels were expensive to run because in order to make sure inmates remained in their stalls and did not stop to gossip, teams of guards had to be constantly watching.

When it came to building Wandsworth, to save money, dozens of labour or crank machines were installed in cells. With these, convicts had to turn a handle fixed to a drum, which scooped up sand from a tin and tipped it back in. It was mind-numbingly boring and anybody failing to make up to 15,000 revolutions a day faced punishments that included not being fed. In addition, convicts discovered it didn't pay to annoy warders, who could tighten up the machine and make it harder to turn by merely adjusting a screw. Hence why prison officers became known as 'screws'.

Once the prison surgeon had ruled them fit enough, men might spend three months at a time turning the handles. If they behaved themselves, they might then be sent to work at gardening, carpentry, tailoring or shoemaking.

Miscreants might also find themselves thrown into one of the punishment cells, the 'dark', 'segregation' or 'solitary' cells – nowadays universally termed 'The Digger' – where the total absence of light left offenders disoriented. Very often they were given only bread and water, resulting in them losing between one and three pounds of body weight a day.

Before the Bishop decided a new jail was needed, the punishment cells at Durham were a cold, miserable hell in which men and women offenders were often left in pitch darkness chained to the floor. The segregation unit at Dartmoor was a row of damp, dank rooms, the walls glistening with moisture, and the thickness of the walls made communication between inmates impossible.

Prisoners might spend weeks on end in solitary confinement, their warders not even breaking the monotony by speaking. A few almost relished this misery; many others couldn't stop themselves from breaking prison rules and being thrown into solitary cells, or facing other penalties that included losing remission, not being allowed to mix with others, receiving punishment diets that left them constantly hungry and, worst of all, being flogged.

A survey at Pentonville, which operated the 'separate' rule, showed that in 1854, a total of 263 prisoners were officially punished, one man a remarkable twenty-four times in the year and another twenty-three times. It was probably not surprising that the most common offence – occurring 171 times – was communicating with other inmates by slipping them notes, talking during exercise periods or tapping out coded messages on walls or water pipes. That was followed by 149 instances of disobedience, such as refusing to work or attend prison school or exercise; 102 examples of talking or whistling in school; eighty-three of disturbing prison routine by shouting, whistling, or singing obscene and other songs; sixty-four of deliberately destroying prison property; thirty-three of obscene communications or drawings on books and chapel stalls; and the same number for misbehaviour in chapel during services; thirty instances of fighting; twenty-nine of using bad language to officers; twenty-five of boring holes in cell walls and windows; twenty-two of stealing food; fourteen of being caught with tobacco; and a variety of others that included feigning suicide, trying to escape and assaulting prison officers.

Prison officials had the power to inflict a whole range of punishments, and during that year inmates were sent to punishment – 'dark' – cells 534 times, more than half of them having the additional misery of being put on a restricted diet. Mostly they spent just one or two days in the dark cells, but in a handful of cases the sentence was up to three weeks there. Other penalties included having their books taken away or not being allowed to work – their only chance to talk with other prisoners – and in one case at Pentonville, an inmate was ordered to be flogged. He endured a horrendous thirty-six lashes.

At one time official beatings in prison were common and feared. Offenders were 'married to the three sisters' by being tied to a triangular wooden stand; they could be stripped naked and lashed on the buttocks, or stripped to the waist and beaten on their backs. The instrument of pain might be a simple lash or whip, a birch consisting of a bundle of birch twigs tied to a handle and soaked in water to make them more supple, or the hated cat o' nine tails, which wreaked considerably more pain and damage. Sometimes two birches might be needed in case the twigs of one became too damaged during the beating. Individual prisons usually made up their own versions and at Dartmoor, for example, an especially brutal weapon weighing 450 g and more than a metre long caused extreme pain and was known as the senior birch.

When it came to sending men and women to prison, judges were given some guidelines as to how long sentences should be, to at least give a sense of consistency, but the number of strokes dished out in floggings, lashings or whippings varied enormously. In 1841 George Barker of the Horse Artillery was given 150 lashes after a court martial convicted him of stealing a piece of sponge from a colleague. He was just seventeen.

No one was too young to feel the sting of the lash. Joseph Charmom was only eleven when he received a whipping for stealing peas in 1872. If his hiding was meant to be a deterrent, it failed, because within a few months, four feet five-and-a-half inches tall Joseph was locked up with murderers and rapists in Wandsworth Prison for six weeks for stealing a hen.

Some men took their punishment in silence, gritting their teeth as they heard the swish of the lash coming down on their naked flesh. Others could not stop screams of agony, their humiliation loud enough for all to hear and very often causing unrest among fellow prisoners. A report in 1864 described the flogging of two men at Durham Prison with the cat o' nine tails:

Two men, who were convicted at the Durham Assizes of garrotte robberies at Sunderland and sentenced, the former to five years and the latter to ten years penal servitude, with twenty lashes each, underwent the punishment of flogging at the County Prison. The instrument of punishment is described as of a formidable-looking nature and was manufactured by a sailor who is undergoing imprisonment in the jail. The first lash was received with comparative equanimity by each prisoner, but, on the second, the yell of deep and excruciating agony which burst forth is represented as indescribable. Their cries continued during the whole of the punishment, and these, together with the sight of the mangled backs of the sufferers and the clotted skein of the cat, made up a spectacle of horror overpowering to those who witnessed it. When the punishment had been inflicted, the prisoners were taken down and removed to the prison infirmary in a state of complete prostration.

Accounts such as these meant reformers and politicians pressured for greater control over the degree of punishment that could be passed down. In 1883 Parliament laid down firmer rules, but they would not have helped the Sunderland men. It could even be argued they got off lightly because from then on courts could order under-eighteens to be given up to twenty-five strokes of a birch or the cat o' nine tails. Reformers argued such punishment meant the pain inflicted on victims was unreasonable. During a debate in the House of Lords about proposed changes to the law, Lord Esher pointed out these rules would allow a judge to 'order a flogging of fifty lashes three times – all to be administered within six months of conviction. A man's back would not heal in less than two months, and before he had properly recovered he would be flogged again and afterwards a third time.' Despite his dire description, the birches and cats continued to swish.

That sort of punishment – especially if it was inflicted on a youngster – caused increasing unease, although the right of courts to order beatings would continue for many decades. In May 1895 the playwright Oscar Wilde had been convicted of gross indecency and given two years' penal servitude with hard labour. He spent the early part of the sentence in Pentonville and Wandsworth jails before being moved to Reading, and it was what he saw that resulted in his writing to the *Daily Chronicle* newspaper in 1897:

Sir, I learn with great regret, through the columns of your paper, that the warder Martin, of Reading Prison, has been dismissed by the Prison Commissioners for having given some sweet biscuits to a little hungry child. I saw the three children myself on Monday preceding my release. They had just been convicted and were standing in a row in the central hall in their prison dress, carrying their sheets under the arms, previous to their being sent to the cells allotted to them. They were quite small children, the youngest — the one to whom the warder gave the biscuits — being a tiny little chap, for whom they had evidently been unable to find clothes small enough to fit. I had, of course, seen many children in prison during the two years during which I was myself confined. Wandsworth Prison, especially, contained always a large number of children. But the little child I saw on the afternoon of Monday the 17th at Reading, was tinier than any one of them. I need not say how utterly distressed I was to see these children at Reading, for I knew the treatment in store for them. The cruelty that is practised by day and night on children in English prisons is incredible, except to those who have witnessed it and are aware of the brutality of the system.

There were, of course, many who felt that as well as enduring his stint in prison, Wilde himself should have been flogged. Had he been, he would surely have put pen to paper to rally more support for change. But then it sometimes paid to stay silent. Undoubtedly, William Bowker wished he had. In 1901 he was convicted of robbery with violence. The judge was told that as he was being arrested. Bowker, aged thirty-one, had told his captors, 'Highway robbery means a flogging. Don't let them take me for this, boys. This means something.' Bowker had heard from associates just how drastic a flogging could be, but the judge also heard he made the mistake of warning, as he was being charged, 'This means a bashing. The man that flogs me won't live another day.' One prediction was right, the other wrong. At Pentonville he was strapped to the prison's version of the sisters, and after being bashed with eighteen strokes, dished out by a warder he was not allowed to see, he went off to serve twelve months' hard labour.

Bowker had known what to expect; so did James Edward Spiers. Early in 1930 he was sentenced to ten years' penal servitude after being convicted at the Old Bailey of assaulting a cashier with intent to rob. When his home was searched, police discovered cash hidden in tins that had been cemented into the walls. Spiers, a thirty-seven-year-old carpenter, had an appalling record, and after hearing details of it, the judge added that he was to be given fifteen strokes of the cat. The convict was hauled off for his date with the Wandsworth walloper, but before the rendezvous, he jumped over a balcony from his cell on the second floor, and fell to his death. His shocked wife said: 'My husband was such a happy-go-lucky man. Normally, his nerves were strong and this is the last thing I should have expected him to do. When I met him before he was sentenced I said to him, "My dear, there is only one thing I am worried about, and that is the 'cat'." His answer to that was, "Don't you worry. If I have to go through it I am quite prepared." He was not the type of man to fear physical pain, but I cannot help feeling that the strain of the last few weeks have been too much for him.'

The tragedy renewed calls for flogging to be abolished, but they fell on deaf ears. Not even an admission during a debate in Parliament, that a boy of eight had been flogged with four strokes of the birch, persuaded MPs to change the law. At Dartmoor, hidings were commonplace and led to a frightening build-up in tension between warders and inmates.

Sometimes people felt judges were far too indiscriminate in ordering the men appearing before them to be whipped. Simply being discovered sleeping outside or begging made the poor liable to being tied up and lashed. The sentence of twelve strokes of the birch that was imposed on a fifty-nine-year-old tramp led to an outcry.

Even punishing those who clearly merited a good hiding brought protests. In 1938 David Wilmer was given fifteen strokes of the cat at Wormwood Scrubs as part of his sentence for taking part in a Mayfair jewel robbery. His accomplice, Robert Harley, was told he would get twenty strokes. The deans of Canterbury and St Paul's were among those who signed a letter complaining that in addition to lengthy spells behind bars, the robbers had been told they would be whipped. The letter stated: 'We submit that the approval that has been widely expressed over these sentences is not due to any belief that society has been made safer, but to a deeper emotional satisfaction at the thought of the pain inflicted on these men. It is a fact that people are obtaining enjoyment by reading details of all that this punishment involves, and the moral injury that results overshadows even the physical injury of the men concerned. It is ideal to pretend that these sentences can be justified on the grounds of expediency. If the prospect of a seven years' sentence of penal servitude is not sufficient to act as a deterrent to others, a flogging sentence will not be either.'

The case reared again a year later during a debate in Parliament about a proposal to abolish flogging. 'There is no half way house with regard to the cat,' argued one MP. 'You have either got to use it or abolish. You are demanding that we should retain a penalty which, after the Mayfair case, enabled the whole gutter Press to indulge in those sadistic qualities which disgusted every decent man and woman in the country.' He claimed that by accepting a beating from the cat o' nine tails, convicts had their sentences reduced by two years. His words failed to impress, and floggings continued.

Just how painful was the cat? In an interview about his book, *The Brutal Truth*, not long before his death in 2011, Eric Mason described what it felt like. Eric, big, likeable and brave, had mixed with the hardest. His associates included the Kray Twins, and he was a legend in the London underworld. Eric spent many years in prisons – the majority at Dartmoor, where he built up his muscles in the prison quarry and at the same time developed an intense dislike of the vast majority of screws. Life in prison was, for Eric, a war against authority and the officers who enforced rules. But in an interview with me, he admitted the one time when he almost cried out for mercy was the day in 1954 when he was given twelve strokes of the cat at Wandsworth:

I was twenty-four and had been given a series of beatings by screws. They'd chucked me into the punishment block and left me in my own blood and filth. I was in there for a couple of weeks, and then they decided I was to be given the cat. I was given another couple of weeks to think on what would happen. I knew a few guys who had been flogged and one of them told me I'd feel the first stroke which would numb my back and after that I'd feel nothing. They took me to the laundry at Wandsworth and strapped me to a triangular frame. A big canvas belt was bucked around my middle to protect my kidneys, and my head was pushed through a slip in a canvas sheet that protected my neck. It also meant I couldn't see who was holding the cat. The governor was standing beside me with a doctor and they counted off the strokes. The first one hurt but I'd told myself I wouldn't be feeling anything after that. My pal had got it wrong, though. The second stroke was even worse and they got progressively more agonising after that. After each one I could hear the screw untangling the tails of the cat and getting ready to do his best to make sure the next stroke landed exactly where the previous one had hit me to cause maximum pain. My back only went numb after the last one. But I didn't cry out and I chalked that up as a win to me.

I don't know how I made it back to my cell. Blood was running down my sides and that was the one and only time I came close to giving in and asking for help from the screws. But I stuck it out. In fact, the worst pain came when I went back into mainstream and pals, without thinking, started congratulating me by slapping me on the back.

The cat o' nine tails did not deter Eric from future crimes, and other men were lashed after him. But in 1967, the last birching given to a serving prisoner in England was dished out. The cats and birches were consigned to prison museums.

4

MASSACRE

FLOGGINGS, HARSH conditions and over-zealous guards are often behind trouble in jails. But the spark for the worst atrocity in prison history was the result of homesickness. Disease and sickness due to poor diet and the miserable weather in which the place seemed to be forever shrouded led to the deaths of hundreds of prisoners of war who'd been herded into Dartmoor. A few died trying to escape, shot or bayoneted by the militia who stood guard on the walls, but mostly they suffered from cold, damp and neglect. In those early years more than 1,100 French and 271 American inmates perished at Dartmoor, mainly from pneumonia, exposure, smallpox and typhus. It could be argued that most of those deaths were unavoidable; however, the events of just a few hours on Thursday, 6 April 1815 would arouse feelings of horror and anger on both sides of the Atlantic.

Ever since America declared war on Britain in June 1812, the problem of where to hold prisoners had been a headache for the British government. Most soldiers were locked up in barracks in Canada, but as these filled to capacity, it was decided that captured sailors should be transported to hulks and prisons in England. One of these places was Dartmoor, which saw the arrival of nearly 7,000 American seamen. Armed soldiers patrolled the walls and guarded gates, but inside, the prisoners virtually ran things themselves, organising recreation, discipline and the distribution of food. Troublemakers were still liable to be flogged by their guards, but their hopes of an end to the nightmare were raised by the signing of a peace deal, the Treaty of Ghent, which was ratified in February 1815. When news of it reached Dartmoor, the Americans waited to be told they were on their home. And waited, and waited, and waited . . .

Security on some who gave their word not to escape was eased, but frustration among the vast majority grew. A few men ran away, hoping to make it to Plymouth, where they might land a berth on an American-bound ship. However, even though they were destined to be freed, the authorities wanted those who escaped back. A typical newspaper advertisement in the *Morning Chronicle* on 7 February 1815 announced: 'A reward of one guinea on the recapture of each of the undermentioned prisoners who escaped from Dartmoor prison on the 3rd inst, Caleb R. Holmes, seaman, 25 years of age, 5 feet 9 inches high, stout made, round visage, fair complexion, dark-brown hair, grey eyes and scar on little finger of right hand. John Langford, prize master, 25 years of age, 5 feet 5 inches high, stout made, oval visage, fair complexion, brown hair and hazel eyes.'

The Americans wanted to be home. One of the problems facing Britain was that she was now in the middle of a furious new war with Napoleon Bonaparte and needed all her ships to supply her armies and blockade French ports. Some now-friendly American vessels were heading to the south-west of England, but inside Dartmoor, the atmosphere was growing tenser by the day.

Matters came to a head at about six in the evening on 6 April. Tempers flared and soldiers opened fire, leaving seven Americans dead – including a boy aged fourteen – and thirty-five injured, some seriously. After a two-day inquest that same month, the jury returned a verdict of 'justifiable homicide' on the dead. The *Lancaster Gazette* and *General Advertiser* reported: 'Several of the thirty-five that were wounded are not expected to survive. One of the unfortunate men was sitting smoking his pipe and coolly observing the tumultuous conduct of his comrades. About the time when the Somerset Militia fired first, he was desired to be removed from his situation, when he observed that he had no hand in the row and should stay where he was. He did so and fell with the rest.'

By the time of the inquest, a commission of inquiry had already been set up with orders to investigate who did what, and to do so quickly, such was the mounting rage as word about the massacre spread across the Atlantic. It reported on 26 April, and here are extracts from the findings:

During the period which has elapsed since the arrival in this country of the account of the ratification of the Treaty of Ghent, an increased degree of restlessness and impatience of confinement appears to have prevailed amongst the American prisoners at Dartmoor, which, though not exhibited in the shape of any violent excesses, has been principally indicated by threats of breaking out if not soon released. On the 4th of the month in particular, only two days previous to the events, the subject of this inquiry, a large body of the prisoners rushed into the market square, from whence, by the regulations of the prison, they are excluded, demanding bread, instead of biscuit, which had on that day been issued by the officers of the depot; their demands, however, having been then almost immediately complied with, they returned to their own yards, and the employment of force on that occasion became unnecessary.

On the evening of the 6th, about six o'clock, it was clearly proved to us, that a breach or hole had been made in one of the prison walls sufficient for a full-sized man to pass, and that others had been commenced in the course of the day, near the same spot, though never completed. That a number of the prisoners went over the railing erected to prevent them from communicating with the sentinels on the walls, which was of course forbidden by the regulations of the prison, and that in the space between the railing and those walls they were tearing up pieces of turfs and wantonly pelting each other in a noisy and disorderly manner.

That a much more considerable number of the prisoners was collected together at that time in one of their yards near the place where the breach was effected, and that although such collection of prisoners was not unusual at other times (the gambling tables being usually kept in that part of the yard), yet, when connected with the circumstances of the breach, and the time of day, which was after the hour the signal for the prisoners to retire to their respective prisons had ceased to sound, it became a natural and just ground of alarm to those who had charge of the depot. It was also in evidence that in the building, formerly the petty officers' prison, but now the guard barrack, with stands in the yard to which the hole in the wall would serve as a communication, a part of the arms of the guard who were off duty were usually kept in the racks, and though there was no evidence that this was in any respect the motive which induced the prisoners to make the opening in the wall, or even that, they were ever acquainted with the fact, it naturally became at least a further cause of suspicion and alarm, and an additional reason for precaution. Upon those grounds Captain Shortland appears to us to have been justified in giving the order, which about this time he seems to have given, to sound the alarm bell, the usual signal for collecting the officers of the depot and putting the military upon the alert.

However reasonable and justifiable this was as a measure of precaution, the effects produced thereby in the prisons, but which could not have been intended, were most unfortunate and deeply to be regretted. A considerable number of the prisoners in the yards where no disturbances existed before, and who were already within their respective prisons, or quietly retiring as usual towards them, immediately upon the sound of the bell rushed back from curiosity (as it appears), towards the gates where, by that time, the crowd had assembled, and many who at the time were absent from their yards were also, from the plan of the prison, compelled, in order to reach their own homes, to pass by the same spot, and thus that which was merely a measure of precaution, in its operation increased the evil it was intended to prevent.

Almost at the same instant that the alarm bell rang (but whether before or subsequent is upon the evidence doubtful, though Capt. Shortland states it positively as one of his further reasons for causing it to ring), some one or more of the prisoners broke the iron chain, which was the only fastening of No. 1 Gate, leading into the market square, by means of an iron bar; and a very considerable number of the prisoners rushed towards that gate, and many of them began to press forward as fast as the opening would permit into the square. There was no direct proof before us of previous concert or preparation on the part of the prisoners and no evidence of their intention or disposition to affect their escape on this occasion, excepting that which arose by inference from the whole of the above detailed circumstances connected together. The natural and almost irresistible inference to be drawn, however, from the conduct of the prisoners by Capt. Shortland and the military was that an intention on the part of the prisoners to escape was on the point of being carried into execution; and it was at least certain that they were by force passing beyond the limits prescribed to them, at a time when they ought to have been quietly going in for the night. It was also in evidence that the outer gates of the market square were usually opened about this time, to let the bread wagons pass and repass to the store, although, at the period in question, they were, in fact, closed. Under these circumstances, and with these impressions necessarily operating upon his mind, and the knowledge that if the prisoners once penetrated through the square, the power of escape was almost to a certainty afforded to them, should they be so disposed.

Capt. Shortland, in the first instance, proceeded down the square towards the prisoners, having ordered a part of the different guards, to the number of about fifty, only at first, though they were increased afterwards, to follow him. For some time both he and Dr McGrath endeavoured by quiet means and persuasion, to induce the prisoners to retire to their own yards, explaining to them the fatal consequences which must ensue if they refused, as the military would in that case be necessarily compelled to employ force. The guard was by this time formed in the rear of Captain Shortland, about two-thirds of the way down the square; the latter is about one hundred feet broad, and the guard extended nearly all across. Captain Shortland, finding that persuasion was all in vain, and that although some were induced by it to make an effort to retire, others pressed on in considerable numbers, at last ordered about fifteen file of the guard, nearly in front of the gate, which had been forced, to charge the prisoners back to their own yards.

The prisoners were in some places so near the military, that one of the soldiers states that he could not come fairly down to the charge, and the military were unwilling to act as against an enemy. Some of the prisoners were also unwilling and reluctant to retire, and some pushing and struggling ensued between the parties, arising partly from intention, but mainly from the pressure of those behind preventing those in front from getting back. After some little time, however, this charge appears to have been so far effective, and that with little or no injury to the prisoners, as to have driven them for the most part quite down out of the square, with the exception of a small number who continued their resistance about No. 1 Gate. A great crowd still remained collected after this in the passage between the square and the prisoners' yards, in the vicinity of the gate. This assemblage still refused to withdraw, and according to most of the English witnesses, and some of the American, was making a noise, hallooing, insulting, and provoking, and daring the military to fire; and, according to the evidence of several of the soldiers and some others, was pelting the military with large stones, by which some of them were actually struck. This circumstance is, however, denied by many of the American witnesses, and some of the English, upon having the question put to them, stated, they saw no stones thrown previously to the firing, although their situation at the time was such as to enable them to see most of the other proceedings in the square.

Under these circumstances the firing commenced. With regard to any order having been given to fire, the evidence is very contradictory. Several of the Americans swear positively that Captain Shortland gave that order, but the manner in which, from the confusion of the moment, they describe this part of the transaction is so different in its details that it is very difficult to reconcile their testimony. Many of the soldiers and other English witnesses heard the word given by some one; but no one can swear it was by Captain Shortland, or by any one in particular, and some, amongst whom is the officer commanding the guard, think, if Captain Shortland had given such an order, that they must have heard it, which they did not. In addition to this, Captain Shortland denies the fact; and from the situation in which he appears to have been placed at the time, even according to the American witnesses, in front of the soldiers, it may appear somewhat improbable that he should then have given such an order. But, however, it may remain a matter of doubt whether the firing first began in the square by order, or was a spontaneous act of the soldiers themselves, it seemed clear that it was continued and renewed, both there and elsewhere, without orders; and that on the platforms, and in several places above the prison, it was certainly commenced without any authority. The fact of an order having been given at first, provided the firing was, under existing circumstances, justifiable, does not appear very material in any other point of view than as showing a want of self-possession and discipline in the troops, if they should have fired without order.

With regard to the above important consideration, of whether the firing was justifiable or not, we are of opinion, under all the circumstances of the case, from the apprehension which the soldiers might fairly entertain, owing to the numbers and conduct of the prisoners, that this firing in a certain extent was justifiable, in a military point of view, in order to intimidate the prisoners, and compel them thereby to desist from all acts of violence, and to retire as they were ordered from a situation in which the responsibility of the agents, and the military, could not permit, could not permit them with safety to remain. From the fact of the crowd being so close, and the firing at first being attended with very little injury, it appears probable that a large proportion of the muskets were, as stated by one or two of the witnesses, levelled over the heads of the prisoners; a circumstance in some respects to be lamented, as it induced them to renew their insults to the soldiery, which produced a repetition of the firing in a manner much more destructive. The firing in the square having continued for some time, by which several of the prisoners sustained injuries, the greater part of them appear to have been running back, with the utmost precipitation and confusion, to their respective prisons, and the cause for further firing seems at this period to have ceased. It appears accordingly that Captain Shortland was in the 'market square', exerting himself and giving orders to that effect, and that Lieutenant Fortye had succeeded in stopping the fire of his part of the guard.

Under these circumstances, it is difficult to find any justification for the continuance and renewal of the firing, which certainly took place in the prison yards and elsewhere; though we have some evidence of subsequent provocation given to the military, and resistance to the turnkeys in shutting the prisons, and of stones being thrown out from within the prison doors. The subsequent firing rather appears to have arisen from individual irritation and exasperation on the part of the soldiers who followed the prisoners into their yards, and from the absence of nearly all the officers who might have restrained it; as well as from the great difficulty of putting an end to a firing when once commenced under such circumstances.

Captain Shortland was from this time busily occupied with

the turnkeys in the square, receiving and taking care of the wounded. Ensign White remained with his guard at the breach, and Lieutenants Avelyne and Fortye, the only other subalterns known to have been present, continued in the square with the main bodies of their respective guards. The time of the day, which was the officers' dinner hour, will, in some measure, explain this, as it caused the absence of every officer from the prison whose presence was not indispensible there – and this circumstance, which has been urged as an argument to prove the intention of the prisoners to take this opportunity to escape, tended to increase the confusion, and to prevent those great exertions being made which might perhaps have obviated a portion, at least, of the mischief which ensued. At the same time as the firing was going on in the square, a cross fire was also kept up from several of the platforms on the walls round the prison where the sentries stand, by straggling parties of soldiers who ran up there for that purpose. As far as this fire was directed to disperse the men assembled round the breach, for which purpose it was most effectual, it seems to stand upon the same ground as that in the first instance in the square.

But that part which it is positively sworn was directed against straggling parties of prisoners running about the yards, and endeavouring to enter in the few doors which the turnkeys, according to their usual practice, had left open, does seem, as stated, to have been wholly without object or excuse, and to have been a wanton attack upon the lives of defenceless, and at that time, unoffending individuals. In the same, or even more severe terms, we must remark upon what was proved as to the firing into the door ways of the prisons, more particularly that of No. 3 prison, at a time when the men were in crowds at the entrance. From the position of the prison and of the door, and to the marks of the balls which were pointed out to us, as well as from the evidence, it was clear this firing must have proceeded from soldiers a very few feet from the door way, and although it was certainly sworn that the prisoners were at the time of part of the firing at least continuing to insult and occasionally to throw stones at the soldiers, and that they were standing in the way of, and impeding the turnkey, who was there for the purpose of closing the door, yet still there was nothing stated which could in our view justify such excessively hard and severe treatment of helpless and unarmed prisoners when all idea of an escape was at an end.

Under these impressions we used every endeavour to ascertain if there was the least prospect of identifying any of the soldiers who had been guilty of the particular outrages here alluded to, or of tracing any particular death at that time in the firing of any particular individual, but without success; and all hopes of bringing the offenders to punishment should seem to be at an end.

In conclusion, we have only to add that whilst we lament, as we do most deeply, the unfortunate transaction which has been the subject of this inquiry we find ourselves totally unable to suggest any steps to be taken as to those parts of it which seem most to call for redress and punishment.

The stern words of the Commission did nothing to appease American anger, which was worsened when it was discovered that four American seamen had been taken from Dartmoor and forced into serving on British warships. Although they were freed when the vessels docked at Gibraltar, one American newspaper summed up the growing ill feeling over the Dartmoor massacre had sparked between the nations that had been until comparatively recently father and son: 'It is lamentable that peace, in form, does not produce reconciliation at heart. England seems still sour, sullen and hostile. The butchery of American prisoners at Dartmoor, after peace was known to exist, the imprisonment of four American sailors since that event. We cannot doubt that our Government will profit by experience and settle accounts with England before delay increases the score.'

It was not just the tragedy that sparked the repatriation process into life. The government needed room at Dartmoor to house thousands of French prisoners captured as Napoleon Bonaparte was finally brought to heel at Waterloo. Among the hordes who arrived – some for their second term of imprisonment – as the Americans were going home were many who had been wounded during the battle. Jackson's *Oxford Journal* reported on 8 July 1815: 'The French exhibited at their successive debarkations and on the different marches to prison the same frivolity, the same thoughtlessness which has always characterised the French nation. They made themselves extremely merry with the round hats of the Royal Marines who escorted them, addressed the spectators in the most vivacious manner and talked of Davenport Depot with the familiarity which a former residence must have induced. Many of them observed that they knew the road to Dartmoor better than the Marines did.' Other newspapers were less light-hearted. Stormed one: 'The American prisoners who we recently released at Dartmoor, in marching from that place, passed a body of French prisoners as they were conducted to that depot. The Americans halted and saluted the French with a shout of "Vive l'Emperor", but this salute was not returned by the latter who continued their march in sullen silence.'

At least the French would not have to suffer long at Dartmoor. By January newspapers were reporting that Captain Shortland had been ordered by the London government to arrange for ships to take the men home. When they left, Dartmoor stayed empty until late October 1850, when major reconstruction work had transformed the damp walls into a home for 400 convicts, but the atmosphere among those destined to be kept within its cells would remain one of unhappiness and frustration.

In 1861, following a riot at Chatham Prison, an inspection at Dartmoor revealed: 'It appears that the convict establishment is in a more disorderly and insubordinate condition than the prison at Chatham, where the mutiny lately occurred. The officers of the establishment here have been assaulted time after time in a most desperate manner, and it was only a few days since that a plot for a general rising was opportunely discovered and consequently prevented. The prison inspector had visited the place and distributed the usual remedies, the "cat o' nine tails" and "starvation". But it is said that these desperate villains, during the time they were being flogged, uttered expressions of savage exultation and defiance.'

Time would show that things did not improve.

5

PORRIDGE RIOT

IN A RANKING OF THE worst riots in British prison history, Dartmoor takes the top two places, with the 1815 massacre followed by an appalling mutiny in 1932. There have been many other mutinies or riots, but none as widespread or sinister as the events of 24 January 1932. A newspaper reporter at the time gave this account:

Amazing scenes were enacted at Dartmoor Prison when over one hundred convicts attacked the warders, set the prison on fire, attempted to capture the governor and were fired on, seventy being injured. Trouble had been brewing at the prison for over a fortnight and it came to a head yesterday morning when, after creating an uproar in their cells, a number of the prisoners threw their porridge over the warders. The uproar became so great that it was decided to allow the prisoners out for exercise. As soon as the men were together, the struggle started, a number of the convicts attacking the warders with improvised weapons.

For over two hours there was a stern struggle between the convicts and armed warders. A dozen warders were seriously injured.

As though following a pre-arranged plan, a group of convicts dashed off to the Governor's office in the centre of the prison and, raking out the coal fire, set light to the building. In a very few minutes flames were leaping over the prison and were visible for miles around. Fifty policemen were sent out in motor cars and military details ordered to turn out, over one hundred soldiers parading in fighting equipment and steel helmets and two machine gun squads. A terrific struggle raged inside the prison. Convicts attempted to escape in all directions and over a hundred of them tried to scale the high boundary wall. The warders, however, had anticipated this move and, armed with rifles, occupied every vantage point. They were forced to shoot and for over two hours the noise of rifle reports mingled with the crackling of the flames. Practically every resident in Princetown was enrolled as a special constable and given a rifle.

In March, thirty-two convicts went on trial, charged under an Act of 1861 that: 'On the 24th January 1932 at Princetown in the County of Devon, being riotously and tumultuously assembled together in the disturbance of the peace, did feloniously and unlawfully pull down or destroy, or begin to demolish, pull down or destroy, a building devoted to public use, or erected or maintained by public contribution.'

The hearing was sensational, not least because it was clear that widespread flogging was responsible for most of the ill feeling among the prisoners. During the cross-examination of an aptly named warder called Ernest Birch, he was asked if he was responsible for splitting open the head of convict Thomas Davis, a thirty-three-year-old chauffer who was accused of slashing another officer before being knocked senseless.

'I do not know,' replied Birch.

The next question, 'Do you know how many ribs of his have been broken?' resulted in the same response. The interrogation continued.

'Can you tell me how many men have been flogged in the prison through your reports?'

'No, sir.'

'Have you lost count of them?'

'I expect I have.'

'How many times have you been assaulted?'

'About four times.'

'Is that a record for an officer to be assaulted four times?'

'No, sir.'

Another warder told how up to eighty convicts had stormed the Governor's office armed with pick shafts, sledgehammers, iron bars and stones. On their way to the trial, the convicts had been heard singing, 'Pack Up Your Troubles In Your Old Kit Bag' and 'Tipperary', and during a lunch break at their trial, each of the accused was given a cigarette, prescribed by the prison doctor 'as a sedative'. Five of the accused had something to sing about when the trial ended. They were cleared. But others were given sentences totalling nearly 100 years, which they were told they would have to start serving once they had finished their current stretches.

Thomas Davis, thought to be the ringleader of the mutiny, got twelve years, and Mr Justice Finlay told him: 'You yourself said that you intended to mark the man whom you attacked, and to mark him for life.' Davis' was the heaviest sentence and while others had been just as involved in the rioting, the jury begged for mercy on behalf of some.

John Jackson, an engineer, aged thirty-eight, had been jailed for six years in 1921 for highway robbery and was ordered to be given fifteen strokes of the cat. He had been sent to Dartmoor in 1930 for ten years after an armèd robbery on a post office. A senior police officer told the judge: 'He is an intelligent, determined and violent criminal and unscrupulous to a degree. He will go to any lengths to dominate his fellow criminals.' However, there were reasons why the judge wanted to show Jackson mercy.

During the trial, warder Frank Sims Milton said he had been in the school with a teacher when the mutiny started, and they found themselves being invaded by a horde of raging convicts, who'd screamed: 'Kill every one of them. Spare none.' It was only the intervention of Jackson and London bookmaker Charles John Sparks that saved their lives. So while others were getting longer sentences, Jackson, a father of seven children – one of them blind – was told he would have to serve an extra six years.

Sparks, aged thirty, had been serving five years at Dartmoor for conspiracy to steal and for being a habitual criminal. The judge was told: 'He lived with the sister of an associate. This woman is known as the "Bobbed-Hair Bandit". He is concerned with smash and grab raids. He escaped from Manchester prison but was recaptured on the following day. He is known to the police as one of the motor bandit-type, without the slightest regard for other people's life and property. He and Jackson have been associated for many years and he is a leader of criminals as Jackson is. When he was at Wandsworth Prison, the Bobbed-Hair Bandit was in a motorcar outside with other criminals. They had ropes which they threw over the wall. One man got away, but was arrested afterwards. Sparks was caught just as he was going to climb out of the prison.' The bookmaker was given an extra four years.

There were other occasional glimpses of mercy being shown. Edward James, a twenty-nine-year-old fitter from London, was a member of the same gang as Jackson and Sparks. 'He is a most desperate criminal,' the judge heard. 'Their gang worked from the Elephant and Castle neighbourhood and used stolen cars to commit housebreaking offences and smash and grab raids throughout the country. After his conviction he was brought to Dartmoor and on the way down in the train attempted to escape. One of his confederates jumped out of the train and killed himself.' However, the jury had been told James had saved three lives during the mutiny. The judge told him: 'That induces me, in spite of your lamentable record, and despite the prominent part you played in these deplorable events, to pass a much more lenient sentence.' James was given a further eighteen months.

Another ringleader, seaman Joseph Conning, thirty, was given an extra ten years, as was Joseph Ibbeson, aged thirty-one, who told the judge as he was about to be sentenced: 'The prosecution has been tampered with. It has all been made up against me.'

Paedophile Frederick Smith, thirty-six, a stoker, received eight years after the judge told him: 'You have a disgusting record. I have no doubt you were a prominent ringleader.' William Mason, thirty-four, a tailor, was given eight years, as was Thomas Hollows, a thirty-one-year-old labourer; mechanic James Horn, thirty-three, received another twenty-one months, and fireman Patrick Kavanagh, thirty-eight, fifteen months.

One of the most remarkable cases was that of labourer Harry Stoddart, aged thirty-eight, who, during the Great War, had been taken prisoner by the Germans, escaped, made his way back to Allied lines and won the Military Medal for his role in the recapture of a village. After hearing about his Army exploits, despite his being a ringleader in the mutiny, the judge gave him four extra years.

Songwriter James Del Mar, thirty-one, was told he would serve a further eighteen months; baker Alexander Muir, thirty-two, three years; painter Joseph Taylor, thirty-three, three years; and schoolteacher Thomas Elliott Dewhurst, thirty, another three years. 'You played a somewhat contemptible part in this miserable affair,' the judge said. Another paedophile, salesman Walter Francis Moore, forty-two, was given three years.

Harry Burgess, a labourer, aged forty-one, had been serving in the Army in France during the Great War when he was sentenced to death for desertion before being reprieved and given penal servitude. He received an extra three years. When the judge gave him another three years, George Garton, a labourer, aged forty-three, told him: 'I thank you, my Lord, for giving me such a fair trial.' Labourer Frederick Roberts, twenty-six, had already tried escaping twice from prison, once only being forced to come down from a roof after a fire hose was turned on him. He received a further three years. Patrick Cosgrove, twenty-nine, a tailor, received twenty months and Sidney Tappexden, thirty, a porter, six months.

William Gardner, a twenty-nine-year-old carpenter, had been shot and severely wounded during the mutiny. The judge felt sorry for him and let him off with just a further six months.

During the trial, prisoners repeatedly complained about the number of floggings doled out at Dartmoor. But the beatings there continued, and while the reputation of the mutineers followed them as they were transferred to other prisons throughout England, it was obvious administrators elsewhere had determined that the lessons of Dartmoor and the consequences of over-zealous punishment would not deter them from continuing with regular floggings.

Resentment over these beatings led to major trouble at Wandsworth on the afternoon of 26 May 1954. In one of the crowded workshops, convicts were sewing mailbags in resentful silence, brooding over the flogging of two of their number from the day before. Suddenly the peace was shattered as two inmates, Scot William Dair and Thomas Edward Harris, leapt up, grabbed hammers and began laying into one of their guards. Other warders ran in to rescue their colleague, at which time three other convicts joined Dair and Harris. It was clear a full-scale riot was about to erupt, and it was only prevented from getting out of hand by the ringing of the alarm bell and the arrival of more guards. Realising their planned uprising was not attracting more support, the five rebels barricaded themselves into a storeroom while the workshop was cleared. Appeals for the mutineers to give up peaceably were ignored, and after an hour and a half they were charged by warders. In the brutal and bloody melee that followed, all five were injured together with twenty-one warders, five of whom needed hospital treatment.

An immediate investigation started, at which some convicts hoped to gain favour and extra remission by giving details of what was originally intended to be a major rising at which inmates would take control of the prison. The result was that the five principals were charged with mutiny and a sixth with incitement to mutiny, charges that carried long prison sentences. Following the inquiry, however, only Dair and Harris were singled out.

Corporal punishment had been abolished in 1948, but flogging was still allowed in prisons for serious attacks on staff, which meant that in July both were strapped to the sisters and flogged with the cat, Dair getting eighteen strokes and Harris six.

The day of the cat in England was dying out, but after its abolition in 1962, many called for it to be restored five years later when eighteen inmates went on the rampage in Durham Prison's top-security E Wing. This part of the jail had been opened in the early 1960s. It was thought to be escape-proof and housed some of the most desperate and dangerous men in the English prison system. By 1967 inmates included Moors murderer Ian Brady, armed robber John McVicar, police killer John Whitney, Great Train Robber Buster Edwards and men convicted of spying. Early in the year, resentment against warders erupted into violence. It all began when a prisoners' football disappeared. Staff claimed they knew nothing, but as is so often the case in prisons, a molehill grew into a mountain.

Inmates went on food strike over the missing ball, ignoring pleas for them to return to normal routine. Growing tension finally exploded, and eight E Wing inmates locked themselves into three cells, daring guards to come in to force them out. Three more joined the lock-in, then a further eight. The stand-off was only brought to an end when officers in riot gear and carrying batons smashed into the first three cells, overpowered the convicts inside and dragged them out. Realising they were outnumbered, the others gave up. It had lasted a day and a half, and while the ringleaders found themselves in solitary confinement, then separated after being transferred to other jails, they could at least claim a minor victory. At an inquiry in March, a committee of magistrates, appointed by the Home Office, agreed to hear evidence from twenty prisoners, who took the opportunity to air grievances about conditions that included food, restrictions on visiting – most of the E Wing inmates were from the London area, causing major problems for families and friends wanting to see them – and lack of recreational amenities.

Many of those same grievances were raised again in 1979 at Wormwood Scrubs. At that time, the prison system held dozens of men and women given very long sentences for offences connected to terrorism resulting from the Troubles in Northern Ireland. It was widely felt that the Scrubs was not equipped to hold men who felt particularly bitter towards the English State and who, in many cases, simply felt they ought to be serving their sentences in Northern Ireland. There were regular fights with English inmates, who were bitter over their fellow countrymen and -women and soldiers being killed and maimed in bomb attacks. The resentment increased with what many saw as frivolous grousing by the Irish inmates over such apparent trivialities as prison toothpaste, which, they complained, was gritty and caused the inside of their mouths to bleed, and the poor selection of toiletries such as deodorants and tissues. Some among the IRA contingent were convinced prison officers constantly picked on them, seeking to have them punished through a reduction or loss of privileges. There were half a dozen incidents in which officers were briefly taken hostage before being released.

It was obvious the growing tensions were about to boil over. The first incident was a rooftop protest, followed by a peaceful sit-in by inmates of D Wing, and then a full-scale riot in August, in which more than forty inmates and prison officers were injured. It was brought to a stop by a special team of prison officers known as the MUFTI – Minimum Use of Force Tactical Intervention – Squad. Yet what actually happened, and the bizarre reason for the outbreak, did not emerge until in 1982, with the publication of a report into the trouble, which made it plain there had been an attempt at the prison to cover up major shortcomings.

In the report, the Home Office admitted management at Wormwood Scrubs had lost authority and control. Even more damning was that a senior official of the prison service found *prima facie* evidence of criminal assaults on prisoners by prison officers. According to the report, Wormwood Scrubs governor Norman Honey and senior members of his staff gave an 'incomplete and misleading' version of the riot 'which made more believable allegations of brutality and of a deliberate cover-up'.

The trouble that August day began when warders started removing makeshift weightlifting equipment from cells. These consisted of broom handles with containers filled with water and sand on each end. When inmates complained, they were told the equipment could be used for weapons, and protestations of innocence by inmates were ignored. It was enough to spark real trouble, and soon word was spreading throughout the wing that a full-scale protest was about to begin. In no time the situation was out of hand. Senior prison staff were told the prisoners had weapons including rails ripped from landing staircases.

Reinforcements were called in from Wandsworth and Pentonville; the sight of coachloads of extra warders turning up armed with staves and riot shields caused panic. According to the report, seven minutes of confusion and chaos left thirty prisoners hurt, most of them with head injuries, and eleven officers needing treatment. Later, inmates told investigators that prisoners on the upper landings were forced to run a terrifying gauntlet through the MUFTI Squad and were smashed about the head and body on their way to their cells. Despite the seriousness of the incident, it was nearly a month before Home Office officials were told how many prisoners had suffered injuries.

And yet, according to the inquiry team, it could probably all have been avoided if a simple public-address announcement had been made, ordering prisoners to go back to their cells before they were attacked. The Home Office thought of holding a public inquiry, but it was decided that would only prolong the tension at the prison. That same concern was the reason why it took so long for the investigators' findings to be made known. There was a long delay too in announcing no warders were being charged, although the Home Office at least admitted, 'Mistakes were made at Wormwood Scrubs and important lessons must be drawn from them.'

6

FLIGHT TO FREEDOM

HARDLY ANYBODY IN prison wants to be there: that's why jails are designed to keep inmates in. But the reality is that no jail is escape-proof, and convicts have displayed remarkable ingenuity in devising ways of getting out. One of the legendary getaways was that of Scottish hardman Willie Leitch. While being held at Edinburgh's Saughton Jail in 1967, he spotted a group of local athletes exercising near the prison. Quick as a flash, Willie stripped to his vest and shorts, snatched a tin of boot polish and painted a number on his back, then grabbed a ladder and scaled the prison wall. As the runners jogged past, Willie joined in and kept on running. He was even waved through a police checkpoint after the alarm was raised. He was eventually recaptured, but became known as 'The Saughton Harrier'.

Four years later, Willie got clear in even more spectacular circumstances, this time from Craiginches Jail, in Aberdeen. He laid a series of springy wooden planks into a seesaw, leapt from a roof and was bounced over the prison wall, clearing it by ten feet and landing in the governor's cabbage patch. He was on the run for six months, spending some of that time hiding in the loft of an unwitting prison officer's home.

Going up, up and away was also how robbers John Kendall and Sydney Draper decided to get away from Gartree nick in Leicestershire in 1987. Their plan was ingenious. Accomplice

Andrew Russell hired a Bell 206 Longranger helicopter, saying he wanted to do an aerial survey. When the pilot neared Gartree, where scores of inmates were playing football in the exercise yard, Russell pointed a gun, forcing him to land the machine. Kendall and Draper were waiting and clambered on board while other cons prevented astonished screws from intervening. Kendall was caught ten days later, but Draper stayed on the run for more than a year. All later got lengthy stretches, Russell copping the heaviest punishment, of ten years. He ended up in Whitemoor Jail, Cambridgeshire, where he joined a group of IRA prisoners in an escape in 1994, in which a prison officer was shot.

Former schoolteacher Brian Lawrence was another who schemed an astonishing escape by helicopter. Sentenced to a minimum twenty-one years for committing one murder and planning two others, Lawrence plotted from his cell at Parkhurst on the Isle of Wight. He used lemon juice to write codes hidden in Sudoku puzzles and sent them to a couple of accomplices, who hired a chopper with part of the £500,000 Lawrence was raising by selling a quarry. During a 2010 music festival, when dozens of other helicopters would be in the air, the aircraft was to land in a section of Parkhurst not covered with the netting that most jails had fitted after the Gartree incident and whisk Lawrence away. However, his hopes of reaching Spain were scuppered when a sharp-eyed prison officer spotted the expression 'more heat, less light' in one of the killer's letters and warmed up one of the puzzles, revealing the secret messages. Lawrence knew police could quickly seal off the Isle of Wight in the event of an escape from its prison complex, which was why he tried flying away. That was also the idea of three other inmates who dreamed up a daring plan in 1994.

Keith Rose and Glaswegian Andrew Rodger were both convicted murderers. The third member of their gang was Matthew Williams, a former genetics and microbiology student, whose crimes included leaving a bomb in a Liverpool street packed with Christmas shoppers, trying to poison his family by injecting sodium chlorate into a tin of tomatoes and stealing enough cyanide to wipe out 300 people. Williams had tried escaping previously. As he was being driven to Parkhurst, he threatened a prison officer with a hypodermic needle he claimed was filled with AIDS and had to be battered by other guards with truncheons.

The freedom bid of the trio became a major scandal and resulted in the then head of the prison service being fired. Appalling prison security allowed the three to unlock a door during an exercise period, cut through a mesh fence and scale the prison wall with a steel ladder Rodger had secretly made from stolen goal posts right under the noses of guards. Rose was a qualified pilot, and they made their way to an airport, hoping to steal a light aircraft, but couldn't get a plane to start. They hid out, intending to steal a boat and get to mainland Britain, but five days after their escape, they were spotted by an off-duty prison officer and recaptured. All had long stretches added to their existing sentences.

Paramilitaries in Northern Ireland didn't bother with the niceties of trying to steal aircraft or organising helicopter rides. Their preferred method of escape was much more direct. In 1983 at the Maze Prison in County Antrim, thirty-eight Republican inmates – half a dozen of them armed with handguns – snatched the lorry carrying their dinners and smashed their way to freedom, shooting two guards and injuring another, who died from a heart attack. One escaper drowned and half were soon recaptured, but many were at large for years, during which time a handful were killed by security services or Loyalist paramilitaries. It was the biggest mass escape in British prison history.

Spurred on by that success, the IRA decided to attempt another mass escape, this time in 1989, by blowing up one of the walls surrounding Belfast's Crumlin Road Jail with a huge bomb carried in a JCB digger. Stolen cars for fleeing inmates to use were parked nearby, but the plan came to nothing when the digger had a puncture.

The use of smuggled guns was rare in prison escape attempts but happened occasionally. As Nessan Quinlivan and Pearse McAuley were being escorted back to their cells at Brixton Prison from Mass in 1991, McAuley produced a small calibre handgun from a training shoe, fired several shots and forced warders to hand over their keys so the pair could reach the prison yard. There they scaled the seventeen-foot-high wall by piling a wheelbarrow on top of a dog kennel. In the street outside they forced a prison officer at gunpoint to give them his car, and after driving less than 200 yards, they shot the driver of another motor and hijacked his car. They were both arrested in the Republic two years later.

Three years later, shots were again fired, this time at Whitemoor, when five IRA Volunteers and Andrew Russell climbed two high walls and a steel mesh fence. The escapers had two handguns and a prison officer was shot and slightly wounded. All six were quickly recaptured and both guns recovered. But that was not the end of the story. Russell and fellow escaper Danny McNamee sued the prison service, claiming they had been beaten up after they were caught, and both were awarded damages – Russell £2,500 and McNamee £5,000.

Simeon Langford decided that if he couldn't go over the wall, he'd simply go through – the same method used by an escaping inmate in the highly praised film *The Shawshank Redemption*. Langford was on remand in Exeter Jail in 2011, alleged to have assaulted staff at another jail, and fed up waiting for his day in court, he made his freedom bid. The judge at his trial described what happened: 'There was a routine inspection and brick dust was found beneath the outside wall and after a search of your room, officers found plastic cutlery with screws attached, sheets and paint. You had concealed what you were doing with papier-mâché. This was an ingenious and inventive attempt but was doomed to failure.' Because Langford had already spent so much time behind bars, he was given a short sentence.

From time to time convicts go to remarkable lengths in attempts to escape. In 2010 Michael O'Donnell hit on the idea of getting himself taken to hospital so he could escape from the ambulance taking him there. He told pals on the outside about his plan, then sliced off part of his ear. The ambulance was attacked by his co-conspirators, and O'Donnell fled. Not long after being recaptured, he hanged himself in his cell at Forest Bank Jail, Salford, Cheshire.

Andrew Farndon cut himself across his shoulder in 2013, told staff at Highpoint Jail in Suffolk he was the victim of an attack and was taken to hospital, where pal Gary Cowan pointed a gun at three guards and both ran off. They were caught in Scotland.

Prison staff are often blamed – sometimes with justification – when inmates escape, so it was hardly surprising when they decided to take no chances with Britain's most notorious convict, former armed robber Charles Bronson, a one-time circus strongman. Eyebrows were raised when Bronson took up knitting at Wakefield Jail in Yorkshire. 'I'm knitting a scarf,' he told curious staff, who watched as the scarf grew and grew. When it reached forty-five feet it was confiscated, Bronson claiming the reason given by prison staff was that he was planning to use the scarf in an escape attempt.

Prisoners escape because they want to be free. But not armed robber Timothy Stern. As his time for release neared, he was moved to Leyhill open prison near Bristol to get used to having greater freedom. Stern immediately absconded and made his way back to his old nick, high-security HMP Bullingdon in Oxfordshire, where he knocked on the door and demanded to be let back in. Staff refused, and so Stern sat outside and waited for police to arrest him. 'My family live near Bullingdon and I want to be near them,' he said.

Associates of the Great Train Robber Charlie Wilson went one further than Stern. They actually broke into a jail to get him out because it was widely believed Wilson had been treasurer of the audacious hijack and knew the whereabouts of much of the £2.6 million proceeds of the crime. Wilson had been jailed for thirty years and sent to Winson Green Jail near Birmingham. Four months later, in the middle of the night, a three-man gang climbed over the wall of the jail and, using a duplicate pass key, opened a series of doors, allowing them onto the landing and giving access to Wilson's cell. The patrolling guard was knocked unconscious, Wilson's door was unlocked and he was given a pile of civilian clothing into which he changed before being hustled to freedom, climbing over the main wall up a ladder. Wilson fled to Canada, where he stayed on the run for four years before being recaptured.

His escape raised questions as to how the plotters managed to get hold of the duplicate key. It also prompted a discussion in Parliament, where Lord Molson said:

I do not make any point of the unfortunate escape of Charles Frederick Wilson, the train robber, because that was obviously an extremely carefully and skilfully planned enterprise by the same people who had planned the Great Train Robbery. I do not think that one can reasonably complain when so much ingenuity has been used by such extremely able men in carrying out a rescue, if it is successful. I am sure all these escapes are a matter of great public concern. Too small a proportion of the known criminals in this country are convicted. With all the difficulties that legal procedure and evidence puts in the way of a conviction, when people are convicted and rightly sentenced to imprisonment, it is really a very serious matter that there should be so many escapes from prisons of all kinds. These escapers are dangerous, as is shown by the records of these men. They are a great danger to the people who live in the vicinity of these gaols, especially to the aged, to women and to those who are not able to defend themselves.

When a man has broken out of gaol he usually commits some offences, whether it is trespassing or stealing food and clothes, or taking and driving away a car, or perhaps something even more serious than these offences.

I understand that there was one case where a convict escaped from an open prison with the wife of one of his warders. In other cases, prisoners have escape while enjoying recreation, which is a part of the reformative treatment, or while working outside of prison or, as on a large number of cases, when they have gone to hospital for examination or treatment, whether they were really suffering from an ailment or suspected ailment or whether that was part of the method adopted in order to escape.

7

MOTHERS IN SHACKLES

FOR ALMOST FORTY YEARS, until her death at the age of sixty in 2002, Myra Hindley was the most hated woman in Britain. Her role in the Moors Murders, the appalling slaughter of five children aged between ten and seventeen, ensured she would never be safe whether in or out of prison. Newspapers regularly published photographs and news stories about Hindley, meaning she would be instantly recognised and at immediate risk if she was ever set free. It was no surprise then that when Hindley plotted to escape from Holloway Prison, she planned to head six thousand miles away, to Brazil in South America.

Hindley was, in fact, lucky to be alive and in Holloway. She and her co-conspirator Ian Brady could have been hanged. Just two years before the vile pair killed the last of their victims, Edward Evans, aged seventeen, in October 1965, Henry John Burnett had been hanged at Craiginches Prison in Aberdeen for murder. But in November 1965, a month after their arrest and while they were on remand awaiting trial, politicians passed the Murder (Abolition of Death Penalty) Act 1965, which suspended the death penalty for murder in England, Scotland and Wales for five years and replaced it with life imprisonment. Hanging on the mainland was finally abolished in December 1969.

There is nothing unusual about lesbianism in women's prisons, and Holloway was home to many, like Hindley, who were sexually active and facing extremely long sentences. A former official at the jail claimed many officers there were gay and involved in sexual relationships with inmates or fellow guards. Hindley was no exception. Her crimes were so horrific that most females were repulsed by the thought of giving her love and comfort, but some others were attracted by her sheer notoriety. If anything could be said to be conventional about Myra Hindley, it was that before her jailing she had a male lover in Glasgow-born Brady. But their fusion was the formula for real evil.

There were five known victims of the pair: Edward Evans, Lesley Ann Downey, aged ten, John Kilbride, twelve, Keith Bennett, twelve, and sixteen-year-old Pauline Reade; but at Chester Assizes in 1966 they were only charged with murdering Lesley Ann, John and Edward. The then Attorney General, Sir Elwyn Jones, gave a taste of the sort of horrors that would spill out during their trial. 'In association with all these killings, there was present not only a sexual element but an abnormal sexual element, a perverted sexual element,' he told the jury at the outset. As the dreadful story of torture and sadistic killing unfolded, the tragedy became known as the Moors Murders because the bodies of Lesley Ann and John had been discovered in shallow graves on Saddleworth Moor in the South Pennines. The trial ended with Brady being convicted of all three murders and Hindley of killing Edward and Lesley Ann. Both were jailed for life.

As the years passed, Hindley moved through a succession of prisons and a handful of occasional female lovers. Immediately after the trial she had unsuccessfully appealed against her conviction. She and Brady kept in touch by letter for a time, but five years into her sentence she wrote to him for the final time to ditch him, because her affections were elsewhere. Hindley had been introduced to attractive, dark-haired Holloway Prison warder Patricia Cairns, and for both, it was a case of love at first sight. Cairns would later claim she had no idea of Hindley's evil background. She had missed the sensational press coverage of the Moors Murders trial because at the time she was a Carmelite nun living in an enclosed convent and effectively cut off from the real world. During the late 1960s she began questioning whether her faith was strong enough to bind her to life in a convent and left to join the prison service. But by then the frenzy over Brady and Hindley had calmed down.

Cairns and Hindley began exchanging letters and finding excuses to meet in the prison chapel, during games of table tennis and even in cells. They believed their relationship was a secret. In fact, it was well known among other inmates and quietly supported by some gay staff, who knew what it was like to experience the general distaste for lesbians and sympathised with the lovers. When rumour of the relationship reached the prison hierarchy and the killer was asked for an explanation, Hindley reacted angrily to what she said were 'mendacious and wicked allegations', and claimed Cairns had simply been giving her 'considerable spiritual help'. Her explanation was accepted. An entry in Hindley's prison file recorded that, 'As a prisoner she presents herself as a very disciplined, very controlled person anxious never to transgress prison rules.'

It was the deepening of their love that led to the most sinister escape plot in the history of Holloway. Brief snatches together would never be enough to satisfy their desire for one another, but it was another inmate, Maxine Croft, who came up with an idea that had already crossed their minds. Croft pointed out a fact that was obvious to everyone: that it was only a matter of time before their affair reached the ears of senior staff, who would have to take a course of action to end it, including sacking Cairns and turfing Hindley off to another jail. They only had a future if they escaped, she told them. The idea grew as, one by one, solutions were found to each problem. How to get out? Simple, Croft said: Cairns had access to prison keys, so why not make an impression of the master keys and use them to unlock doors and gates? How to get away? Easy. Croft was a forger and promised she could provide bogus passports, visas and even money. Where to go? Brazil, where nobody knew them and there was no extradition agreement in place that could put them at risk of being returned to the UK in the unlikely event of their being discovered.

It was now that the scheme would take a new and more dangerous turn. Hindley's cellmate at Holloway was Anna Mendelssohn, a writer and political activist who had been arrested in 1971 by detectives investigating the Angry Brigade, an anarchist group who carried out a series of bomb outrages in Britain. A police raid had uncovered machine guns, gelignite and ammunition. She had been remanded to Holloway, an experience she hated, and which left her sick and troubled. Mendelssohn had links to the terrorists, and in 1972 she was convicted of conspiracy to cause explosions and possessing armaments. She was jailed for ten years and, back at Holloway, empathised with anyone wanting to escape from that hellhole.

Meanwhile, Croft had not been idle. With the help of Cairns, she had made plaster casts of three keys and had the impression of a fourth in a bar of soap. A crony on the outside had already agreed to use the moulds to make metal replicas of the keys and waited for the postman to deliver a package containing the impressions. Security at Holloway itself was poor, but elsewhere in London it had been stepped up as a result of a series of letter bombs and explosions perpetrated by the IRA. Those explosions included a car bomb that exploded outside the Old Bailey in early 1973, injuring 200 people, one of who died as the result of a heart attack brought on by the blast. Among those arrested following a huge police dragnet were sisters Dolours and Marian Price from Belfast. Before their trial they had been held in Holloway and went back there to start life sentences and made it clear they did not want to stay in England.

The effect of the IRA terror campaign had been to step up checks on parcels for potential letter bombs. During one of these checks the package containing the key impressions aroused suspicion. It was opened and police were informed. Investigations led to Holloway and the certainty that an escape was being organised. Secretly, detectives began infiltrating the prison and scrutinising staff with the inevitable result that the relationship between Hindley and Cairns was discovered. Cairns was put under surveillance. Her every movement was monitored and a report by a senior police officer would reveal a chain of contacts that linked Hindley and the escape attempt to the Price sisters. One day, detectives watched as Cairns met a woman in a London snack bar. This woman was an occasional visitor of Hindley's at Holloway. She was also known to have helped an Angry Brigade sympathiser who was already on the police radar as having IRA contacts in Belfast and had at one stage shared the dock with Mendelssohn. And Mendelssohn was a close friend of Hindley.

The plotters meantime continued with their planning, totally unaware the police net was closing about them. Once the keys were made and sent back to them, they would use them to get outside the cell blocks and, using a ladder, clamber over the outer wall and in a waiting motor head to Heathrow, where they would take a late-night flight to South America and start a new life of freedom. But suddenly it all came to nothing. Worried at the prospect of the IRA becoming involved in a mass escape from Holloway, police swooped. Cairns was arrested, and in 1974 she was jailed for six years for conspiring to help Hindley escape. The conviction meant she lost her job, but despite a ban on either woman ever again having contact with one another, Hindley sent her coded letters which went unanswered.

In 1987 the grave of Pauline Reade was discovered on Saddleworth Moor, but Hindley died in 2002, aged sixty, still in prison and taking with her to the grave the whereabouts of the body of Keith Bennett. Cairns served four years of her sentence and when she was freed moved to the north of England to live alone.

The prison service had come close to a major catastrophe and it found itself having to fight off claims of incompetence later, in 1994, when three women who had been remanded to Holloway – one of them facing a murder charge – escaped. They had sneaked off from a party of inmates as they were being escorted back to their cells from the exercise yard. The trio smashed a window and climbed though it on the roof of the jail swimming pool, which allowed them to reach the outside wall. Climbing over it, they simply walked off. Police warned the public all the escapers were dangerous. They were soon recaptured, but the incident meant that Holloway personnel were taking no chances, even if it meant the jail finding itself in the centre of a full-scale controversy.

In 1996 it was revealed that a woman remanded to Holloway while she was pregnant, had given birth in hospital after being forced to spend much of her labour shackled to her bed. Mary Newburn of the National Childbirth Trust, said: 'We should not be shackling women who are having babies. It is archaic and completely inappropriate. To start your motherhood in shackles is terrible.' It was admitted that while the woman had not been shackled in the delivery room, immediately she went out to the toilet or to make a telephone call, prison staff shackled her. According to the prison service: 'If you are capable of getting up and walking downstairs and making a telephone call, there is a possibility you could escape.'

The row escalated when it was confirmed that it was policy to shackle pregnant women. During a lively debate in the House of Commons, the then Minister of State for Prisons, Ann Widdecombe, defended the practice: 'Some Members may like to think that a pregnant woman would not or could not escape, but unfortunately, that is not true. In a recent case, a prisoner who was four and a half months pregnant jumped from a first-floor window during an antenatal appointment. In a further incident, a male prisoner who was diagnosed as completely

71

paralysed jumped up and ran away as soon as his bed watch was withdrawn. The prison service has a duty of care to the mother, but that must be balanced against the needs of the service to keep all prisoners – including pregnant women prisoners – in secure custody. I am satisfied that the policy is right.'

When it suspected another escape might be on the cards, the prison service made it plain it was taking no chances. Sandra Gregory was working in Thailand as an occasional English-language teacher when she ran short of money. In 1993, as she was about to leave the country, she was searched at Bangkok's Don Muang Airport and found to be carrying heroin. She was sentenced to death, but this was first commuted to life imprisonment and then reduced to twenty-five years. In June 1997 she was transferred to Britain to complete her sentence and held at Holloway, where she was put under close surveillance. Almost immediately her antics caused concern. She posted out her passport and jewellery, and prison security staff noticed how she appeared friendly with a man who regularly struck up a conversation with her, even though he was visiting another Holloway inmate. Although there was no firm evidence of an escape plan, Gregory was moved to Foston Hall in Derbyshire. But even there, staff had concerns about her and she was again moved, this time to top-security Durham Prison. Gregory did get out of prison without serving her full term. Following impassioned pleas by her family, she was pardoned by the King of Thailand in 2002 and set free.

In 2009 Holloway staff were left with red faces and described in a *Sun* newspaper headline as 'Porridge Oafs' after admitting the jail was the setting for the escape that never was. A full-scale search was mounted when a check revealed remand prisoner Aishatu Ishaku was missing. It was thought she had literally walked out of the prison by tagging on to a visiting church group. Police were notified, ports and airports warned to be on the lookout for her, helicopters scrambled to search the streets around

Holloway and tracker dogs were brought in. Five days later she was recaptured – still inside Holloway. Aishatu had saved up a supply of food and water and sneaked into the roof space of the education centre. The searchers had looked everywhere – except Holloway.

8

DEATH ON THE MOOR

ESCAPE PLOTS WERE not, of course, confined to Holloway. Every jail has its stories to tell of how determined and imaginative escapers could be. Getting out of Dartmoor Prison, for example, was easy; the problem was how to get off the moor. From the very earliest days when it held American and French prisoners of war, men did runners, but without outside help to get them food, warmth and transport, their chances of showing a permanent clean pair of heels were remote. It was a grim, terrible place, and even back in 1964, during a Parliamentary debate, it emerged there were plans to close it and build another elsewhere. Little wonder inmates ran off – a fact about which Lord Molson complained, saying,

In former days, Dartmoor owed its security to two factors. In the first place, the warders were perfectly ready to use their carbines and sabres; the prisoners knew this, and they seldom had to use them. The other factor was the terrain. Some sixty years ago Dartmoor was a wilderness, scattered with bogs, wild and almost trackless. To cross Dartmoor then without a compass and a really good map was not only difficult but dangerous. Today things have altered. The warders have become so humane. Public opinion insists on such humane conduct from them – I do not complain of it, but it is a factor of which we must take account – that if, at

74

the end of a long, arduous chase, one warder gets a little rough with the prisoner he has recaptured, there is an inquiry and public opinion is brought into play.

Then Dartmoor's character has altered. It is now crossed by excellent roads and many – too many – tracks. There are forestry plantations where a man may hide. There are landmarks in the shape of television masts and telegraph wires. And, above all, the bogs, I am informed by those who know them better, are drying up. It is not nearly so difficult or dangerous for an escaped prisoner to make his way across Dartmoor. Consequently, the authorities of the prison have to face this dilemma. They have to decide whether to keep a man in all day in the terrible circumstances of that old-fashioned prison – and that is a soul destroying thing to do – or allow him out on working parties in the knowledge that almost any day on Dartmoor a mist may descend and make it easy for him to escape. More and more men are escaping from the Moor.

Are all possible precautions being taken? I am under the impression that every time a prisoner escapes 'walkie-talkies' are hired and issued to the police who have to search Dartmoor. I should have thought it more sensible to make them a permanent part of police equipment. Now tracker dogs; why do we not keep tracker dogs at Princetown? Surely that is an obvious precaution. Is enough use being made of horses on the moor? There are hunts all round the moor. Has anybody thought of enrolling huntsmen and Masters of Hounds as special constables? Is enough use being made of the experience gained in guarding prisoners of war during the conflict? Have we turned new and first-class intelligence agencies on to this problem or are the Home Office content to go on in the old way, I wonder?

Often the 'old way' was to make a cursory search once a man was discovered missing, but then to let nature take its course with the cold and wet, the dangers of bogs and lack of cover wearing down the runaway until he gave himself up. Even if a man managed to make it off the moor, there were untold and frequently unexpected problems facing him. Typical was the plight of three young convicts who were being held at Dartmoor in 1850 prior to being transported. Not fancying spending at least the next ten years in Australia, they escaped and headed for Plymouth, snatching sleep behind the shelter of walls and living on raw turnips and even corn. Their plan was to reach London, where they were confident they could easily be lost among the swelling population. All was going well until they arrived at a toll gate, and without money to pay they were forced to head for the nearby town of Ashburton, where locals immediately realised from their unkempt appearance the trio were on the run. They were arrested and sent back to jail.

The ever-present damp affected not just inmates and warders; it also soaked into the walls leaving some sections crumbling and vulnerable to anyone with a sharp tool such as a knife or spoon. In the winter of 1876, anxious to get out and spend Christmas with his family, a convict began hacking away at the wall of his cell. His weeks of secret toil brought him to within inches of freedom until, in late December, the hole was discovered. The only reward for his efforts was a flogging.

Beatings, being locked in solitary confinement in irons and forced to spend weeks on end on a bread-and-water diet were regular punishments for misdemeanours. Not surprisingly, convicts felt bitter and resentful. None more so than Joseph Denny, a persistent thief from London, who in 1881 had been sent down for eight years for theft. When the judge at the Old Bailey sentenced him, Denny shouted, 'Why don't you send me to the gallows? I'll commit murder before I'm done.' He was sent to Dartmoor, where warders, mindful of his threat, kept a close eye on him. Possibly because of his promise to kill, Denny was picked on and bullied by guards, but belligerence and refusal to obey instructions were cited as the reasons for his being put on bread and water for long spells and regularly chained up. Denny argued he was penalised because he was coloured. Staff must have been glad when he was freed and went off to sea. But he continued to sulk and harbour a grudge against the chief warder over his treatment. Finally, he snapped and in August 1890, carrying a knife and matches to start a blaze, he broke into Dartmoor, hell bent on murdering the officer. Luck was against Denny. Although he managed to climb the perimeter wall using a clothesline, his foot tangled in a wire that set off an alarm bell. Within minutes he was found in an outhouse and battered before being formally arrested and handed over to the police.

Some men were so desperate to escape Dartmoor's miseries that they would try getting away even though warders were armed. Not all were lucky. In late 1896, under cover of approaching darkness and fog, William Carter and two other convicts fled from a working party that was being marched back to the jail. Guards opened fire, killing Carter. His companions were caught soon after. And it wasn't only the warders who killed. Escapers ran a gauntlet of bogs that could suck a man under in seconds, as well as old mine workings and defunct quarries. In 1951 convicts Frank Cook and Walter Smith took advantage of the early December darkness, low cloud and a mist that reduced visibility to a few feet to disappear. Within minutes the alarm had been sounded and bloodhounds were brought in to join the police and prison officers' search. The escape had been carefully planned, but the pair quickly lost their way, and as they blundered around, twenty-four-year-old Cook first lost sight of his companion then heard a scream and a crash. Shouting out Smith's name, he heard faint cries and eventually found himself on the edge of a cliff face, part of a worked-out quarry. At the foot of a 100-foot drop he found twenty-six-year-old Smith, semi-conscious, unable to move and in extreme pain. Cook could have abandoned his friend and made his way off the moor but, instead, he frantically looked about for help, eventually stopping a motorist who, probably unsurprisingly after being confronted by a bedraggled stranger in the darkness, refused to return to the quarry with Cook, but instead promised to get an ambulance. He did, and police and ambulancemen found the stricken man, who was taken to hospital with severe back injuries. Cook was returned to Dartmoor.

Eight years later, another escape came to grief in near identical but more tragic circumstances. It would feature one of the most colourful characters ever to see the inside of the grim prison walls. Dennis Stafford could have grown up to be a successful businessman or a show-business entrepreneur. He had the brains and the looks. Born in the East End of London, his dad Joe was an on-course bookmaker and pub owner, while mother Margaret had been born a Roman Catholic but, to please her husband, converted to Judaism. The Staffords were near neighbours of the Kray family and as a teenager Dennis had his first run-in with Ronnie and Reggie when he witnessed a dance-hall fracas prompted by the twins. The glitter and thrill of London's vibrant nightlife were magnets to a young man desperate to make an impression, but being a regular clubber, he needed money, and so Stafford turned to the underworld and crime. Inevitably, he was jailed after being caught with a handgun during a break-in. He went off to Wormwood Scrubs to begin a seven-year sentence but escaped and, realising he was bound to be recognised if he remained in London, he headed north to Newcastle-upon-Tyne. It was the beginning of a relationship with Geordieland that would ultimately lead to a sensational crime that is still a major talking point in the region.

Newcastle too had its own colourful nightlife and soon debonair Stafford was a popular and familiar face. He splashed out money made from a series of frauds, but the brash cockney man-about-town soon interested the local police, who sent his photograph to detectives in London. Tipped off by pals in the capital, he was about to be collared as an escaped prisoner when Stafford did another runner, this time to Trinidad, where he basked in the baking sun. But it was not only the police who missed him. So did one of his girlfriends, who sent him a telegram begging him to come home. Detectives had waited for her to make a move, and when she did her message was intercepted. Stafford was arrested in Port of Spain and extradited back to Britain. At Newcastle-upon-Tyne Assizes, he was given another seven-year stretch for conspiracy to defraud, and hauled off to Dartmoor.

On the moor he teamed up with another con, William Joseph Day, and soon the pair were plotting an escape. They were determined not to fall into the same trap as others who had got away easily enough only to lose their way and become bewildered in the darkness and fog. With the help of other inmates, they put together a home-made compass made from a bottle top, drawing pin and razor blade, and on 5 January 1959 they made their move. For weeks the two men had been secretly filing through iron bars over a workshop window. Now they climbed through and, using a scaffolding pole as a ladder, heaved themselves over the outer wall, setting off onto the moor in torrential rain. Day's freedom was short-lived. As they ran along a road, the pair saw approaching headlights and flung themselves over a fence. On the other side was a reservoir. Day plummeted in, while Stafford's fall was halted by a post holding a lifebelt. He would later tell pals he had leapt in to try to save Day, who screamed he couldn't swim, but had been unable to reach him. Suddenly, Day's cries stopped. Stafford dragged himself out and made for Plymouth. At Roborough, eight miles from the jail, he broke into a garden shed and stole clothing, leaving behind his brightly coloured prison jacket, then stole a car and headed east, stopping to contact an associate in Poole, Dorset. His eventual destination was London, where he believed his dad was ill and needed his son. The stolen motor was dumped near Poole, from where Stafford continued on to warmth and safety.

Police stations all over Britain were alerted to be on the lookout for two men. But six weeks after the escape, workmen carrying out routine maintenance of the reservoir spotted a body. When frogmen recovered it, Day was identified. Where was Stafford? London, Newcastle-upon-Tyne, abroad? He appeared to have vanished into thin air, but his cocky confidence betrayed him. Instead of lying low, he returned to his old ways, and on 20 February he was spotted by an old school friend – who happened to be a police officer. Stafford went back to jail, locked in solitary confinement, from where the authorities were certain there was no escape. He was moved around a series of jails while he served out the remainder of his sentences. But it was after he was legally released that the real drama of Stafford's story would unfold.

Stafford had only been able to get off the moor by finding dry clothes and a motor and then a helpful pal. Just how much of an ordeal Dartmoor could be was shown in 1963 when convict Henry Bramley literally walked away from the jail in thick mist. He endured a remarkable six days on the moor in rain, sleet and freezing temperatures, eventually wandering to Tavistock, just seven miles from the prison, where he knocked on the door of a local couple and announced he wanted to give himself up because he was so cold and exhausted. A survival expert commented: 'To be out on the moor in appalling weather in January and to still be alive after almost a week is remarkable. Bramley must have had an astonishing determination to get away, and it was this that probably kept him going when most others would have quit much sooner.'

Just how sapping the conditions on the moor could be was explained by ace escaper Walter 'Angel Face' Probyn to Paul Buck, author of *Prison Break: True Stories of the World's Greatest Escapes*. According to Probyn, who disappeared from a working party outside Dartmoor in August 1964, everyone was afraid of the terrain and the climatic conditions of the moors themselves: 'If you kept to the roads you were picked up. If you ventured off the roads you fell into a bog or went around in circles, particularly in the pitch darkness of night.' Probyn made sixteen escapes from prisons all over Britain.

His wife, Beryl, had urged him to serve out his five-year sentence, imposed for shopbreaking, in Dartmoor, but he would have none of it after getting wind that she was being pestered by a former boyfriend. On the day he made his move, Probyn was a member of a working party renovating prison officers' houses at Princetown. As a fog descended, he simply hoisted a bag of plaster onto his shoulder and walked off. Once out of sight, he dumped the bag and, using a compass smuggled in to him some time earlier, set off. The alarm was quickly raised and a series of roadblocks were set up. Probyn almost wandered into one, but after five days, by which time he was confident the search would have been scaled down, he telephoned a relative, who arrived with a car packed with dry clothes, food and drink. Probyn was on the run for seven weeks before he was arrested after an incident in Poplar, London. Shots were fired at police as they moved in, having spotted Probyn and Beryl in a shop. He was remanded to Wormwood Scrubs, from where he tried to escape, and claimed he was badly beaten up, suffering a broken arm. The following February, Probyn was jailed for a further twelve years.

Probably the simplest escape from Dartmoor was that of Frank 'The Mad Axeman' Mitchell on 12 December 1966. Mitchell, a giant, broad-chested strongman, was as mad as the proverbial Hatter. He had been certified insane and spent time as a patient at both Broadmoor and Rampton hospitals. His 'Axeman' tag stuck after he absconded from Broadmoor in 1958 and forced his way into the home of an elderly couple, threatening them with an axe until he was overpowered by police and jailed for life. He was sent to Wandsworth and then Dartmoor, where, as the years passed, his behaviour seemed to improve. He was even thought to be sufficiently trustworthy to be allowed to join outside working parties. The truth was that despite remarkably lax treatment, Mitchell was deeply and increasingly frustrated at not being given a release date, and he made his restlessness known in letters to his old friend Ronnie Kray, who he had met at Wandsworth.

Kray reckoned the twins could improve their image within the underworld by doing Mitchell a favour, and came up with the idea of helping him escape and then publicising his case. In the spring of 1966, Mitchell was overheard telling three visitors, 'I want to be home for Christmas,' and one had replied, 'You won't be here for Christmas.' He was urged to continue giving the impression of being a model prisoner and of making sure he was a member of outside working parties. And he did. He was often left unsupervised to a degree where he wandered off with another inmate and visited local pubs. The prosecution at the later trial of nine men accused of helping Mitchell escape pointed out: 'It is quite clear he had ample opportunity to communicate with persons outside the prison.'

Many would later wonder how the prison hierarchy continued to allow convicts outside to work because by 12 December eight inmates had run off from working parties. As it was, on that day Mitchell and four others, under the direction of one officer, were outside on the moor when the weather closed in. They took shelter in a hut until a lorry arrived to take them back to the prison. The weather could not have been better for the escape plan that had already been hatched. With no sign of improvement, Mitchell asked permission to take bread to a herd of wild ponies the party had seen earlier in the day. He was told to go ahead, but when the lorry arrived just under an hour later, there was no sign of him. By then, he had been met by two men in a hired Humber car and was speeding east towards London.

As 100 Royal Marines joined in the hunt for the Axeman, their quarry was already safe and warm. A flat had been organised, but Mitchell was about to discover he had exchanged the relative freedom of Dartmoor for a room where he was guarded round the clock by minders provided by the Krays. After a week, with his frustration mounting, Mitchell was provided with a woman companion, an attractive blonde club hostess named Liza. It was love at first sight, but even that was not enough to calm him, and he felt Ronnie Kray was ignoring him. He threatened to call on the twins, which posed a problem. If he was spotted and recaptured then the Krays' role in his escape might well be discovered. Something had to be done, and so Mitchell was promised he would spend Christmas with Ronnie.

On 23 December a van pulled up outside the flat. Mitchell was bundled inside and immediately a number of shots rang out. One Kray associate was heard to tell another: 'They gave him four injections in the nut.' Mitchell was never seen again. A number of men, including the Kray twins, were charged with his murder, but acquitted. So was underworld hardman Frankie Fraser. Once found 'Not Guilty', he could not be charged again and so Fraser felt sufficiently safe to later admit he had shot Mitchell, whose body was tied up with chicken wire and dumped in the English Channel. Nine men went on trial charged with helping Mitchell escape. Most were cleared, but Reggie Kray and Wallace William Garelick were convicted and jailed.

No sooner had the politicians expressed irritation over the apparent ease with which inmates were able to get away from Dartmoor than alarm bells were ringing once again. On Boxing Day 1966, five prisoners took their keys after tying up two warders, let themselves out of the gymnasium and got over the outside wall after climbing onto a bench and a table. Raymond Hanney, twenty-six, was caught within a couple of hours, and John Kenneth Johnston twenty-seven, four days later as he wandered over a railway bridge. It was the capture of the next two that caused hilarity.

Mark Owens, aged thirty-two, and twenty-eight-year-old John Thompson had reached Ashburton, ten miles from the prison, after stealing a car, when they decided to lie low at a local farm and hid themselves in a pile of straw. Unfortunately for them, one of the escapers left his leg sticking out. It was still there when two youngsters wandered in, spotted the leg moving and shouted. The boys had been playing 'Cops and Robbers' and immediately Owens and Thompson emerged and gave themselves up. They told the police who were called to the farm they had not eaten since the escape and had lost a stone and a half each.

James Moray, twenty-six, was the last to be netted. Freezing, hungry and wet, he had taken shelter in a telephone kiosk when he was caught in the headlights of a police patrol car. He tried running off but was rugby tackled.

'I'm glad it's over,' he said. 'Can I have a shave and something to eat?'

9

A DAY AT THE RACES

WANDSWORTH WILL forever be known as the prison which let Great Train Robber Ronnie Biggs slip away. His escape and astonishing life that followed are the stuff of high drama. To many, Biggs was a hero simply because of the ease with which he was able to laugh off all efforts at recapture by police, and even a band of kidnappers. While his exploits are a storyteller's dream, comedy writers will have a field day with the adventures of bookmaker Charles Simpkins.

In August 1898 Simpkins was being taken by train to Wandsworth Prison by bailiff Leonard Packer, who had arrested him over unpaid debts. Clearly the two men got on well, so much so that when they reached London's Clapham Junction and discovered they would have to wait for the train to Wandsworth, Packer suggested that rather than hang about in a station waiting room, they nip over the road to a nearby public house and wait there instead. Simpkins was more than happy to agree, and once inside, the two men had quite a session, knocking back a series of brandies and soda. The warmth of the drinks increased the spirit of conviviality, and when Simpkins proposed the pair of them adjourn to a nearby horse race meeting where he could borrow money from his brother-in-law, a well-known jockey, to pay what he owed, his captor was more than happy to agree. The bookmaker sent off a telegram to his relative, asking if he would loan him money, and while they waited for a reply, at least six Wandsworth trains came and went.

Finally they decided to make tracks for the racecourse, but by the time they made it back to Clapham Junction, the station was packed with other race-goers. When the train pulled in, Simpkins showed his drinking companion a clean pair of heels, disappearing among the crush. Packer had to admit he had lost his prisoner. However, there was worse to come when Packer was hauled before a judge. The prosecutor demanded he pay Simpkins' debts because had he not let him escape, these would have been settled with the loan from the jockey. After the judge heard about the bizarre booze-up he ruled Packer should cough up because he had been negligent by not taking Simpkins straight to Wandsworth Jail and instead going into the public house with him, thereby letting him escape. 'You have not shown the proper strictness required of a person with such important duties to carry out,' the judge told him. The case brought laughter in court.

Smiles were what Robert Mackenzie intended to leave behind when he escaped from Wandsworth in 1901. Sadly his exploit ended in tragedy. Mackenzie, aged twenty-seven, was serving eighteen months with hard labour after being convicted of burglary. A persistent offender, he had a reputation as a prison comedian, and decided to cheer himself up by disappearing and then writing his own version of his escape. He was determined not to be locked in a cell on a top-floor landing – having been placed high up to discourage him from attempting to break free – and began patiently hacking away at an outside wall.

Mackenzie somehow managed to make a thirty-foot-long rope from tar twine and sneak it into his cell. Finally on the verge of breakthrough, he sat down to write an account of the drama before taking the final step to freedom. After his escape was discovered, warders found a note in his cell. It read: 'Great was the surprise and excitement in Wandsworth Prison this morning when it was ascertained that an old stager had found his way through two feet of brickwork by means of a knife, which he had cheated the warders of cleverly when they were collecting tools. The prisoner was a determined man. He had once before tried to make his escape when undergoing eighteen months and would have succeeded then had not a fellow prisoner given him away to a warder. The cage is empty, the bird is flown. I'm off to the place where I am known.'

Unfortunately for Mackenzie, he did not make the destination for which he hoped. Having broken through and secured one end of the rope to a bed in the cell, he climbed though the hole he'd made, but suddenly the rope snapped and he plunged thirty feet to the ground, landing with a sickening crash and dying from a broken back and fractured skull.

During the trial of the 1932 Dartmoor mutineers, the police referred to the 'Bobbed-Hair Bandit', a mysterious and brazen gangsters' moll who had been spotted by bookmaker Charles John Sparks hanging about Wandsworth during an escape attempt in 1930. The prisoner had been caught before he could get out, but a clever plan drawn up by the woman had ensured freedom for his friend James Turner. Two men had hidden a long rope and a ladder in preparation for climbing over the Wandsworth prison wall, but the success of their escape depended on timing, and on their woman accomplice being in the right place at the right time. She was waiting in a hired car below where they would clamber down the wall. Having scaled the wall successfully, Turner quickly joined her, but Sparks, his fellow inmate, was spotted by warders and grabbed. The Bobbed-Hair Bandit and Turner sped off, but knowing police would be on the lookout for a couple, one of whom would be wearing distinctive prison clothes, she had brought a set of civilian clothes into which Turner changed. He was then dropped off at a pre-arranged hideout. The Bobbed-Hair Bandit then abandoned the getaway motor, and collected a second car that she had hired. Soon after, she rejoined Turner.

Newspapers reporting the escape revealed: 'The man's

description has been circulated to all stations in the country as well as to the ports. In addition, all the seaside towns have been asked to keep a special watch on day excursion boats to the Continent, in case he should attempt to leave the country in this way.'

By getting Turner away and safely into his hideout, the woman had already done the job for which she had been well paid, and left Turner to his fate. Confident his best chances of staying out of the clutches of the police would be by not travelling far, he had been driven to his hideout in Peckham, seven miles from Wandsworth. But his freedom would not last long. An underworld rival betrayed him, and he found his safe house surrounded by police merely five days after the breakout. Desperate to avoid recapture, he leapt through a second-floor window into a garden but fell and injured himself and was quickly grabbed. Turner went back to jail swathed in bandages. The Bobbed-Hair Bandit remained at large.

So did Ronnie Biggs. He was free for almost thirty-six years and only went back to jail because he gave himself up. The Londoner was a member of the gang that held up the Glasgow to London mail train in August 1963 and stole a staggering £2.6 million. The theft was the result of supreme planning, but carelessness meant fingerprints were left at their hideout and gradually police reined in the thieves. In 1964 Londoner Biggs was jailed for thirty years and went off to begin his sentence at Wandsworth.

With so much money waiting for him on the outside, he was determined from the minute he passed through the jail gate to be free. The escape of fellow gang member Charlie Wilson only four months after his conviction prompted fears that security on the robbers would be stepped up, making escapes more difficult, if not impossible. Biggs waited for the dust to settle, but quietly began planning freedom. He teamed up with fellow inmates Eric Flower, serving twelve years for robbery, and Paul Seaborne, who was close to completing a four-year term. The trio took careful note of how surveillance on Biggs was tighter, but they realised too that there was a potential weak spot in the prison's security. During exercise periods prisoners mingled together. If one made a break, others could mill around, making it difficult for warders to move in. The plan would be developed with the help of small-time London villain Ronnie Leslie. Two other inmates, Robert Anderson and Patrick Doyle, would also join the plot.

Money was no problem. Biggs' share of the train robbery haul was £150,000, enough to pay for an escape, a facelift and a new life on the other side of the world.

The escape itself, on 8 July 1965, was a model of daring, perfect timing and simplicity. In mid-afternoon, Biggs, Flower, Anderson and Doyle were among fourteen inmates in the exercise yard being watched over by four officers. All seemed quiet and normal, but on the other side of the twenty-foot-high prison wall, the drama was developing. A green Ford Zephyr and a red furniture van slowly drove along the side of the wall and parked. The van had an odd-looking platform on the roof. Suddenly, things happened. One man emerged from the platform carrying a rope ladder and a steel ladder. He pushed the steel ladder up to the top of the wall and threw the rope ladder over. As he did so, a masked accomplice emerged from the Zephyr. He carried a shotgun.

In the yard, one of the officers looked up, and to his amazement, he saw a head emerge from the other side. Suddenly a rope ladder dangled into the melee of prisoners. Instantly four men were scrambling over the wall, as guards struggled vainly to get through the crowd of other inmates.

The escapees raced up the rope and were helped down the steel ladder and ushered into the van through the roof. There, changes of clothing waited. When everyone was accounted for, the Zephyr sped off.

Biggs and Flower were hidden by friends until the initial splurge of publicity calmed down. Biggs then headed first to Brussels and later to Paris, where it had been arranged for him to have plastic surgery at a private clinic. During weeks of painful recuperation in Spain, where he read of the recapture of Anderson and Doyle, he was joined by his wife, Charmian.

In an exclusive interview with me in 2010, Biggs recalled: 'Even before I was arrested, I told myself that if I was caught, no jail was going to hold me. There was no way I was going to grow old in a prison cell with so much waiting for me on the outside. I knew that even with plastic surgery, there was always going to be a chance that no matter where I went in Europe or the United States, somebody could recognise me. I needed to get as far away as possible. I remembered reading about all those war criminals who had disappeared in South America, and that part of the world was an option. The worry was that because I only spoke English, language might cause problems. I thought of settling in New Zealand, but it was small, and I reckoned I'd stick out like a sore thumb. In the end, there was really only one place to go, and that was Australia.'

There was no way he could journey to Australia under his real name, so he arranged to be given a false passport and other documentation under the name of Terrence Furminger. His family travelled separately, and in Sydney, Biggs was reunited with them. There, Eric Flower joined them. Worried by constant reports that police in Britain believed the runaways to be in Australia, they moved first to Adelaide and then Melbourne. By 1969 Flower had been arrested and was taken back to London and prison. Seaborne and getaway driver Leslie were both jailed for their role in the escape, while Biggs, his money virtually all gone, fled to South America, settling in Brazil. A Scotland Yard detective arrested him there in 1974, but was forced to leave empty-handed when Brazilian authorities refused to extradite the robber. Seven years later, a group of freelance adventurers snatched him and sailed him to Barbados, intending to take him to Britain. But a Barbados court ruled he had been seized illegally and once again Biggs was set free, returning to Brazil.

Fed up with having no money and needing better care for his deteriorating health, he voluntarily came back to Britain in 2001, spending eight years in jail before being released on compassionate grounds. In the rare interview with me before his death in 2013, Biggs said: 'I escaped from prison, but my real sentence was knowing I could never go back home to hear my own language spoken, to wander into a London bar and have a drink with my friends. In the early years I was constantly thinking that every morning when I woke up it would be my last day of freedom because the threat of being given away was always there. It just needed a careless phone call, a slip in a letter or a word out of place. Eventually that worry died away. The fact was, I might have been free, but my sentence was the longest of any of us.'

Biggs had made it to freedom from the exercise yard. In 1990, the same area was the scene of another dramatic escape attempt, but this one was foiled by the courage of a prison officer. That year, five inmates produced masks and forced their way into the exercise yard, where they hauled the driver of a mechanical digger out of his cab. Their plan was to smash their way out of jail with the digger, but they hadn't factored in one of their guards, who drove a truck to block their route. Vicious hand-to-hand fighting with prison staff ensued. One officer was badly cut when he was smashed over the head with a bottle, while another had his arm broken.

Most convicts who escape and manage to stay at large for months or even years ultimately find themselves back behind bars as a result of betrayal by a rival or even a one-time friend seeking to collect a reward. Irish-born James Hurley, however, was caught because his electricity bill was unusually high. Hurley was the most wanted man in Britain from the moment he escaped in 1994. He and other inmates were on their way to Wandsworth in a prison bus when the passengers began fighting an accompanying officer, who had moved in to break up a row. Hurley was shackled to another prisoner but produced a

91

knife and forced one of the guards to unlock his handcuffs. He promptly vanished into London's rush-hour traffic and spent the next thirteen years on the run.

Police had a special reason for wanting Hurley back behind bars. He had killed one of their own, acting as getaway driver for a gang carrying out an armed robbery on a security van in 1988. The raid happened to be seen by brave off-duty policeman Francis Mason, aged twenty-four, who tried to stop the robbers but was shot dead in the back at point-blank range. Hurley, Perrie Wharrie and Charles McGhee were tracked down by detectives and jailed for life.

After he fled from the bus, Hurley was helped by friends to Ireland. He later settled in Spain, but with a £30,000 reward being offered for his recapture, he was forever looking over his shoulder and decided to move to a farm near The Hague, Holland, where an astonishing stroke of bad luck resulted in his recapture. The authorities tipped off police that the premises were using a remarkably high amount of electricity, often a sign that a building or room was kept hot to grow cannabis plants. Police raided the farm, but while Hurley cursed his bad luck, the police must have thanked their stars for their good fortune. Instead of cannabis, they found Hurley and a huge cache of Class-A drugs. A Dutch judge sentenced Hurley to six years and as he served out his sentence in Holland, British authorities successfully applied for his extradition. He was returned to London in 2001 to complete his life sentence.

10

THE SPY

THE CEMENT USED IN the do-it-yourself build at Wormwood Scrubs was hardly dry before it was being scraped away by one of the amateur builders, convict John Bourke. With three of the five blocks finished, thirty-one-year-old model prisoner Bourke never gave trouble and was trusted enough to even be allowed to work outside. But the crafty con was not all he seemed. From the building tools available to work with, he sneaked three pieces of circular iron, and in the privacy of his cell high up on one of the top landings, he started hacking away at a newly built outer wall. It was slow work, but over almost a year he had just about hacked out a hole big enough for him to drag himself through. Yet he still faced frightening obstacles. Breaking through the last few inches would mean making lots of noise; he was thirty feet up; trigger-happy armed guards patrolled inside and outside the prison; and he would need to somehow scale the twenty-foot-high outer wall. Even if he got away, he would be wearing distinctive prison clothing. Desperation, though, gave him the courage to go on. Only eighteen months into a twelve-year sentence of hard labour, the future was bleak. Freedom seemed the only answer, and Bourke was convinced he could achieve it.

What happened on the night of 1 September 1883 might easily have provided the idea for the remarkable escape featured in the movie *The Shawshank Redemption*, made more than a century later.

When a storm swept across London, Bourke used the crash of thunder to cover the sound of the thuds as he smashed through those final inches. He had already ripped up his bedding to make a rope and fixed one end to a table. Painfully, he heaved himself through the hole, dragging a set of spare clothing with him. His progress down the rope was slow as he watched for any sign of guards and their guns. Once on the ground, he crept towards the outer wall where, incredibly, scaffolding stood unguarded. In a moment he was over and hiding under a canal bank while he waited for the storm to clear. In a deserted hut he changed into dry clothes and vanished into the night, making history as the first man to escape from the new jail.

There were some who might wonder why Bourke was not happy to complete his sentence at the Scrubs. A newspaper report of 1889 painted this glowing picture of conditions there: 'The gaol-birds have constructed their own cage, and with all the modern improvements that experience has taught the authorities to be necessary. It is in every respect a model prison – doubtless the best, as well as the newest, of all the convict establishments – and Commissioners and Directors of Prisons are to be heartily congratulated on the forethought and calculation which has brought this "house of sorrow" into existence and for having abolished some of the old-fashioned, unhealthy prisons in consequence.'

Just two years later came a very different account of life at the Scrubs when a terrifying mutiny was the cover for an attempted mass escape. This time a report in the *Birmingham Daily Post* told how convicts rioted. The newspaper blamed major defects in the self-built jail. The mutiny, it said:

was of a most alarming character, and might easily have been attended by loss of life and the escape of some of the most desperate ruffians in England. While the prisoners were at chapel, the place was, in a moment and by a pre-concerted signal, transformed into pandemonium. The disturbances continued with shouting, whistling, yelling and volleys of obscene language. It culminated in the prisoners almost as a body rising and making for the door. Its gravity may be estimated by the fact that contingents of men had to be drafted from the other London prisons to assist in restoring order and removing more than a hundred of the ringleaders to other prisons.

It is no secret to the Visiting Magistrates that Wormwood Scrubs prison has been in a state of veiled rebellion for some time back, and the wonder is that the crisis has been delayed so long. Many causes have contributed to produce this deplorable result and unquestionably one of the most important is the defective structure of the prison itself. Unlike the prison at Pentonville, Wormwood Scrubs is a series of detached blocks over which it is impossible to exercise satisfactory supervision. It is also so badly constructed that the corridors are swimming in water after every shower, and this water often finds its way into the prisoners' cells. In addition to this, there is no proper drainage in the exercise yards, with the result that wet weather deprives the prisoners of outdoor exercise, sometimes for days together.

But the most dangerous features of the prison are the ventilators and the chapel. The chapel is so constructed that once outside it the prisoner has only the outer wall between him and liberty, and the ventilators in the cells are so imperfectly devised that they serve the purpose of speaking tubes between one prisoner and another. The management of the prison is also questionable. Large numbers of old and hardened criminals are placed in the charge of young and inexperienced warders, who are utterly unable to cope with them. With all these evils working together, the outbreak is not at all astonishing, and it is in the interests of public security that the Home Secretary should sift the matter to the bottom with the least possible delay.

However, it was clear lessons had still not been learned in 1898 when an escape bid was condemned in a report as 'a striking example of the laxity or worse prevailing at Wormwood Scrubs Prison'. Convict Joseph Morris had been allocated cell 37 on level 3 of Block A. It was supposed to be inspected twice a day and given two weekly spot checks, yet Morris was still able to hack a hole in his wall big enough to crawl through. His plan was to lower himself into the outside yard and climb the wall to freedom. He would have got away but for an inmate in the floor discovering lumps of brickwork falling into his ventilator grille and snitching to officers. Even after this tip-off, it was four hours before warders acted and discovered Morris was within inches of breaking through the two-and-a-half-foot-thick wall. In his cell was a rope ladder. The report following this discovery pointed out that the hole in the wall was directly opposite the spyhole in the cell door through which guards were meant to peep at regular intervals to see if the incumbent was up to no good. Senior staff who questioned Morris were astounded to be told he had been hacking at the wall for five weeks without being discovered. He was thrown into solitary confinement for two weeks on a bread-and-water diet while a junior officer was fined ten shillings for negligence. Prison authorities tried hushing up the appalling series of blunders.

Morris's escape attempt seemed ridiculously easy, yet it was nothing compared with the simplicity with which convict James Allright made his getaway a couple of years later. Allright, a trusty (a prisoner whom guards trusted with certain tasks), was in charge of the bakehouse and the cook's kitchen, overseeing other inmates as they prepared food. One morning he turned in for work as usual, but ten minutes later a warder realised he was missing. The alarm was sounded, but Allright had already flown the coop. He had simply gone outside, broken a light chain holding ladders, taken one and used it to climb over the outer wall. Hearing the alarm and seeing him drop to the ground, passers-by gave chase. It was hard not to realise he was a convict. Allright was wearing the distinctive grey prison outfit marked with broad red arrows. Despite his garb, being spotted and a huge search of the area ensuing, he was free for hours before being sighted by a police constable, who hared after the runaway. Realising he was about to be caught and dragged back to jail, Allright decided to make the ultimate attempt at escape from prison life by throwing himself under the wheels of a passing bus, but the policeman grabbed him at the last second, saving his life.

More than thirty years later, in 1937, another policeman dashed the hopes of convict Robert Walsh, whose carefully planned breakout from the Scrubs came to grief after only half an hour of freedom. Walsh was spotted at 11 a.m. sprinting off from the outer wall. The alarm was raised and prison staff were joined by police as they scoured streets surrounding the prison. The owner of a sweet shop just a mile off saw how the escape ended. He told a reporter, 'A policeman who lives opposite was in his shirt sleeves and slippers when he saw the man. Throwing off his slippers in the street, he ran after the man in his socks and succeeded in overtaking him.' A warder told another reporter, 'Walsh is complaining about the barefoot robbery of his freedom.'

Walsh was probably at large for the shortest time of any escapee. On the other end of the spectrum is George Blake, who disappeared from Wormwood Scrubs on October 22 1966 and is still at large after almost fifty years. His is undoubtedly the most famous escape from Wormwood Scrubs, and it was one that rightly angered the British security services especially, because Blake was a spy.

Dutch-born Blake had been a highly respected interrogator for MI6 during World War II. He was ordered to set up a network of British agents in Korea, but in 1950 was captured by North Korean troops and held by communist forces for three years, during which his early sympathies for communism were strengthened by reading the works of Karl Marx while in prison. By the time of his release, he was secretly a committed Marxist, his beliefs cemented by anger at seeing Korean villagers bombed by American aircraft. He was posted to Berlin to recruit Soviet soldiers to work as double agents, but instead told the KGB he wanted to work for Russia and passed on details of British and American spying operations, betrayals that resulted in the assassination of a number of MI6 agents. However, the tables were turned on Blake when a defector exposed his activities on behalf of the Russians, and he was arrested.

After a trial held in secret at the Old Bailey, he was convicted in May 1961 of five offences of spying and jailed for a total of forty-two years. There were some who felt the sentence was too savage, and in Wormwood Scrubs Blake met three of them: Irishman Sean Bourke, serving seven years for sending a biscuit tin filled with explosives to a detective against whom he had a grudge; anti-nuclear campaigner Michael Randle; and former antiques dealer Pat Pottle, who had been jailed for eighteen months for organising demonstrations at a United States Air Force base. In *The Blake Escape*, published in 1989, Randle and Pottle revealed how the plot to free him and get him out of Britain had been devised and carried out.

The idea of escaping had first been discussed at a music appreciation society meeting in Wormwood Scrubs. Blake had said that if any of the men were willing to help him get free once they had been released they should contact the Russian Embassy, say they brought greetings from 'Louise' and put a coded advertisement in the *Sunday Times*, the hidden message indicating whether or not any plan would have Russian backing. Blake even drew a map showing a point on the wall of the exercise yard where a rope ladder should be thrown over on a pre-arranged time and day.

The plan eventually settled on was for Blake to smash glass and a bar from one of the windows in his D Block, slide onto a roof and drop into the yard, then climb up a rope ladder that he would make and clamber over the prison wall.

The plotters borrowed money to buy a car that would take

Blake away, but fears that security would be increased threw their plans into doubt, and the spy moved to another jail after a breakout attempt by six inmates in June 1966. That brought calls for a full review of security at Wormwood Scrubs but, thankfully from Blake's point of view, he was not transferred. He remained upbeat about his escape plans and while Pottle, Randle and Bourke set about raising more funds and looking for sympathisers willing to hide the spy in their homes after the breakout, he began making his rope ladder with knitting needles as the rungs. Escape equipment including wire cutters, a two-way radio and even a car jack – to be used to help break the toughened glass on the window – were smuggled into the Scrubs. All seemed to be going well, but on 12 August 1966 the plotters were horrified at the potential consequences of a terrifying incident outside the prison that was initially thought to be part of a major escape.

Three plainclothes police officers were patrolling the area in an unmarked motor when they spotted an old blue estate car with three men sitting inside it. The car was parked up close to the jail walls. It looked suspicious, the sort of situation to cause alarm. The officers suspected the three were waiting for a signal to pick up escapees. In fact, they were checking over the guns they planned to use in an armed robbery. The officers decided to investigate, using as the excuse the fact that the estate car had no tax disc. They were thirty-year-old Detective Sergeant Christopher Tippett Head, Detective Constable David Bertram Wombwell, aged twenty-five, and their driver, Police Constable Geoffrey Fox, forty-one, who knew the area and many of the local villains operating in it well.

Fox told his companions he recognised one of the trio as career criminal Jack Witney. Head and Wombwell walked over to question Witney, and as they did, one of the passengers, Harry Roberts, pulled out a Luger pistol and shot Wombwell through the eye. The officer fell dead and Head ran towards the police car, only to be shot by Roberts. As Head lay dying in the street, the third man, John Duddy, produced another gun and shot dead Fox, who slumped over the steering wheel. Unexpectedly, his foot jammed on the accelerator, causing the motor to jump forward and over the body of Head.

The three killers drove off, but a passer-by, alarmed by their speed and thinking he might have been watching the getaway of a prison escapee, took down the registration number and passed it on to the police, leading to the eventual arrest of the murderers.

The slaughter of these three men who had simply been doing their jobs caused nationwide outrage. Hanging had been legally suspended by Parliament a few months earlier, but now there were calls for its restoration and for major criminals – including murderers and spies – to be kept in much harsher conditions. Once again the shadow of a prison transfer that would have ended Blake's escape hopes loomed. But nothing happened, and on the evening of 22 October 1966 while most of the inmates and many of the guards were watching a weekly film show, Blake escaped – just as he'd planned. He broke his wrist jumping from the prison wall as Bourke waited below, but it was treated in secret by a sympathetic doctor. He was kept at a series of addresses, including the homes of Randle and Pottle, before being driven to the Continent hidden in a camper van. He gave himself up to East German authorities and from there was handed over to the Russians, who installed him in a flat in Moscow and gave him a KGB pension.

After publication of their book, Randle and Pottle were charged at the Old Bailey with complicity in his getaway. They pleaded 'Not Guilty', arguing they were right to help Blake because his long prison sentence was cruel and could have led to his suicide. The jury cleared both men. Bourke died in Ireland in 1982 and Pottle in 2000. Blake still lives in Moscow.

11

ESCAPE TO A LIFE SENTENCE

HAD GEORGE BLAKE not escaped, he would probably have spent the rest of his life behind bars, longer than those given life sentences. Michael Purcell ran off because he couldn't wait to begin what was usually regarded as a life sentence of a different kind. In January 1967, the twenty-two-year-old had been briefly allowed out of Wormwood Scrubs to remarry his former wife, Patricia, at Hammersmith Register Office. After making his vows, he evaded his warder escorts by taking to his heels wearing a pair of Chelsea boots. His honeymoon from prison life didn't last long, however. He was recaptured later that night. A Register Office official said, 'The last thing anybody saw was him kissing his wife goodbye and getting into a car with two escorts.'

As the Northern Ireland Troubles spread to the mainland, top-security jails such as Wormwood Scrubs were warned they would be holding terrorists given long sentences. With few exceptions, these men did not regard themselves as ordinary criminals but as political prisoners, and in any case, the majority insisted they were entitled to be imprisoned nearer their families in Northern Ireland. Their demands were backed up by disturbances, arrests and the occasional escape attempt.

Gerard 'Gerry' Kelly was a strict adherent to the Republican belief that as a soldier taken prisoner it was his duty to try to break free. He had escaped from Belfast's Crumlin Road Prison in the 1960s and then from Mountjoy Jail in the Republic. In 1973, IRA bombs exploded in London close to the Old Bailey and the Ministry of Agriculture, leaving one person dead and injuring scores of others. Kelly was convicted of causing explosions and conspiracy to cause explosions and given two life sentences plus twenty years. When his insistence on moving to a jail in Ulster was ignored, he went on hunger strike and then in 1974 made a dramatic escape attempt that was only foiled when he was spotted on the outer wall of the Scrubs. A few months later, he was moved to the Maze Prison, from where he took part in the 1983 mass escape. Kelly went on to become a prominent Ulster politician.

Just how determined paramilitary organisations were to free their men was discovered when police searched a Republican bomb factory following a siege in London. In December 1975 four members of the Provisional IRA, chased by police, burst into a flat at Balcombe Street and took the couple living there hostage. After a six-day stand-off, the four surrendered and were later given long prison sentences. But documents found in the bomb factory caused major concern, because among them were details of a plot to attack Wormwood Scrubs and free scores of inmates. The homes of warders would also come under attack while other Provisionals' targets included the Queen's Gallery in Buckingham Palace, the British Museum, University College, London, power and water-pumping stations and Army establishments.

The documentation showed just how vulnerable prison staff were. But the need for constant vigilance was demonstrated in February 1992 when a shocking example of carelessness allowed a dangerous criminal to abscond. Warders at the Scrubs were awaiting the arrival of convicted murderer John Paul McFadyen, who was being transferred there from Full Sutton Jail in Yorkshire. He never arrived. The killer had been given a life sentence after shooting dead a drugs courier on a lonely moor outside Glasgow. It was decided to move him south in a private-hire taxi, driven by a woman with two warders acting as guards. McFadyen should have been checked before leaving Yorkshire, but on the journey he suddenly produced a knife, forced the warders out and ordered the woman to drive him to Euston, in North London, where he disappeared. He was only caught five months later, when he became caught up in a bar brawl and police were called.

Sometimes the ease with which prisoners were able to flee sounded almost ridiculous. Staff at the Scrubs had warned that part of the jail where inmates worked had no security cameras, yet convicts were still allowed there to help work on a refurbishment contract run by a private firm. In July 1995 Gary Johns and Anthony Coughtrey had been members of a work party when they tied up the civilian workman in charge of them, and then used a blowtorch to cut through a perimeter fence and flee. Both were convicted killers sentenced to life imprisonment, and questions were asked as to why they had been allowed into the area and left in the charge of a civilian. What made the lax security even more unacceptable was that a few months earlier warders had found a tear-gas canister in an inmate's cell. Coughtrey and Johns were recaptured and given further sentences for escaping.

The following year, Wormwood Scrubs was at the centre of a major alert surrounding Irish crime lord John Gilligan. He had been targeted for regular publicity by journalist Veronica Guerin, and when she was shot dead in broad daylight on the outskirts of Dublin in late June 1996, he and his associates became prime suspects. However, the killing had infuriated politicians and fellow journalists, and even disgusted others in the brutal drugs-riddled Dublin. Police set out to smash Gilligan's crew, and after receiving threats from other gangsters, Gilligan decided to hide out in Amsterdam. He flew first to Heathrow, where he was arrested after customs officers discovered he was carrying £330,000 in a metal case. Authorities in Dublin announced they would seek his extradition over the Guerin slaying, and Gilligan was remanded to Wormwood Scrubs. He had been there only a few days when he was suddenly moved away. The reason was a tip-off to the prison service by MI5 that some of Gilligan's gang were on their way to London to organise a plot to free him – and money would be no object. He spent three years in other English jails before being returned to Ireland, where a court acquitted him of murdering the reporter.

Of all the Wormwood Scrubs escapes, could any have been as simple as that in January 1999 of Anthony Lavene? The wealthy, bearded sixty-one-year-old had been remanded to the jail on a cocaine-smuggling allegation. The daily visiting sessions were always busy. Warders needed to be on the alert as visitors mingled with inmates. Lavene simply took advantage of the confusion. He shaved off his beard so he would not be recognised and, as visitors began leaving, pulled on a white shirt and a pair of black trousers to give the appearance of a guard. Then he simply strolled outside to freedom. It was the stuff of legend, and the exit through which he had walked became known as 'Lavene's Door'.

Or was the simplest escape of all that of expert burglar Steven John, known as 'Raffles' because of his penchant for stealing from the rich? It must surely have been the most obvious. The father of five was facing a long prison stretch after police raided one of his homes and discovered a hoard of jewellery and high-class goods stolen from top hotels and apartments in London. He was sent to Wormwood Scrubs to await his sentence, but had no intention of extending his stay at Her Majesty's pleasure.

When he complained of being ill, prison officials decided to send him to hospital. He was handcuffed and shackled but the cuffs were taken off when he asked to go to the toilet. John was not seen again. The thief, described by a policeman as 'the smartest burglar I have ever known', somehow managed to free himself from his remaining shackles and climb out of the toilet window. He was sentenced to six years in absentia.

12

JOHN McVICAR

THERE ARE COUNTLESS reasons why men and women want to escape from prison. On Wednesday 9 February 1859, a number of newspapers reported on an incident the previous Thursday, in which a convict had escaped from Durham Prison, '[A]nd has not since been heard of. Great excitement was caused in the town next day on the occurrence being made known, the officials declaring that they are totally unable to account for his obtaining possession of the means by which he made his escape.' James Gray, aged twenty-one and a shoemaker serving twelve months' hard labour for highway robbery, had shown a clean pair of heels after a breakout that displayed courage and determination. 'He had got through a skylight, having previously secured a quantity of rope sufficient to let himself down from the roof. As a new wing is in course of erection he had ample means at command to scale the high wall which surrounds the prison,' explained the *Daily News*.

Why had he fled? The *Daily News* had the answer the following day: he simply wanted some fun and female company. The paper revealed, 'Gray was captured at half-past 11 on Saturday night, in a low beer-house, Hartlepool. Mr Hodgson, a warder in the prison, in company with some policemen, found him treating some lewd women with glasses of rum; he made no resistance. He was safely deposited in his old quarters on Sunday.'

Escapes usually require a degree of thought and planning. In September 1869 – ten years after Gray's escapade – pitmen Thomas Shield and Robert Screener managed to get out of the prison, but it was soon obvious they had not thought out the entire plan. Shield had every reason to want to get away. He was facing a murder charge, and if convicted, he would certainly be hanged at Durham. Screener was serving a short sentence for a minor theft. The two men found themselves in adjacent cells in the newly built south wing. Inmates were not supposed to communicate with one another, but Shield and Screener had somehow broken this rule and discussed breaking out, because they each sneaked workmen's tools stolen from the wing builders into their cells.

On the night of Sunday, 11 September, the pair waited until the final check of the night by warders at eight o'clock and then got to work. They used the stolen tools to hack away the stonework between their cells until one could crawl through to join the other. Then they dragged an iron bar from the cell window and smashed the glass. They had already worked out how to reach the ground twenty feet below. Stripping off their clothes, they ripped the prison uniforms and underwear into strips, knotted these together, tied one end to one of the remaining window bars, wriggled through the gap and slid down the makeshift rope. It was now that the plan hit an obvious snag. The idea had been to shake the clothes rope free and don what they could to cover their modesty. Unfortunately, the knot around the bar had been too firm. Despite shaking and pulling them, the clothes would not come free, and they found themselves in the prison yard virtually stark naked.

Should they give up and go back to the relative comfort and warmth of the wing? If this was an option they considered, it was rejected because they carried on, discovering a scaffolding pole which they used to shin up and onto the top of the twenty-foot-high outer wall. Just as they were about to jump to the ground the pole fell, the din rousing another prisoner in one of the lower landings, who called warders. The alarm was sounded. By now Shield and Screener were climbing a second eight-foot-high wall and reaching freedom.

Despite their near-naked bodies being bruised and bleeding, and their skin having ripped on the rough walls, they vanished into the night, no doubt hoping they met no one on their separate ways. Shield reached the home of his brother on the outskirts of Durham, where he was recaptured the following night, and Screener was found soon after and returned to Durham prison.

Shortly before Christmas that year Shield went on trial for his life. It was said by the prosecution that he had been arrested first time around following an altercation. Drinking in a local inn, he had 'offered to fight the best man in the room'. The challenge was taken up by a man named Ralph Reed, and as they fought, Shield produced a knife and fatally stabbed his rival in the neck. Other witnesses said Reed had started the fight, and the jury found Shield guilty of manslaughter, meaning he escaped the hangman's noose. Instead, he was jailed for twenty years.

The story of the makeshift clothesline that became part of prison lore was entertaining and served as a lesson to all would-be escapers. It was certainly remembered by a young Welshman in May 1880, but what was remarkable about his escape attempt was that he had only two months left to serve before his release. Noticing a window between his cell and the corridor running along the outside of his door had been left open, he waited for it to be shut by guards. When it stayed open, he decided to escape, and somehow sneaked two long ropes into his cell. Despite regular patrols past his cell by three warders on duty throughout the night, the Welshman managed to climb through the window into the corridor. He waited until the coast was clear, then silently climbed up a staircase to the top landing of his wing. Quietly removing tiles, he was able to get onto the roof and open a skylight, to which he tied one end of the ropes, throwing the other over the high prison wall. Freedom beckoned. He needed only to lower himself down the rope, but just as he was about to begin, he was spotted by a warder patrolling outside. The guard set off the alarm.

A report into the escape attempt said, 'Meanwhile the prisoner had not been inactive and surmising that he had been recognised, he hastily made his way back to his cell and on the governor and warders entering they found him apparently fast asleep. There was, however, sufficient evidence to show that he had attempted his escape.' He was later given a longer stretch for his exploit.

Durham's most sensational escape remains the breakout of armed robber John McVicar. Yet that of local man Ronnie Heslop seven years earlier, in March 1961, was just as dramatic. On remand facing charges of stealing from a lemonade factory and attempting to crack the safe of a government office, Heslop feared that if he was convicted, he would be looking at a very long sentence. He'd snuck a teaspoon and knife from the prison kitchen, and used them to get out of his cell via a ventilation grille. From there he managed to clamber over the outer wall and onto the roof of the adjoining courthouse. Next he climbed down and fled. He realised his best chance of getting away from the town and the swarms of police and prison staff who would be searching for him was to cross the River Wear, snaked through the city. Police set up checkpoints on bridges and roads, ruling those out as crossing points. But for the young, fit serving soldier, the prospect of escape outweighed the dangers of entering the swollen river. He dived in. Swimming the Wear allowed him to get clear to the safety of friends. He was on the run for six weeks before being discovered and sent back to Durham and into solitary confinement and the standard bread-and-water diet.

It was McVicar, however, who made headlines and, eventually, a movie about his remarkable escape. Worried by a series of prison breaks, the government decided to follow a tactic employed by the Germans during World War II, which was to put troublesome captives together in one escape-proof cocoon – in that case, Colditz

Castle in Saxony. In Britain, the spot chosen to hold the bad eggs was grim Durham Jail. In 1965 the authorities opened E-Wing, confident they had created an escape-proof unit. Among the early occupants were McVicar and Walter Probyn, both of whom had previously escaped. In 1966 Londoner McVicar fled from a bus carrying him to Parkhurst Prison. He was on the run for four months and after his recapture was sent to E-Wing. Probyn was a prolific escaper.

Just as Colditz turned out to be a guards' nightmare in which escape followed escape, E-Wing was, from its inception, a major trouble spot bedevilled by riots, complaints about poor conditions, unrest among staff and even sightings of the ghost of a former inmate stabbed to death two decades previously by another prisoner. It all came to a head when McVicar, Probyn and convicted murderer Joey Martin disappeared on 29 October 1968.

McVicar had been jailed for fifteen years in February 1967 and was given a further five years in July that year for conspiring to rob an armed security van. Probyn was serving a twelve-year stretch for the incident in which shots were fired at police, and it was he who discovered a false wall in the E-Wing shower room hiding a shaft. They worked out that this shaft would give them access to a small exercise yard, where from they could climb to the roof of the adjoining courthouse or the main prison wall. To create a hole big enough for a man to crawl through, brickwork had to be removed from the false wall. It all should have been straightforward, but as McVicar said in a television interview, a major snag appeared in the shape of Charlie Richardson, boss of a terrifying London gang: 'Richardson had this streak in him. Basically he'd torture people, anyone who crossed his path. He said he and one of his associates would become part of the escape plan.'

The solution sounded easy: simply to refuse to take Richardson and his pal along. But Charlie had already come up with a proposal McVicar and Probyn could not refuse. He would start digging his own tunnel in the shower room and make his project so obvious that it was bound to be discovered, thus sparking off a minute search for evidence of other digging that was sure to lead to McVicar and Probyn's secret being uncovered. McVicar explained, 'By digging out, that would have created mayhem and the guards would have found our hole. So we had to bring them in, and now there were four of us.'

For three weeks McVicar and Probyn, helped by another con who had indicated he would not be escaping with them, removed bricks to dig through to the shaft. They flushed rubble down toilets and mixed and painted papier-mâché to cover their hole. Martin agreed to join them and all three made hooks and ropes to help climb walls once they reached the exercise yard, and civilian clothes to cover their prison-issued outfits. The three had decided not to take Richardson and his friend with them. It was a risky strategy, one reason for their decision being that they felt Charlie had too high a profile and his disappearance would be discovered within minutes.

So on the night of 29 October, while Richardson and his friends were on an association period during which they could mix for recreation such as watching television, the trio made their move. McVicar said in his television interview, 'We went without telling Charles Richardson. We double-crossed him.' However, as they crawled into the shaft, the Richardson group realised what was happening. 'They heard the noise, and Richardson started shouting, "You bastards, you bastards." It was like to tell the warders we were escaping. We were into the exercise yard in less than a minute. Alarm bells were going, warders shouting and screaming, torches, that sort of thing. It was obviously going to be a hard go.'

In an instant, McVicar and Probyn had reached the top of the outer wall. 'We looked over and there were about forty warders stringing out along the bottom of the wall. They were shouting, "There they are! There they are!" But we kept going.'

Martin had already been caught in the exercise yard. The others made it to the roof of the courthouse, where they split up. Probyn realised the game was up and waited for warders to take him back into custody. His capture briefly switched attention from McVicar, who took advantage to leap from the roof of the court building. He landed in gardens, and hearing prison officers run past, he decided to simply follow them before literally walking off in another direction. To his astonishment, he realised he was passing a police station. 'When I heard them rushing past I thought, "I could get out now and you couldn't stop me." None of them could catch me and they're not armed, so the only thing that can stop me is a bullet. I remember running past one guy. He just looked at me and I thought, "What can you do? You can't do anything." I was that confident.'

McVicar had no idea where in Durham he was. He began running again and found himself tumbling down an embankment and confronted by the River Wear: 'Suddenly I was treading on air. I thought I'd broken something. I went into the water very gingerly. I could hear a bit of a manhunt, dogs and stuff, and I thought, "They can't catch me." I decided to stay in the river, but then thought, "I can't swim for ever." I was going to drain myself of energy, and I got so cold I crawled out.'

As he began looking for somewhere to hide, McVicar was unaware that a remarkable coincidence would prove a huge factor in his continued freedom. A few miles to the south, homesick Billy Ferris from Glasgow had absconded from a young offenders' institution at Wetherby and was heading north, determined to reach Scotland. In his biography, *The Hate Factory*, Ferris recounted the astonishing story of how he was eventually caught hiding up a tree by a huge contingent of police, who were confident they had, in fact, cornered McVicar. By the time the searchers realised they had the wrong quarry, an exhausted McVicar had reached the town of Chester-le-Street, to the north of Durham, and was hiding in an outhouse.

'I had overreached myself physically and mentally and didn't have any reserves. Physically I was depleted and mentally I was as well,' he said. He found a telephone kiosk and rang a friend in London, who arranged for gangland friends to motor to the north-east and collect him. Three days after he broke out of E-Wing, he was in a car being driven south. He said, 'It was a great, great feeling that I'd done it. I didn't know what was ahead of me. I was eventually going to run out of steam, get caught or killed.'

He became Public Enemy Number One. A reward was offered for his recapture, but he was always sure his freedom, hiding out in London, could never last. In the distrustful environment of the underworld, where friendships were often fleeting and flimsy, betrayal would be the most likely source of his downfall and, sure enough, a one-time associate tipped off police as to where the runaway was living. In November 1970, just over two years after his escape, armed Flying Squad detectives surrounded a two-bedroom flat in London's Blackheath and crept cautiously in to arrest a surprised McVicar, who made no effort to resist. There were two scantily-clad women with him, one of them his wife, Shirley. He was returned to prison and given an extra two years for escaping. In jail, McVicar studied and emerged to become a respected journalist and writer. The story of his escape was told in a successful film, *McVicar* (1980), featuring pop singer Roger Daltrey in the lead role.

McVicar's degree of determination to be free was equalled by another armed robber, Simon Bowman, whose sheer audacity was astonishing. In May 1992 Bowman fled from Durham Prison with two friends. Two months later, he was tracked to a house at Upchurch in Kent. Police secretly set up a base in the next door building and surrounded the house for two days, while they prepared to storm it. When they moved in, they discovered it was empty. But there were red faces galore when Bowman was found. He had been hiding under a bed – in the police base.

In April 1994 Bowman fled from officers escorting him from Garth Prison in Lancashire to a hospital appointment. He flagged down a taxi and asked the driver to take him to his native north-east, a 170-mile trip that would cost £220. The cabbie lost his way near Ripon, North Yorkshire, at which point Bowman popped out and asked a police-car driver for directions. When the taxi stopped for fuel, Bowman fled without paying. He was eventually caught and imprisoned at Durham, where he later found himself at the centre of a major scandal after a pistol and ammunition were found hidden in the segregation area of the jail. The discovery followed a tip-off from another inmate that Bowman was about to use a weapon in an escape bid. He was given another seven years for his involvement in the breakout plot.

13

LETTER FROM A RUNAWAY

IF UNDERWORLD GANG leader George Hackett had a crystal ball, he would never have set his mind on escape. Instead he would have stayed in his solitary cell at Pentonville Prison and quietly done his porridge. The motto of any old-time criminal is simply: if you can't do the time, don't do the crime. George's version was quite different: do the crime and don't do time.

In December 1859 the *Daily News* reported:

Few felons have created more interest of late years at the London police courts. In the annals of crime in the City there does not appear a more determined and desperate character. He began his career of crime with smuggling. He then attached himself to a gang of desperate marauders and the amount of depredation they committed was enormous. Burglaries, street robberies, and in fact almost every conceivable crime save murder, perhaps was perpetrated by them with the greatest impunity. Possessing themselves with light chaise carts and swift horses, they drove about the principal streets of the metropolis, and the respectable style of the parties and the vehicles disarmed all suspicion. No uncommon occurrence was it for them to drive up to a warehouse, effect an entrance by skeleton keys, and bringing out the plunder, place it in their cart, and drive off. They had been repeatedly detected driving through the streets in the City, and suddenly stopping by a wagon containing bales of silk, etc, remove some of the property, and drive furiously away.

This nineteenth-century version of a high-speed getaway had made Hackett and his gang relatively well off. Unlike some, though, who squandered their share of the proceeds on drink and loose women, he put by a nest egg for the day when he would need to buy his way to freedom. Luck seemed to be on his side. Sure as the fledgling police force was that Hackett masterminded a series of raids, there was never sufficient evidence to arrest him. Like most crooks, though, Hackett didn't know when to stop, and the inevitable came when a workman spotted him with three accomplices plundering a London store and galloping off at speed in a light cart. A few weeks later, he was seen but badly beat up a police constable who tried to seize him. Not long after, however, as he and his gang waited with two carts outside a warehouse, police arrived in force, and after a fight the crooks were arrested. Before his trial Hackett vanished from a prison cell. The *Daily News* revealed, 'The authorities instituted inquiries and it turned out that a turnkey had received a large sum of money to effect his liberation, and the officer was discharged.'

Now every constable in London was on the lookout for the man who had almost killed one of their colleagues. In May 1859 Hackett was seen on London Bridge by a policeman 'lying at the bottom of a cart. The officer immediately stopped the vehicle and called upon Hackett to surrender, who obeyed the order by jumping out of the cart, and endeavoured to get away. The officer overtook him in Thames Street and a desperate struggle ensued. Hackett drew a formidable life preserver and by beating the constable over the head nearly murdered him. The bystanders, fortunately, secured the fellow.'

Convicted of trying to murder the constable, Hackett was sentenced to fifteen years' transportation and sent to Newgate gaol in London, to wait for a convict ship to take him to Australia.

Never one to give up, he plotted an escape, only to be foiled. He was moved to another jail but once again was found to be planning a getaway. 'For his better security,' said the *Daily News*, 'he was removed to the Model Prison at Pentonville; and after two attempts, he succeeded in getting out of the gaol under circumstances that have led the authorities to suspect that some of the turnkeys had been tampered with.'

The manner of his escape showed just how determined Hackett was to be free. A quick look around Pentonville convinced him the most vulnerable part of the prison was the chapel, where convicts were kept during services in the individual wooden stalls designed to prevent them seeing or talking with one another. That brief period of solitude, intended to let men ponder on their sins, also gave a desperado like Hackett time to escape into the wider world. How he did it needed ingenuity and daring.

According to the *Daily News*:

It appears that by some means he managed to wrench off the spring of the door of his cell to form a crowbar. He concealed about him a weight, and the sheets and rope of his bed, which he must have wrapped round his body under his clothes. As soon as he was conducted to his seat, he must have slipped down off his seat on to the flooring, and by the jemmy and weight forced out the boarding. Having got under the gallery, he met a serious obstacle in the shape of a zinc ventilator, but this, armed with his crowbar, soon gave way, thus enabling him to descend to a small closet beneath. A window with trifling protection afforded him access to the parapet wall a few feet below. Gaining it, he proceeded along to one of the main walls, 50 or 60 feet long, communicating to the governor's house. Reaching the end he, by some stratagem, got on to the roof of the house, a height of more than six feet from the wall. Having obtained this point, all obstacles were apparently at an end to him. He divested himself of the prison clothing, save his trousers and blue shirt, and left them with the crowbar, rope, sheets, etc on the roof and by sliding down one of the gable end walls, got clear out of the prison.

The authorities would not see twenty-two-year-old Hackett again. But they would both hear of and from him. A few days after he disappeared, a letter from him arrived in the office of the Pentonville governor. Cheekily, he had written, presenting his compliments, 'and begs to apprise him of his happy escape from the gaol'. He was, he said, in excellent spirits, and could assure the governor it would be 'useless for his men to pursue him'. He was 'quite safe and in a few days intended to proceed to the continent to recruit his health'.

This remarkable story would, it emerged, become even more astonishing. Instead of heading straight off to Europe, Hackett waited for the heat to die down, going into hiding in the London area with relatives and friends and planning for a future far from the capital, aided by associates, who set about raising enough money to ensure a safe getaway. Londoners found themselves encouraged to invest in raffles and concerts, but were discouraged from inquiring about the purpose of the profits. In fact these were to buy a passage for Hackett and his wife on the weekly steamer that sailed from Liverpool to New York. Now it was time to use the nest egg he had saved. In America he went to a New York bar run by an old friend from London who found the young couple a place to stay. The runaway felt so safe he even wrote again to the Pentonville governor, telling him not to waste time on further searching for the escaper. 'I am in New York in perfect health and spirits,' he said, adding, 'I hope you are the same.'

His escape had made him something of a celebrity, but old habits die hard. In September 1851 he broke into a house in the Newark area, was caught and remanded to jail, where he was warned to expect a sentence of at least ten years. Inevitably, Hackett tried to escape, but he and a fellow convict were caught, a large knife found strapped to one of his legs. 'Every man has his day, and George and me will have ours yet, for our lives ain't worth much in this way,' said his companion. Maybe Hackett wished he had stayed locked up in Pentonville. In 1855 he was executed in New York for stabbing dead a gaoler at the prison. Hackett was finally free.

An inquiry into his hair-raising disappearance from Pentonville had cleared staff of allegations they had been conspired to help the convict in his escape. But senior prison management remained suspicious that some warders were open to bribes. It was a feeling supported by an odd case that came before a magistrate at Clerkenwell in March 1853, when Pentonville warder John Taggart was accused of breaching the rules by smuggling in a letter for convict Henry Thompson, who was waiting to be shipped to Australia after being sentenced to seven years' transportation. His crime? Stealing a watch.

Thompson and a fellow convict claimed Taggart had approached them and offered to take letters to and from friends and family members in exchange for money. Once the arrangement began, said the convicts, Taggart even smuggled in beer and food. But Thompson shopped the warder to senior staff because, he complained, he had been locked in a dark, dank cell for three days, during which Taggart did not come near with a meal or a drink. And, he alleged, Taggart had kept money he was supposed to have handed over to the convict. Most serious of all was his accusation that the warder promised to help him escape – for a price. Taggart was convicted and told that unless he paid a £50 fine – an astronomical amount at that time – he would be ordered to serve six months' hard labour, kept in the same cells into which he had recently been locking other men. He was given a week to come up with the money, and when he returned to court, he admitted raising such a sum was impossible. He went back to prison.

The inventiveness of criminals never ceased to amaze. In March 1856 Peter Simpson and Henry Nicholls, both serving long sentences for burglary, vanished from their cells. In the prison workshops they had made and repaired shoes, and each day when the time came for them to go back to their cells, they hid pieces of twine and wax, patiently tying and knotting them together until they had made a rope ladder. After they were locked up for the night, the two men somehow managed to open their cell doors, creep along a landing, lift open a heavy metal trap door and climb onto a roof, using their flimsy ladder to get down and then clamber up walls until they were free. 'Their miraculous escape has thrown the whole of the prison authorities into a state of bewilderment,' reported *Reynold's Newspaper*.

Getting out was only half the problem, of course. Staying free was another matter. Often escapers had accomplices waiting to whisk them off to a safe house where they could lie low until the search was scaled down; others could head for the safety of family members. Those with neither friends nor family to help them needed money to stay one step ahead of the searchers.

Not having funds was the predicament facing Henry Edmonds when he broke out of Pentonville in May 1859. How he solved his problem was both remarkable and hilarious. American-born Edmonds had, at one time, been a respectable commercial traveller, but when business dried up, he turned to crime, robbing a tavern and being jailed for six years. In Pentonville he was a model prisoner, one who always behaved himself, and as a result warders tended to pay less attention to him. Left undisturbed and unchecked in his cell, he tore up his bedding and made himself a jacket and pair of trousers. Too many men had been caught simply because they were spotted wearing distinctive prison uniforms on the outside. Being trusted, Edmonds was given one of the few perks available by being allowed to join a gardening party. It meant surveillance was slack. As a result, he was able to sneak off unseen. He had previously hidden a rope and a metal hook and with these he hauled himself to the top of the twenty-five-foot-high outer wall.

What happened next might have been a scene from an early black-and-white silent movie. According to the *Hull Packet and East Riding Times*:

Here occurs what appears a remarkable part of the case. The point where he got over is not more than 20 or 30 yards from the Caledonian road, and he had to drop into a side road, along which persons are always passing and children playing. He was seen by several persons when he came above the wall, but being dressed in white he was thought to be some bricklayer or whitewasher employed in the gaol. It seemed that he had some difficulty in getting the rope over to descend, and to make short work of it he dropped down a distance of perhaps 15 or 20 feet, and falling on his hands lacerated them, and they bled freely. For a moment or so he appeared to have been stunned by the fall; he, however hastily got up and walked down the road into the Caledonian road. He then hailed a cab and telling the driver he had had some dispute with his mates, and had got the worst of it, directed him to drive fast towards London. The driver states that he had no suspicion that the man either by his dress or manner, had escaped out of prison. As they got nearer town he directed the driver to proceed to Greek Street, Soho and at a pawnbroker's he pledged some false teeth which he wore for 7s. paying the cabman 3s. for his trouble. Edmonds then disappeared and nothing has been heard of him since.

Henry Edmonds was prepared to sacrifice his teeth. Eleven years later, in September 1870, convict William Newham risked his life for freedom. Just after seven in the morning, while convicts were getting into line to continue building a new wing at Pentonville under the watchful eyes of guards armed with rifles, Newham, aged forty-five, sneaked away. He knew warders would be busy handing out tools and allocating men to their various jobs and, counting on them being distracted, used building poles to climb on top of the outer wall. At this point he was spotted by a prison officer, who shouted at him to come down. When the convict showed no signs of obeying, the guard took aim and shot at him. Fortunately for Newham, the bullet missed, but it left him in no doubt that within the next few seconds more warders would be trying to kill him, and so he dropped to the ground, and to the astonishment of passers-by, hared off.

14

ESCAPE WITH A BIBLE

EVERY ESCAPE RAISED questions as to whether warders had taken money to turn a blind eye or deliberately commit an act of seeming carelessness. So it was hardly surprising that eyebrows were raised over the breakout of Joseph Surrey in February 1871. The housebreaker waited in his cell for the daily supper ration to be dished out, preparing to take advantage of a procedure that never varied. The guard would slowly progress along the landing corridor, opening each cell, handing the inmate his supper and telling the convict to push the door to, so that a spring lock would secure it. Surrey appeared to follow this instruction, but a report revealed that he made sure his door did not lock. As soon as the guard continued along the corridor to the next cells, he crept out and simply walked to freedom. Building work was still going on, and with ladders, planks and poles lying about, Surrey was easily able to go over the outer wall to freedom, leaving the guard to answer difficult questions.

An investigation showed appalling security lapses. After the escape a few months earlier of a fellow convict friend of Surrey, a policeman had been put on patrol outside the wall which the housebreaker had then followed. He claimed he saw nothing. Visiting magistrates, conducting an inquiry, found this odd, as they discovered a brick lying in the road outside with a message attached to it, making it obvious Surrey had thrown it to his friend, telling him when he would escape. The warder who dished out supper was suspended, and the day after he vanished, Surrey's prison clothes were discovered wrapped in a bundle in the Strand.

Just how many blind eyes were being turned at Pentonville was the question asked after an amazing escape attempt in October 1880. There was nothing particularly unusual about the method. Patrolling warders heard noises and eventually narrowed them down to the cell of thief Henry Garratt, who had decided to shorten his ten-year sentence by bashing a hole in the outer wall and creeping through. It was what the guards discovered when they opened his door that caused a sensation. Neatly laid out on his bed was a complete burglar's kit for breaking through the thickest walls, including a drill, a series of drill bits, two saws, six steel knives, a jemmy and a rope made from thread. A report raised the obvious issue: 'How, and under what circumstances, the tools were placed in the hands of the convict remains a mystery. This discovery would seem to add colour to the suspicion that trafficking to a large extent is carried on.'

Of all the items used in escape attempts from Pentonville, though, none was as shocking or as surprising as that of a convict registered as Henry George Foreman in 1896. The story of his escape would have a sensational ending, as would the last years of this astonishing man's life. At seven o'clock one October Sunday morning, warders rousing the inmates wondered why they were met with only silence when they banged on the door of Foreman's cell. Entering, they discovered the answer: a hole in the wall and no sign of the convict. A massive search began. When a rope ladder with wooden rungs and bricks tied to each end so that it could be held down once across the wall was found in the outside yard, officials surmised Foreman was clean away. Newspapers reported how new evidence emerged to back up this belief. One report explained: 'A house in the neighbourhood had been entered by burglars in the early hours of the morning, and money and wearing apparel had been stolen. No doubt the man had got rid of the prison attire, arrayed himself in the missing garments, and gone back into the world with his freedom. The hue and cry was widely spread, the missing clothes described, and constables were posted in every direction. Foreman's old haunts were ransacked, and his pals cross-examined, but there was no tidings of him anywhere.'

Desperate for clues, prison officials and police re-examined his cell and made a discovery that horrified them. It was clear that, from its size, the hole must have taken months to make. The *Pall Mall Gazette* reported:

> Foreman had a Bible in his cell, from which he had removed leaves here and there so that they should not be' missed. With these he covered up the gradually widening aperture, whitening them with lime, thus rendering the place indistinguishable from the rest of the wall. Probably he moistened the lime he removed and then applied it to the pages of the Bible, which again adhered together at the edges so as to present an unbroken surface. It would be curious to know how he managed to make this singular wall-paper adhere. Then the bricks had to come away. But how was he to get rid of them? The bewildered officials who inspected the cage after the bird had flown gave it up. It was suggested that the pillow and mattress should be inspected carefully. Mixed with the contents of this pillow was a great quantity of fine powder. The bricks had absolutely been ground to dust and so distributed in the pillow that it was only discovered upon being opened. Most of the laths of his bedstead were gone. They had been cut into cross pieces for the ladder.

Yet the most amazing feature of the escape was yet to come. While police hunted outside the jail for sightings of the runaway, a renewed and minute search was ordered of the prison itself. Gradually, warders worked upwards, and finally Foreman was found on the roof of the laundry. He hadn't even made it out of Pentonville.

The *North Eastern Daily Gazette* reported:

In the gutter of the laundry the wretch was found nearly dead with cold, hunger and exhaustion but was discovered lying unconscious in a gutter. Baffled in his great and ingenious fight for freedom, he seemed to have clambered up there and lain down to die. Death, at any rate, would have given him the freedom denied to unceasing and deliberate toil, for in the condition in which he was found he could hardly hope to have strength enough to repeat the desperate effort. Now the care of the officials was not to capture him but to save him and get him down alive. The poor fellow returned to consciousness only to realise how completely he had lost the fruits of his immense and patient ingenuity.

Just as the plotters in Robert Louis Stevenson's *Treasure Island* had failed after using a page from a Bible to cut their dreaded Black Spot, many convicts wondered if Foreman's abuse of the Holy Book almost cost him his life. Little did they know that, years later, that question would once again be asked.

Investigators knew how Foreman had managed to get out of his cell, but the disappearance at the beginning of October 1898 of George Smith, aged twenty-one, was a total mystery. At six in the morning a warder saw him in his cell. Half an hour later, when another warder went to check, he discovered the door open and the villain gone. Nobody could work out how this young Houdini had managed to get free when the door was locked and bolted on the outside. Three weeks later, Smith was caught by a watchful policeman, who suspected he was about to burgle a store.

'I know I am wanted,' said the convict, who ran off again as he left the dock and was being taken to a horse-drawn police van. He was caught for a second time by a posse of police, who gave chase on foot and horseback.

Apart from a handful of convicts who were never again found, most men who made it out of Pentonville illegally were eventually caught and, knowing they were likely to get a hefty extra sentence for escaping, they came up with all sorts of excuses. Arthur Bayley, who broke out in October 1925, told judges, 'I did it to save the honour of a girl who was expecting a child, and whom I wanted to marry. I was justified in escaping and taking the law into my own hands. I had great reasons for doing it, and I ask you to give me another chance and I will be a better man.' His words impressed the learned judges, who decided not to add to the five years he was serving at the time of his escape for being an habitual criminal.

Throughout its history, a regular trail of convicts made their way over the prison's outer walls, but the manner in which Julien Chautard fled in 2009 is one of the most unique of any escape. The French-born criminal had been jailed for seven years for arson and was driven in a security van to Pentonville to start his sentence. Ten minutes after arriving with a group of other new arrivals, he somehow slipped away from security staff without being noticed. When the van left Pentonville, thirty-nine-year-old Chautard was with it – not 'on' or 'in' but 'under'. He had wriggled beneath the vehicle and clung to the chassis literally by his fingertips. Somehow nobody noticed that he was missing, and it was only hours later that a headcount of inmates came up one short. A major search of Pentonville drew a blank, then someone remembered noticing a shadow beneath the van as it drove off, but by then he was gone. The van was checked and his fingerprints and bootprints discovered.

Chautard could well have remained on the run, but after talking to his family in France, he contacted police three weeks after his escape and gave himself up.

Very occasionally there is sympathy for escapers, as there was with Foreman. That is certainly the case with convicted murderer John Massey, who has been in prison since shooting dead a pub bouncer in London in 1975. In 2012 old-age pensioner Massey made his third escape, this time by using a makeshift rope to climb the outer wall of Pentonville, the same method used by men a century and a half earlier. The motive for his break was to visit his ailing mother after he was told she had been calling out his name. On an earlier occasion he had wanted to be at the bedside of his dying father, who had visited his son at prisons up and down the land. 'I could not fail him or my mother,' Massey said in a letter to a newspaper after his capture. 'To do so would have buckled my shoulders with the guilt of unspeakable things to come.' His last escapade ended after just two days, when he was arrested at a house close to the home caring for his mum. Once again, he was banged up in jail. 'We think of sentences in the old days as being savage, but were they any harsher than John's?' one of his friends queried during a radio interview.

The *Guardian* newspaper, in a lengthy article about Massey, declared, 'If criminal connections are anything to go by, John Massey, who escaped from Pentonville prison on Wednesday, will not be short of people to help him evade capture.' Ex-prisoner and prison campaigner Charles Hanson pleaded, 'Release John now and allow him to live out his final years in the peace. Stop the intimidation and brutality.'

15

HANGING CHAIR

FROM TIME TO TIME men with a confident air of authority would be admitted to Holloway, Durham, Pentonville and Wandsworth jails. They would carry small overnight carpetbags, and along with the usual items needed by the traveller, there would be three tools of their chilling trade: a hood, a set of leather straps and a length of rope. These were government-appointed hangmen, and when they departed, the prison population would be depleted by one or, very occasionally, more. Between 1800 and 1900 almost 4,000 men and women legally ended their days swinging on a rope in England, Scotland and Wales.

A merciful reduction in the list of capital offences saw the number of executions diminish from one a week in the early 1800s to one a month by the time of the last hanging in 1964, and the Murder (Abolition of Death Penalty) Act 1965, which brought down the curtain on legal executions, made hangmen redundant.

In their day, hangmen were celebrity figures. William Marwood, who sent 176 men and women to their maker in a decade as official hangman, even gave out his own business cards bearing the words 'William Marwood Public Executioner'. These would become much sought after by collectors of the bizarre. He took his work seriously, believing he had a duty to see off his victims with speed but without pain, and developed the technique known as the 'long drop' to avoid distressing scenes in which condemned convicts were slowly strangled or even decapitated. But even such an aficionado of the art of perfecting death could get it wrong. And just as today's celebrities have their detractors, so did the hangmen.

On 9 August 1856, up to 15,000 spectators turned up in pouring rain at York Castle to watch the noon execution of William Dove, who had poisoned his wife with strychnine in a wine glass. 'Tell my poor mother I die happy,' said the doomed man.

Before the ceremony, a number of men had replied to advertisements offering the job of hangman to dispose of the unfortunate Dove. One enthusiast wrote, 'Dear Sir, Seeing in The Paper your advertise for a hang man I will Engage With you. My age is 22 year. Height 5 foot 8 inches. Weight 13 stone 6 pounds. Agent to the Insurance Company London. It is from several Friends at Leeds that i hang the convict Laying at York Castle Mr Dove answer will oblidge.'

Newspapers describing the execution referred only to the 'executioner' and did not give his name, leading to speculation as to who had been given the job. According to some reports, 'The convict, having been put under the fatal beam, the executioner placed the cap upon the convict's head, and proceeded to adjust the rope round his neck. This was done with great deliberation, owing probably to the fact that the executioner was a debtor in the Castle, who had volunteered to perform the revolting duties.'

The claim that the hangman was a criminal was not wholly surprising. It was not unknown for hangmen to come from the ranks of villains. Pasha Rose's career ended in 1687 on the same Tyburn, London, scaffold where he had himself executed victims after he was sentenced to death for housebreaking; John Price had the job for four years until he was hanged for murdering his mistress; James Coates was waiting at York to be transported for stealing when he was offered and accepted the post of executioner; and his successor, Nathaniel Howard, was a fellow convict.

But days after Dove's hangman was named – a debtor named

Thomas Askern, a novice hangman – a furious row broke out. A letter in the *Leeds Mercury* claiming to be from a local schoolmaster named Pears said it had not been Askern; others wrote saying some of the debtors imprisoned in York Castle who didn't like Askern had put his name forward simply to make him unpopular. Another, purporting to be from Askern himself, furiously warned the paper's editor, 'I wrote to you cautioning you not to use my name as that of the executioner of the late William Dove. Notwithstanding that caution, you took the liberty of using my name. I should have authorised my lawyer to commence legal proceedings against you.'

Matters warmed up as Pears denied writing to the newspaper, but the 'was it Askern or wasn't it' argument was settled by another letter, this time from another debtor, who wrote, 'An investigation has been made by the governor regarding an assault by Askern, who had broken a heavy stick over the shoulders of a debtor for having pointed him out as the hangman. I may add that from half past ten to a quarter past twelve on the 9th, Askern was nowhere to be found; we suspected him and one of our number saw him draw the bolt.' His role finally confirmed, Askern cleared his debts and went on to act as hangman for twenty-one years.

Sometimes dislike of the hangman boiled over into outright threats. In March 1856 William Bousfield, aged twenty-nine, was hanged at Newburn, London, for murdering his twenty-six-year-old wife, Sarah, who he suspected of having an affair, and also their three children, Ann, Elizabeth and John. Police discovered Sarah in the Soho, London, family home with her throat cut; the children had been stabbed with a chisel. Bousfield claimed he could not remember committing these terrible crimes, and reporters noted that while in the condemned cell, 'the prisoner persevered in maintaining a sullen, morose and dogged demeanour, pretending at times to have no recollection of the murder, and that the whole was a dream to him.'

Fearing a suicide attempt, prison officials at Newgate ordered warders to keep a close watch on the murderer, but less than forty-eight hours before he was due to be hanged, Bousfield suddenly threw himself head first into the little fire burning in his cell. 'The turnkey immediately rushed upon him and forced him back,' said the *Daily News*. 'But not until the lower part of the face and neck was much burned from his neckerchief having caught the flame. In a short time, from the livid and swollen appearance of the face, he became a hideous spectacle.' There had already been some public sympathy for Bousfield, and when word spread about his terrible burns, there were calls for him to be spared. These pleas fell on deaf ears. But now hangman William Calcraft became the target for Bousfield's supporters, and for those opposed to hanging. He received a letter signed by the 'Kent Street Roughs', telling him to get a helmet and wear it because if he carried out the execution he would be shot, 'to put an end to any more executions'.

The letter terrified Calcraft, but it was Bousfield who would suffer as a result. Normally a hanging was relatively straightforward. The prisoner was pinioned, marched to the scaffold, his legs tied together, the hood and noose placed around his or her neck, and with the pull of a lever a bolt caused the little trapdoor on which the victim stood to collapse and the condemned person fell to his or her death. Bousfield's hanging was complicated – not just by the hangman fearing he would be shot dead at any moment, but because, as a result of his injuries, the prisoner had to be sat in a chair and carried by four warders to the scaffold, all the while frothing at the mouth. What happened next was a total farce, as the *Daily News* described:

The chair being placed under the fatal beam Calcraft, who appeared in a state of nervous terror, lost no time in putting on the cap and adjusting the noose. As soon as he had fastened the hook to the chain above, he ran down the steps and withdrew the bolt, the chair and the convict falling at the same time. Scarcely two seconds had passed before the wretched culprit exhibited a power and strength truly astonishing to those who had seen him but a minute before. He raised himself upward by sheer muscular strength, and succeeded in placing both of his feet on the right side of the scaffold, and in that position supported himself for several seconds. Calcraft having disappeared the moment he had withdrawn the bolt, one of the turnkeys ascended the scaffold, and threw off Bousfield's legs, when he dropped once more; the yelling of the crowd being terrific. Again the convict struggled, and succeeded in placing both feet on the left side of the scaffold. The sheriffs were horrified, and Calcraft being brought back, withdrew the legs, and for the third time the body fell; yet life was not extinct, for in a few seconds, for the third time, the convict succeeded in planting both his feet on the right side of the scaffold. The cries, hooting, and yelling of the crowd became frightful. Again the legs were withdrawn, and the body for the fourth time suspended, when, by the legs being secured, after a fearful and convulsive struggle of several minutes' duration, life ceased to exist.

Eleven years later, in November 1867, Calcraft was again on the receiving end of threats when he was offered £20 plus his expenses to hang three members of the Irish Republican Brotherhood in front of the New Bailey Prison at Salford in Lancashire. William Philip Allen, Michael Larkin and William Gould wanted British rule in Ireland ended. A police sergeant was killed when Fenians attacked a horse-drawn cart carrying two Brotherhood members, Thomas Kelly and Timothy Deasey, and after being arrested Allen, Larkin and O'Brien were condemned to death.

In the days leading up to the execution, rumours persisted that Fenian gunmen would mingle with spectators and shoot Calcraft on the scaffold. Then just hours before the trio were due to die, the already terrified executioner opened a letter addressed to him and was petrified to read: 'Sir, – If you hang any of the gentlemen condemned to death at the New Bailey prison, it will be worse for you. You will not survive afterwards.' Calcraft immediately sent the letter to the magistrates, whose job it was to oversee the hanging, and he included a note reading, 'I have received enclosed letter. It seems a serious job. I hope you will look after it, and that I shall get safe home again.'

Extra soldiers and police were drafted in; trains were barred from stopping at Salford until after the executions and a local tough was hired to act as minder to Calcraft on the scaffold. His nervousness was not helped when Larkin fainted as the noose was being put around his neck. Calcraft had to hold him up, then as the doomed men stood on their trapdoors Larkin collapsed again. Calcraft immediately pulled his lever and the three fell. A crowd of nearly 5,000 watched as Allen died within a minute, but one reporter recounted, 'The deaths of his fellow criminals was more painful, both Larkin and Gould appearing, from the vibration of the ropes, to struggle. Gould was the next to give up the ghost and about two minutes later the stillness of the rope showed that Larkin too ceased to live.'

Reporters were quick to point the finger of blame. According to one, 'The sufferings of Larkin, however, seemed very great and it was nearly two minutes before he ceased beating the air in ineffectual struggles which made the halter by which he hung quiver and jerk as if any moment it would be broken. It is said, though we know not with what truth, that the hangman had so clumsily adjusted the rope round this culprit's neck that he suffered more than he would have done had the duties of the scaffold been more carefully performed.' There was speculation that the prospect of being shot had made Calcraft careless, but then incompetence was a charge often levelled at him during his forty-five years as official executioner. Yet others, too, were frequently accused of bungling.

In Scotland there were so many complaints in the 1880s that all local authorities responsible for arranging executions had to be told by the government, 'Mention having frequently been called to the public scandal occasioned by the accidents which have from time to time occurred in the execution of capital sentences and by the proceedings both before and after the execution by the person employed as executioner, the Secretary for Scotland has thought it right to bring the following suggestions with a view of preventing as far as possible the objectionable circumstances which have sometimes attended the carrying out of sentences of death.'

One proposal was that Scots hangmen were so incompetent that future executions should be carried out by their English counterparts. Another made the root of the problems obvious: 'In making arrangements with the executioner it would be well, in order to prevent the possibility of grave public scandal, to stipulate that he should be kept under surveillance during the time he remains in the place where the sentence is to be executed, or at all events for the night before the execution. The Governor of the Prison, if desired by the responsible local authority, will provide a lodging within the Prison for this purpose and will strictly limit the allowance of alcoholic liquor to be made to the executioner. It would also be desirable to arrange for his immediate return home after the execution.'

The reference to drink was a direct result of the antics of executioner Bartholomew Binns. A railway platelayer, Binns used to practise his various methods by hanging cats and dogs. He was an assistant to William Marwood, but was thrust into the job of official hangman when Marwood died suddenly in September 1883. Tall and wiry, Binns looked like someone who made death a profession, and was sometimes mistaken for an undertaker. His first hangings were satisfactory. In a busy November he put to death bricklayer Henry Powell at Wandsworth; followed by former Coldstream Guardsman Thomas Day at Ipswich; pitman Peter Bray, aged thirty-two, at Durham; and then stonemason Thomas Riley, aged fifty-five, at Manchester. But by December there were murmurings about his behaviour, and these came to a head on the third of the month at Liverpool when Binns, then aged forty-four, hanged Henry Dutton for the murder of his wife's grandmother.

For two nights before the execution, Binns had been the centre of attention at a pub called the Sessions Hotel, near the site of the scaffold. There, surrounded by drunken mobs of men and women, he proudly showed off the rope and straps he used. After his weekend binge, it was not surprising that on the Monday morning he made a total botch of his work. The victim weighed only nine stones and an experienced hangman would have given him a long drop in order to ensure the dislocation of vertebrae that guaranteed instantaneous and painless death. But Binns miscalculated the length and compounded his bungling by using a rope that was too thick and then placing the noose in the wrong spot on Dutton's neck. As a result, when the trapdoor opened the murderer's body twisted around for two minutes as he struggled for life. It took eight minutes for him to die. A doctor who examined the body said death was due to strangulation, and described the executioner's efforts as 'poor work'.

Lloyd's Weekly Newspaper said, amidst claims the execution had smelled of drink on the scaffold, 'Bartholomew Binns has not kept the public waiting long for a proof of his utter incapacity and carelessness; and of the impropriety of appointing a hangman without even taking precautions as to the regularity of his conduct and his intelligence.' Binns himself protested, 'It is not true I was any the worse for drink. I got straight up out of bed, partook of no breakfast and went to the gaol.'

Despite the criticisms, he was allowed to carry on, but the last straw came with the hanging of Michael McLean, aged seventeen, at Liverpool on 10 March 1884. McLean was sentenced to death for the murder of a Spanish seaman. Binns had turned up in Liverpool on the Saturday and headed straight for a public house. After a lively boozing session, he had gone to sleep at the prison and made such a fuss when warders woke him up that police had to be called. On the scaffold he measured the length of McLean's drop wrongly, and once again placed the knot wrongly. After the hanging he drank freely in two local bars, yet again showing around his ropes and straps before clambering on a train 'apparently very far advanced in liquor', according to newspaper reports. A few days later he was sacked.

16

MONEY FOR OLD ROPE

HENRY ALBERT PIERREPOINT, the first to become a hangman in what became a well-known family of executioners, wasn't sacked for being drunk on the job, but after turning up the worse for drink to carry out an execution in 1910, he was never again used. Henry's condition resulted in him arguing with his assistant, John Ellis, and when the dispute turned violent, warders had to intervene. Ellis formally complained to the Home Office, which removed Henry's name from the official list of executioners.

Henry Pierrepoint was an efficient hangman. Binns was not, but then again, he was not the only bungler. The experienced William Marwood was also guilty of a particularly brutal example of ineptitude when he was hired to put to death shoemaker Edward Deacon from Bristol in April 1876. Deacon had murdered his wife, Amelia, but the hangman was about to inadvertently satisfy the demands of her friends for revenge. It was clear, as he walked to the scaffold, that Deacon was already terrified. A reporter from the *Bristol Post* described the scene: 'A glance at his face showed that he was suffering intense mental agony. But when he first caught sight of the ghastly engine of death the effect produced on him was painful to witness. He trembled violently and those who were near him aver that his hair stood literally on end such was the terror inspired in him by the dread object that met his eye.'

Deacon was right to be afraid. Marwood had looked nervous

on the scaffold, possibly being affected by the shrieks and groans of the victim. He had difficulty in getting the noose in the right position with the result, said the *Bristol Post* reporter, that as soon as the trapdoor opened: 'It was evident from the appalled looks of those who were in a position to see the wretched culprit in the well that some mishap had happened and that the prisoner's death was not so quick as it was expected would have been the case.' It now became obvious that Marwood's error was even worse. He hadn't left enough room below the trapdoor, with the result that as Deacon struggled for breath, he managed to touch the ground with a foot. 'He appeared to be trying to relieve himself of the suffocating pressure on his throat, and once, when the toes of his right foot touched the brickwork, he drew his shoulders back, as if preparing for a mighty effort, and sprang upwards, raising his feet many inches off the ground. He was distinctly heard to breathe. For nearly three minutes the poor wretch fought with death, and then all was still.'

Equally shocking was the execution of John Henry Johnson a year later at Leeds. Johnson had shot a man after a drunken brawl. Come his execution day, all seemed to be going according to plan until the executioner, Thomas Askern, the one-time York debtor, pulled the lever and the trapdoor opened. Down plunged Johnson, but the rope snapped. Askern and the scaffold party rushed down the steps, found the condemned man unhurt, and helped him back up. He had to wait around on the scaffold for ten minutes for another rope to be produced, but even the second attempt to hang him was bungled. Johnson didn't die immediately, but struggled for five minutes before breathing his last.

In addition to the standard fee of a few pounds, there were other perks claimed by hangmen. But on occasion their haste to finish off the victim and collect these led to criticisms of slackness. In 1828 the execution of William Corder by John Foxton at Bury St Edmunds, Suffolk, aroused considerable interest, especially among women, because the doomed man had a huge following of female admirers. He was on the gallows because he had killed one of his mistresses and then run off to London, where he was discovered much later. As he waited with the noose round his neck, Corder was nervous, and with every right, in view of what happened next. One journalist reported that Corder managed to whisper, 'I deserve my fate', but despite his wrongdoing he should have been spared the agony he was about to endure at the hands of an incompetent hangman. According to the reporter:

> Within a minute afterwards the deadly bolt was withdrawn and he was cut off from the number of the living. The hangman, after the corpse had fallen, performed his disgusting but necessary task of suspending his own weight around the body of the prisoner, to accelerate his death. At the same time the prisoner, who appeared to be in the last agonies, clasped his hands tighter together as if he was forming his last prayer for the mercy and forgiveness of offended heaven. Immediately afterwards his arms, which were raised a little, fell – the muscles appeared to relax – and his hands soon sunk down as low as their pinioned condition permitted. But life was not yet extinct; about eight minutes afterwards there was a heaving of the shoulders, a slight convulsion of the frame, an indistinct groan, and then all was still and no further motion was observed.
>
> It is an extraordinary fact, and certainly not to be accounted for on any principle of reason or common sense, that the rope with which Corder was hanged had become an article of arduous competition. I have been informed that it has been sold for a guinea an inch.

Money for old rope wasn't Foxton's only sideline. After up to 5,000 spectators had filed past the corpse – naked except for trousers and stockings, and with the abdomen split open to reveal Corder's muscles – Foxton whipped the remaining clothing off and hurried away to a local hotel to auction them. 'Such was the anxiety to see him that we heard several females boasting that they had been to see him five times after his head had been shaved,' said a correspondent for the *York Herald and General Advertiser*.

There were many cases of condemned people appearing to survive being hanged – at least for a few minutes – because of the incompetence of the executioner. But a handful literally walked away from the scaffold, and of these the most remarkable was Anne Greene, aged twenty-two, who was hanged at Oxford in 1650 for murdering her baby, even though it was stillborn. A prison doctor pronounced her dead but the next day, as students were about to dissect her corpse, they noticed a faint pulse. She revived, was given a pardon and lived another fifteen years.

In 1724 Maggie Dickson was sentenced to death in Edinburgh for hiding the death of her newborn baby. She was hanged at the Grassmarket, and her body put in a coffin and taken off on a cart, to be buried at Musselburgh. But on the way the carters heard loud banging, and when the lid was lifted, Maggie leapt out. Lawyers argued her remarkable rising from the dead was a sign that God wanted her to live, and so she did, for another forty years. A well-known city pub is named after her.

Robert Johnston was sentenced to be hanged for robbery at Edinburgh in 1818. But the trapdoor was not big enough, and as he hung partly through it, magistrates pleaded for a carpenter to make the opening bigger. Johnston continued hanging there as everyone waited, but finally his friends decided he had suffered enough and rescued him. Police and soldiers intervened and won a tug of war for the condemned man. He was hanged for a second time but another blunder meant the rope was too long and when the trapdoor was opened and he dropped his feet touched the ground. He was lifted up and the rope shortened to allow the noose to strangle him.

In fairness, hangmen had to contend with many distractions. It wasn't unusual for the behaviour of spectators to get out of hand, but the conduct of those who turned up for the execution of husband and wife Frederick and Maria Manning at Horsemonger Lane gaol in south London in November 1849 went from being boisterous to frightening. Among them was the author Charles Dickens, who was horrified by what he saw and heard. Appalled too was a reporter from the *Daily News*. The Mannings had been convicted of murdering Maria's wealthy lover for his money, and it had been decided they would be hanged together by William Calcraft.

For almost twenty-four hours before the time they were due to die, crowds had gathered around the gaol, among them handymen who quickly built rough stands so spectators could watch the ceremony. The journalist wrote, 'The proprietors of these stands were busily and incessantly occupied throughout the night of soliciting the patronage of every decently dressed person whom they encountered, clamorously soliciting attention to the strength, security and cheapness of their structures.' Those who could not afford a good view made do with crude jokes, betting on the precise time at which the Mannings would plunge to their deaths, whether they would be hanged together or separately and what the chances there were of a last minute reprieve. Others kept warm by organising 'late dancing parties, and executed quadrilles, polkas or jigs according to their respective taste or capabilities. Nor was the demeanour of their betters, who crowded the windows and platforms, more consonant with the dreadful scene a morbid curiosity had led them to witness. Some, we were told, formed themselves into late card parties and smoking and drinking relieved the tedium of the night.'

Everywhere drinking houses were packed, staying open throughout. 'Hundreds of itinerant basketmen were crying, "Mannings biscuits" and "Maria Mannings peppermints" for sale. A mob composed of the lowest rabble had collected under the drop where squibs and crackers were flying through the air, and every low cry and oath was to be heard.' Pickpockets had a field day. Fights began. A fire started, shrouding the gallows in smoke.

In the prison the final preparations were being made. *Lloyd's Weekly Newspaper* reported, 'While undergoing the dreadful process, Manning asked Calcraft if he should suffer much pain. Calcraft said if he would keep himself still, he would suffer no pain at all.' When it came to Maria's turn to be pinioned, one of the women warders burst out crying. Eventually the unhappy couple were paraded to the scaffold, where they were allowed a brief kiss and a kindly warder let their pinioned hands touch for a final time just before the trapdoor fell. As the crowd dispersed, many of the spectators lay helpless on pavements and roads: some victims of the crush, others simply too drunk to stand up.

Charles Dickens was appalled. He immediately wrote to *The Times*:

Sir — I was a witness of the execution at Horsemonger-lane this morning. I went there with the intention of observing the crowd gathered to behold it, and I had excellent opportunities of doing so, at intervals all through the night, and continuously from daybreak until after the spectacle was over. I believe that a sight so inconceivably awful as the wickedness and levity of the immense crowd collected at that execution this morning could be imagined by no man, and could be presented in no heathen land under the sun. The horrors of the gibbet and of the crime which brought the wretched murderers to it, faded in my mind before the atrocious bearing, looks and language, of the assembled spectators.

When I came upon the scene at midnight, the shrillness of the cries and howls that were raised from time to time, denoting that they came from a concourse of boys and girls already assembled in the best places, made my blood run cold. As the night went on, screeching, and laughing, and yelling in strong chorus of parodies on Negro melodies, with substitutions of 'Mrs. Manning' for 'Susannah,' and the like, were added to these. When the day dawned, thieves, low prostitutes, ruffians and vagabonds of every kind, flocked on to the ground, with every variety of offensive and foul behaviour. Fightings, faintings, whistlings, imitations of Punch, brutal jokes, tumultuous demonstrations of indecent delight when swooning women were dragged out of the crowd by the police with their dresses disordered, gave a new zest to the general entertainment. When the sun rose brightly – as it did – it gilded thousands upon thousands of upturned faces, so inexpressibly odious in their brutal mirth or callousness, that a man had cause to feel ashamed of the shape he wore, and to shrink from himself, as fashioned in the image of the Devil. When the two miserable creatures who attracted all this ghastly sight about them were turned quivering into the air, there was no more emotion, no more pity, no more thought that two immortal souls had gone to judgment, no more restraint in any of the previous obscenities, than if the name of Christ had never been heard in this world, and there was no belief among men but that they perished like the beasts. I am solemnly convinced that nothing that ingenuity could devise to be done in this city, in the same compass of time, could work such ruin as one public execution, and I stand astounded and appalled by the wickedness it exhibits. I do not believe that any community can prosper where such a scene of horror and demoralization as was enacted this morning outside Horsemonger-lane Gaol is presented at the very doors of good citizens, and is passed by, unknown or forgotten.

17

CLEAN SLATE

UNTIL 1961 AND THE passing of the Suicide Act, it was a criminal offence to either commit suicide or try to do so. But many viewed the execution of Thomas Fury at Durham in May 1882 as a clear case of legal suicide. His hanging and the amazing events leading up to it make his story one of the most astonishing in the annals of crime, and for that reason it merits being told in full. In its edition published on the day William Marwood sent Fury on his way to Hell, this was how the *North-Eastern Daily Gazette* summed up the dead man: 'Undoubtedly the man who today forfeited his life on the scaffold was one of the most extraordinary criminals that has ever come within the grasp of justice, and confessedly from the dock, when sentence of death was pronounced, he is a liar, a thief and a murderer.' Even today, more than a century and a half after he died, questions remain as to whether an innocent man walked to his doom.

Fury was a habitual lawbreaker, a thief, but also a police informer. A seaman who often acted as cook, he was an avid reader who spent much of his time at sea studying the Bible and immersing himself in the works of William Shakespeare. In February 1869 Fury was cook on board the bottle schooner *Lollard*. At the time he signed on, he had given the name Thomas Wright, and when the *Lollard* berthed at Sunderland he and a shipmate, John Lawrence, headed ashore in search of a good time, their pockets bulging with sovereigns. Knowing that seamen were prone to getting drunk and ending up being robbed by locals, Fury visited a Sunderland shop and bought two vicious double-edged Spanish-made pointed knives for protection.

Later, he met thirty-year-old prostitute Maria Fitzsimmons in a dockside bar. She was well known to the police for stealing the wallets of her clients. After a lively drinking session, during which Fury gave the woman a muffler, Lawrence went back to the *Lollard* while Fitzsimmons took Fury back to the grubby lodging house room in Baine's Lane, Sunderland, where she entertained customers. After sex they fell into a drunken sleep, but Fury awoke to find twenty-five of his sovereigns missing. In a rage, he accused Fitzsimmons of being the thief, and the pair started fighting. When she scratched his face, Fury suddenly produced one of the knives and launched a frenzied stabbing attack, leaving her dead from a dozen deep wounds, three of them through her heart. An examination later showed her killer had worsened the effect of one stab by then twisting the knife inside the victim's chest. He left with the walls and floor of the room spattered with blood, and his own clothing heavily bloodstained.

When her body was discovered, police began tracing her last movements and were told she had been last seen with a seaman from the *Lollard*. Officers showed the skipper the muffler but were told he did not recognise it.

Shortly before the schooner had finished loading a cargo of bottles from the Candlish factory in Sunderland and preparing to sail for London, Fury had arrived carrying a bundle, telling curious crewmen his face had been cut in a bar-room fight. During the voyage, the captain told Fury about the visit from police, who suspected the murderer was a crewmember. Somewhere off the east coast the bundle – concealing his bloody clothing – was thrown overboard. In London, Fury disappeared – and so did Thomas Wright. He now became known as Henry Charles Cort.

A series of arrests followed, mostly the result of a then

very substantial reward of £100 being offered by police for information leading to the culprit. Rumours pointed officers to a Hartlepool man who had just committed suicide, but he was soon discounted; then London lighterman Peter Connor appeared before magistrates charged with murder, only to be released a day later when he proved his innocence; other seamen were arrested, one as a result of a tip-off by Fury to the seaman's police handler. Over time, several men – James Hayman, David Hawkins, Joseph Lewes and George Legge – were kept in custody while police investigated their movements.

Their plight began to prey on Fury, on whom Lady Luck had smiled. When he won a huge bet on the result of the University boat race, he decided to act. That night, full of drink, he sat down, and in a pocketbook he wrote a full confession to the prostitute's murder. His unsigned statement said the crime was the result of her stealing money, and he was admitting to the murder so that an innocent man, currently held by the police, could be set free. There would be no point in the police looking for him, he said, because by the time they found the book he would be in America and would never return. He even used space to ridicule the police 'for the blindness they manifested while I was in Sunderland'.

Fury left the book at the side of the Serpentine, a popular spot with bathers, not realising that heavy overnight dew would soak it. However, next morning it was found, reasonably dry, by a Fellow of the Royal Geographical Society who was out for an early morning dip. The Fellow handed it to the police, and it was eventually sent to the north-east. Now officers were sure the killer had been on board the *Lollard* and that he was the man who had given his name as Thomas Wright. But where was he? Had he gone to America?

Gradually, interest in the murder of the prostitute faded. It was highly likely the killer would never be found, and for years the case, the muffler and the pocketbook, remained in a box gathering dust on a shelf in the Sunderland police office.

Ten years later, in August 1879, Henry Charles Cort appeared before a judge at the Old Bailey and was convicted of horse stealing and the attempted murder of a policeman. He was jailed for fifteen years and taken to Pentonville to serve his sentence. Slowly the daily grind of the tread wheel and sewing workshops wore him down. In the grim loneliness of his cell, he began writing upon a large slate given to each inmate to communicate with staff, speaking being punishable by a bread-and-water diet. On 13 March 1882, thirteen years after the Fitzsimmons slaughter, the prisoner Cort handed his slate to a warder and asked him to take it to the Pentonville governor. Both sides were covered with what amounted to a complete confession to the prostitute murder, including details of the weapon and the number of wounds that had been inflicted.

It included, 'I killed her by stabbing her several times. I wrote a most insulting note in a pocket-book with directions to the finder to forward it to the coroner of Sunderland, which is also in the possession of the police. On comparing the writing with my past and present sheets it will be found to correspond, and the book would be recognised by all the crew of the *Lollard*.'

Cort wanted to get everything off his chest, and the prison governor must have felt as though he was a priest hearing the sins of a parishioner in the confessional. Cort continued:

There are some others I have to account for but I have selected this case as likely to give the least trouble and expense to the public, whom I have already cost too much, and to which I shall confess as soon as I can obtain materials and leisure previous to my trial, for I see plainly I shall not be able to do so here by reason of being continually under punishment through inability to fulfil my tasks. Therefore sir, if you have the wish to keep that which you appealed to when punishing me . . . a clear conscience, let me beg of you not to deprive me of the little I have remaining by delaying to lay this statement before the proper authorities in order that other people may no longer suffer for my crime. In making this statement, I do so from a strict sense of duty, in my calm moment, not under the influence of passion, my own sufferings causing me to wish to relieve others now suffering by my means; so it remains with you how much longer they are to suffer.

A copy of his statement was sent to Sunderland, where police immediately realised the writer was the murderer. He was transferred north under heavy guard and admitted to really being Thomas Fury. While he waited for his trial at Durham Assizes, Fury read and wrote with a fervour that fascinated his captors.

When it came to his trial and the charge of murder was read out, Fury answered that he was guilty. Yet the only evidence against him was his own confession. He had only to say he had written it in a moment of madness and the police case would have collapsed. Even the judge, Mr Justice Watkin Williams, was moved by Fury's seeming determination to end his life and insisted that the prisoner change his plea to 'Not Guilty' and have proper legal representation. It should be for the jury and not Fury himself to decide whether there was a strong enough case to merit the death sentence. Clearly the judge realised that rather than face the remaining twelve years of his sentence in prison, Fury wanted to end his life. It was a bizarre form of legal suicide. And that was the argument put forward by his counsel, who pleaded for a verdict of manslaughter, but the jury preferred to rely on Fury's own words in the confession on his prison slate.

The *North Eastern Daily Gazette* reported, 'The trial lasted all day, the prisoner being accommodated with a seat in the dock, where he followed the evidence very closely, and at times could scarcely repress laughter. On the prisoner being found guilty, and asked if he had anything to say why sentence of death should not be passed upon him, an unusual scene occurred. The prisoner, without evincing any fear or motion, commencing to read an extraordinary document on drink, crime and the conduct of our convict establishments. Stopped by the judge while reading his statement, he pitched the whole of the manuscript into the reporters' box and appealing to them for publicity.'

Fury was told he would hang, and was sent to await a meeting at Durham Prison with executioner William Marwood. His fifty-page document was published by a firm of printers and attracted huge interest. In it, there were references to Shakespeare, Carlyle, Byron, Plato, the American Bill of Rights, the 'judicious hooker', the Bible, the Prayer Book and even the coronation oath. On 16 May 1882, Marwood walked through early morning sunshine from his lodgings in Durham's Dun Cow Inn to the prison, and at eight o'clock he gave thirty-seven-year-old Fury his final wish: death.

There were many similarities between the Fury case, that in 1891 of fifty-five-year-old agricultural labourer John William Johnson and another in 1950, of Patrick Turnage. Enraged with jealousy, Johnson had shot dead his former landlady on her wedding day. A native of Lincolnshire, he had moved north to County Durham in search of work and around 1874 began lodging with recently widowed Margaret Addison, aged thirty, at Hetton-le-Hole. He was well educated, she respectable, and he became infatuated with her. However, in about 1887 his drinking began to worry her and he was told to leave, the excuse being that his room was needed for her newlywed son and his bride. He found lodgings locally, but then discovered Margaret had a suitor and planned to marry. 'There will be a funeral before a wedding,' he warned in local bars. Then he carefully planned her killing.

He bought a revolver, and on the morning she was due to catch a train to meet her bridegroom, he kept watch on her home and her movements. When he saw Margaret leave, he walked up behind her and shot her twice, the second bullet crashing into her brain and killing her instantly. Then he walked a few yards to a police station and told officers what he had done. A clever defence counsel would have argued for a manslaughter verdict on the grounds that his mind was disturbed by the thought of losing forever the woman he loved. But when he appeared before Mr Justice Wills at Durham Assizes charged with Margaret's murder, the exchange that followed demonstrated his determination to die.

Formally charged, Johnson told the court, 'I am guilty.'

The judge asked, 'You have pleaded guilty to this murder. Do you appreciate the consequences? Do you understand the consequences of your pleading guilty?'

When Johnson told him, 'Yes, sir', the judge persisted in trying to help him, asking if he wanted legal representation. 'I do not wish it,' came the reply.

'You thoroughly understand what you are about?' wondered the judge.

'Yes, sir,' said Johnson. Seconds later the judge had donned the fatal black cap. 'I think you have arrived at a just conclusion in thinking that no investigation would alter, in any respect, the circumstances of this case, and I am not surprised, although it is unprecedented in my experience, that a prisoner should plead guilty to a charge of this nature involving the highest punishment of the law,' he said. Then he sentenced Johnson to death.

At that point the condemned man pulled out several sheets of blue foolscap paper, saying he wanted these to be given to reporters. The judge took them, but refused to pass them on.

While he waited in the condemned cell, Johnson told warders he had prepared a statement explaining why he had shot Margaret and trying to justify the murder, claiming he had a right to her hand after courting her for seventeen years. He was executed by James Billington three days before Christmas 1891.

Almost sixty years later, another seaman pleaded guilty to murdering a prostitute and demanded to be put to death. Patrick Turnage, aged thirty-one, was a merchant seaman who was trawling dockside bars in search of sex in July 1950. He eventually picked up a seventy-eight-year-old prostitute named Julia Beesley. After sex, an argument broke out when he objected to paying, and she was strangled. Detectives quickly tracked Turnage down, who admitted from the outset to being responsible.

Turnage was advised by his lawyers that the prosecution would accept a manslaughter plea and he could expect a fifteen-year sentence, meaning he would be free in ten years. But the bleak prospect of prison life was too much. No matter how hard his legal team argued against him, Turnage insisted it was murder, knowing certain death at the end of a hangman's rope would follow. He told a friend, 'Better to get it over with now,' and was executed in November 1950.

Just as Thomas Fury and John Johnson had wanted to die, Joseph Deans was so anxious to get the business of being hanged over as quickly as possible that he literally ran to his death. Deans' story moved many of his friends, who felt it was the classic tale of a man cheated by the woman he loved. It even brought a lump to the throat of the man called in to execute him, John Ellis, official hangman for twenty-three years.

Deans spent much of his younger life in South Africa, both as a gold miner and a soldier. When he decided to return home to England, he was reasonably well off, with good savings and a comfortable pension. With the prospect of the Great War looming and men being encouraged to enlist in the Army, Deans had no difficulty getting work as a miner near Sunderland. Women found him attractive, not least because he was happy to offer them a good time and to buy them presents, but it was widow Catherine Convery, aged forty-eight, who caught his eye.

Deans lavished his money on her, but his affection for Catherine turned into an ugly obsession. He resented her going out, became angry if he suspected she had looked at another man and then as his money began running out blamed her as a spendthrift, a gold digger. When he became convinced she had another beau, Deans began talking madly of killing her. He carried a photograph of her in his hat, and one night in a bar he showed it to a pal and told him, 'I love every hair of her head. But I'm going to finish her off tonight.'

After seeing her in a bar he chased after her with a razor and axe, inflicting appalling wounds with the axe that almost severed her head. She died a week later while he cut his throat with the razor and then handed himself in to the police, together with the murder weapon. He was convicted of her murder and sentenced to be executed. In his remarkable life story, *Diary of a Hangman*, John Ellis tells how after leaving the condemned cell on the morning of 20 December 1916, Deans set off on his own to the scaffold. 'He was running so fast that it was as much as my assistant could do to keep up with him,' said Ellis. The hangman clearly sympathised with Deans' desire not to hang about. In seconds he was pinioned, dropped and dead.

But of the countless gruesome crimes that led men and women to the Durham scaffold, none were so pitiless as that of twenty-two-year-old Charles William Conlin from Norton near Stockton-on-Tees in County Durham. Factory worker and former Royal Scots Fusilier Conlon murdered his grandparents, market-stall holder Emily Frances Kirby, aged sixty-four, and her husband, Thomas, who was two years younger, then stole their savings and began splashing money about the district. A near neighbour, who was digging for soil in which to re-pot plants, discovered Kirby and Thomas's bodies in a shallow grave under a hedge.

The find was grisly enough, but even more horrible was what a post-mortem revealed. The couple had been battered and strangled – and then buried while they were still alive. There were traces of soil and debris in their throats and windpipes. A witness told of seeing Conlin in the area the previous day carrying a spade. Inquiries showed he had a dodgy past. He had once worked for Emily but was sacked for stealing, a pattern repeated when he was given a job with a local jeweller. When he was arrested, Conlin claimed he could not remember killing his grandparents, but the evidence – including the discovery of Thomas's wallet in the murderer's coat – convinced a jury. He was executed by Thomas Pierrepoint at Durham on 4 January 1929.

The expression, 'Let him have it' featured crucially during the trial for murder in London in 1953 of Derek Bentley and Christopher Craig. In November 1952, Bentley, then aged nineteen, and sixteen-year-old Craig were spotted trying to burgle a warehouse. Craig had a revolver and when a police officer told him to give up the weapon Bentley was said, by police, to have shouted, 'Let him have it,' although he would later deny using the expression. However, Craig fired one shot, hitting an officer in the shoulder, and another which killed Constable Sidney Miles. Both young men were charged with murder, the prosecution at their trial suggesting that by calling, 'Let him have it, Chris,' Bentley was urging his accomplice to fire. Both were convicted of murder. Bentley was condemned to hang, but because Craig was legally regarded as too young to be executed he was ordered to be detained at Her Majesty's Pleasure, serving ten years before being freed. Despite a massive campaign calling for him to be reprieved, Bentley was hanged. In the 1990s, Bentley was pardoned and then his murder conviction was quashed.

But it was not the first time those four simple words, 'Let him have it' had preceded a murder. In February 1940 police constables William Shiell and William Stafford were tipped off about an ongoing robbery at the Co-operative store in Coxhoe, County Durham. They arrived there and saw several men in the act of thieving. As Shiell chased after two of the culprits, he was shot in the stomach. Among his last gasping words were that the gunman's accomplice had shouted, 'Let him have it.'

Three days after Shiell had died in hospital, Vincent Ostler, aged twenty-seven, and twenty-four-year-old William Appleby were arrested in Yorkshire. During their interviews, Appleby admitted they had been the robbers, but, he claimed, he did not know Ostler had a gun, and he denied saying, 'Let him have it.' However, in law, even though Appleby had not fired the fatal shot, he was deemed to be equally guilty and both were charged with murdering the policeman. They were convicted following a lengthy trial and hanged together by Thomas Pierrepoint on the Durham Prison scaffold on 11 July 1940.

18

THE HAUNTED HANGMAN

AT PRECISELY NINE O'CLOCK on the morning of 9 January 1923, at separate London prisons, hangmen launched into eternity Freddie Bywaters, aged twenty, and his mistress Edith Thompson, who'd heralded her twenty-ninth birthday a few days earlier. Edith was literally carried unconscious to the scaffold at Holloway, where executioner John Ellis gently placed the noose around her neck. Four warders held her, and at a signal from Ellis, let go. At that instant he pulled the lever, opening the trap. A few hundred yards away in Pentonville Jail, Freddie, protesting his mistress was innocent, was being put to death by William Willis.

The execution of Edith Thompson continues to be regarded as the most controversial and unjust hanging of a woman in British legal history. One million people who signed a petition demanding she was reprieved had their hopes rejected; warders who witnessed her death were so sickened they quit their jobs; Ellis, a veteran of 203 executions did not believe she should be hanged. In *Diary of a Hangman* he wrote, 'I genuinely hoped she would be saved from my rope.' He resigned as hangman just months after her execution and went on to commit suicide. The case had one more victim. It was the only occasion when a hanging almost resulted in the prison governor being locked up in one of his own cells.

Lively and intelligent, Edith's bubbly brightness had led to her becoming chief buyer for a firm of London milliners. When she was fifteen she met shipping clerk Percy Thompson, three years her senior. They finally wed in 1916 after courting for six years. Edith soon realised she had signed into a loveless, dull marriage. She longed for fun and adventure and found these when she and her husband became friendly with handsome Bywaters, who fascinated her with stories of voyages around the world in the Merchant Navy. Percy fatally invited the young seaman to join them on holiday and then to stay with them. That set off a passionate affair between housewife and lodger, and when Percy discovered them making love, a violent quarrel ended with Bywaters being sent packing. The lovers continued their affair, exchanging dozens of letters when Freddie was at sea, and secretly meeting when he came ashore.

In their letters they not only vowed an everlasting desire to be with one another, but Edith wrote of trying to get rid of her husband by feeding him mashed potato mixed with ground glass and then trying to poison him. 'Be jealous so much that you will do something desperate,' she implored Bywaters. And he did. One night as the Thompsons walked home from the theatre, Bywaters leapt out from behind a hedge and stabbed his rival dead before running off. He was soon caught, because Edith gave police his name and said he was the killer. She revealed details of the affair, but when detectives discovered the love letters and the incriminating contents, she and Bywaters were charged with murder.

At their trial Freddie shouldered the blame, saying Edith did not know he was going to kill her husband. But the judge, Mr Justice Shearman, made his disgust of an adulteress who scorned her marriage vows so obvious that it rubbed off on the jury, who convicted both accused. There was little public sympathy for Freddie, but massive support for Edith, who was convinced, until only hours before her date with death, that she would be reprieved.

On the morning of her execution thousands protested outside

Holloway, many fascinated by the sight of a well-dressed middle-aged woman parading about carrying a placard, proclaiming, 'If these two are hanged, judge and jury are murderers also.' None of the pleadings saved Edith, and the story might have ended with their deaths. But was the establishment so ashamed of what had been done to her that it determined to have the case itself hushed away and put to sleep for all time? An astonishing development was yet to come.

On his way to the scaffold Bywaters had exchanged a few words with the governor of Pentonville, Major Frederick Wallace Hastings Blake. Those words would land the major in very hot water after he retired three years later on a pension of £300 a year. Keen to earn some extra pocket money, he wrote a series of newspaper articles about his experiences, and in one described the final moments of Bywaters. That particular article was read by thousands of Londoners. Part of it was also read out aloud in court in December 1926 when the major appeared charged with breaching the Official Secrets Act, the first-ever case of its kind.

Under the headline 'What Bywaters Said to Me' the major had written about his final meeting with the condemned seaman on the morning of the execution:

The young man shook me warmly by the hand and said, 'It is her I want to speak to you about, sir. I will swear she was not guilty.' I said, 'My boy that is no good now. She was tried and found guilty. She appealed, and there is nothing left. In any case, it would not be a very happy life for her after all that has happened.' He said, 'I cannot bear to think of them mauling her about.' I replied, 'They will be very gentle. Don't think of it. There is only a minute or two left. I should like to hear you say that you are sorry for what you did.' 'I am sorry sir, damned sorry,' said Bywaters, and then the door opened and they, the executioners, came. We shook hands and he said, 'Yes sir, I really am sorry. Goodbye.' And they marched him to the shed and sent him on his last voyage.

Just how seriously the Establishment took the governor revealing Bywaters' final words was shown by the fact that the case was prosecuted by a very senior government law officer, the Solicitor General, who told the jury, 'That statement, whether historically accurate in some respects or not, clearly contained statements referring to a confession or comment made by Bywaters before his sentence and upon the sentence passed upon Mrs Thompson. Last-minute confessions or comments upon the trial or sentence of the court are obviously matters which require the consideration of the Secretary of State himself. It is plainly undesirable that they should be communicated to members of the public. In the first place, they are likely to cause great pain to many persons. It would be against the public interest, I suggest, that when confessions are made at the last moment they should be communicated to the public when other persons involved in statements made will have no opportunity of dealing with them.'

Had Major Blake written the truth? One of the warders there that morning told the court, 'As I was pinioning Bywaters he looked at Major Blake and said, "I'm sorry I murdered Thompson." I had been at more than twenty executions and never heard a man confess before.'

The governor was facing prison, almost certainly in the same jail he used to run. His lawyer said what many outsiders believed: 'Major Blake is brought here as an example. Everybody who can read knows that for years people in eminent places have been publishing and broadcasting in books and articles things that they learned when they were in official positions, things that at the time were deadly secrets but which possibly in the passing of time ceased to be secrets. You may just imagine that the authorities had writhed under it and hated it.'

The judge left the jury in no doubt what was expected of them. They were told, 'If sensationalism and bad taste devour and feed upon information of this sort, and the information is something which ought not to be disclosed, that is a very good reason for putting the law into action. It is nasty to give to the still gaping public three years after the event the last words of a young man sentenced to death. It is an offence against good taste.' They found the major guilty. He was spared jail, but after the judge was told he had been paid £315 for his series, he was fined £250 and ordered to pay the prosecution costs.

After her execution, in accordance with custom, the body of Edith Thompson was buried inside the Holloway walls, but in 1971 during rebuilding work, it was exhumed and this time the authorities agreed it should be reburied elsewhere. She was laid to rest in a Surrey Cemetery and later a headstone was placed at the spot with the inscription, 'Sleep on, beloved.'

If Edith Thompson was unlucky, Ethel Le Neve was fortunate to escape the same fate as her lover, Dr Hawley Harvey Crippen. They were chief players in a real life-and-death drama that reached its climax with a wireless message from a ship's captain, the first time one had been used to catch a criminal.

American-born Crippen, an eye, ear, nose and throat specialist, lost his first wife to a stroke, and after marrying music-hall entertainer Cora Turner, whose stage name was Belle Elmore in 1892, the couple moved to London. Cora made no secret of a string of affairs. She was loud, uncouth, bad-tempered and at times she disgusted her husband, who took his own mistress, typist Ethel Le Neve. When their affair began in 1907, Crippen was forty-five and Ethel twenty-four. Three years later, in late January 1910, Crippen announced his wife had left him and had moved to California, where she had died of pneumonia. Ethel moved in with him and began drawing money from Cora's bank account.

Then Crippen changed his story, claiming his wife had run off to America with an ex-boyfriend, Bruce Miller. Suspicious police searched the home he shared with Ethel and eventually discovered human remains under the brick floor of the basement. It was impossible to identify them, but forensic specialist Sir

Bernard Spilsbury claimed he discovered traces of human tissue bearing signs of an old scar. And that fitted in with an operation Cora was said to have had not long before she vanished. He said too he had found traces of the poison hyoscine, and inquiries revealed Crippen had bought the drug around the time his wife disappeared. By that time, Crippen and Ethel had vanished. Newspaper stories about the police hunt for them, and the offer of a £100 reward, interested Captain Henry Kendall, skipper of the steamship *Montrose*.

As the vessel crossed the Atlantic, Kendall became curious about two of his passengers, a Mr John Philip Robinson and his son. The boy seemed remarkably feminine, and the two acted more as lovers than father and son. What Kendall could see of Mr Robinson matched the description of the man police wanted. But, according to the newspapers, the fugitive had false teeth. The crafty captain invited the Robinsons to dine at his table, told a joke and looked closely as his guest laughed. He sported a set of false teeth. The skipper sent a message to his London office, requesting it was passed on to the police. It was to the effect that he was convinced Crippen and Le Neve were among his passengers, and his slow-moving ship would dock at Quebec in a few days. Scotland Yard dispatched Inspector Walter Dew on a faster vessel, and when the *Montrose* arrived at the mouth of the St Lawrence River, the policeman was there to meet it and arrest Crippen and Le Neve.

Crippen was accused of poisoning his wife and burying her body, and if it was found that Ethel knew about the killing, then the likelihood was that she too would end up on the gallows. The doctor not only said he knew nothing about his wife's death, but claimed the remains found in his basement weren't those of Cora and had been put there by an earlier tenant. And he was adamant Ethel had done nothing wrong.

Initially Crippen and Le Neve appeared in the dock together, and a few days before that initial appearance Crippen wrote to a friend begging, 'Will you please get Ethel a blouse! A crepe de Chine one, with a nice-figured insertion in the yoke and cuff! I want her to wear it at our trial and to be a surprise present from me.'

But then it was decided to try them separately, and Crippen was convicted of killing Cora and sentenced to death. Ethel's trial followed immediately. She was accused of 'assisting Hawley Harvey Crippen to escape from justice at a time at which she knew that he had been guilty of a felony, namely the murder of his wife.' She sat in the dock, her face covered with a veil, while Crippen waited to die at Pentonville prison. Her former landlady told how in late January Ethel had 'come home very ill. She would take no supper but went to bed. Her appearance was that of somebody who had suffered a great shock, who was stricken with horror at something that had happened.' Not long afterwards she suddenly became cheerful, wearing Cora's clothes and talking of marrying the doctor, who was planning to divorce his wife because she had left him for another man.

The jury was told, 'You must ask yourselves whether there was not in her mind some knowledge that Mrs Crippen would never come back. It is quite obvious that she was certain Mrs Crippen would never return.'

But Crippen had continually argued that Ethel could know nothing about a murder, because he didn't either. She was acquitted, and in his condemned cell, knowing she would now survive, Crippen wanted only to end his life as soon as possible. He worried about his cat, Peter. 'Kiss Peter for me and tell him to be good,' he asked a visitor. 'I cared so much for him. My heart has ached so after him.' He took one of the lenses out of his spectacles, intending to cut his throat with it, but a suspicious warder discovered the little plot.

Hangman John Ellis, meantime, was also wishing the execution day would come. He was being plagued with morbid requests for souvenirs. One woman even wrote begging for a scrap of the noose, telling Ellis it would make her 'a lucky talisman'. After his retirement, the executioner revealed Crippen had walked smiling to the scaffold on 23 November, and continued smiling even as the hood was pulled over his head. Crippen left all his property and savings to Ethel.

On the day he was hanged, Ethel boarded a ship and set sail for North America. She lived in Canada for three years before returning to London, changing her name and later marrying and bringing up a family.

Ten months after Crippen was hanged, spinster Eliza Mary Barrow, aged forty-nine, died suddenly at the north London house where she lodged with insurance superintendent Frederick Henry Seddon and his wife Margaret. Miss Barrow was well off, while Seddon was a skinflint obsessed with money. She frequently fell out with her relatives, believing they wanted to get their hands on her savings and leave her broke and homeless. Seddon on the other hand convinced her he could be trusted and suggested an arrangement in which she handed over all her assets to him in exchange for which he would pay her just over £70 a year for the rest of her life, more than enough to pay for her keep and provide small luxuries. He convinced her this would give her the security she sought and mean she would always have a roof over her head. So Miss Barrow signed an agreement to this effect and made a will naming Seddon as executor. Three days later she died suddenly. Despite her wealth, she was buried in a grave with other paupers – this after Seddon haggled with the undertaker to get his price down.

Family members kicked up such a fuss that the body was exhumed and found to contain massive amounts of arsenic. Police claimed their inquiries showed one of the Seddon children, Margaret, had bought arsenic-soaked flypapers from a local chemist and the parents had soaked these in water to extract the poison with which they laced their spinster's food. The Seddons were charged with murder, but from the outset protested their innocence. The only direct connection between them and arsenic was the flypapers, but Margaret, then aged sixteen, claimed at the trial of her parents in 1912 she had never ever set foot inside the chemist's shop. Nevertheless, Frederick was found guilty. His wife, however, was cleared.

Even facing death couldn't stop Frederick from conducting business deals. Just before John Ellis executed him, Frederick was haggling from his cell over the price offered for some of his furniture. When the arguing stopped, he was taken to the gallows in April 1912 – three days after the sinking of the *Titanic* – and Pentonville prison officials boasted that the time between his leaving the cell and dying was just twenty-five seconds. The day after his death his sister received a letter from him. 'I am a victim of a gross miscarriage of justice. My execution will be a judicial murder, for I did not murder Miss Barrow,' he wrote. A century later many are convinced it wasn't evidence that convicted Frederick Seddon but his reputation for being mean.

John Reginald Halliday Christie was a schoolboy at the time Crippen was performing his heinous deed. But the evil of the doctor was nothing compared with the vile crimes of Christie, who turned his home at 10 Rillington Place, Notting Hill, London, into a mausoleum of horror. A pervert who could only get sexual satisfaction with prostitutes, Christie killed some of his victims on the pretext of curing them of bronchitis and other health problems by persuading them to inhale a home-made concoction from a jar. In fact, the container was linked up to the gas supply, and victims fell unconscious, at which point they were strangled. His catalogue of evil was discovered in 1953 when he moved out of the premises and another tenant found a bricked-up alcove in which were the bodies of three women. Police began a detailed search, digging up floors, the garden and an outhouse, until nine bodies emerged, including those of Christie's wife Ethel and the wife and baby daughter of another tenant, Timothy Evans. Christie was hanged at Pentonville in July 1953. He had been tried only for the murder of Ethel, although there was no doubt he murdered at least seven others. He was also responsible for the death of Timothy Evans, who was wrongly convicted of murdering his own daughter Geraldine and hanged at Pentonville in March 1950. Christie was the real killer of the child. As he stepped on to the same scaffold where Evans had died, Christie complained to executioner, Albert Pierrepoint, 'My nose is itching,' at which the hangman assured him, 'Don't worry. It won't bother you for long.'

In 1966 Evans was granted a Royal pardon and his remains, which had been buried in Pentonville Jail, were exhumed and he was given a Catholic funeral and re-buried in Leytonstone, London. But the hanging of this innocent added weight to the increasing arguments against the continuing use of the death penalty and was an important factor in the abolition of capital punishment except for a handful of offences.

Christie's last request – for his nose to be rubbed – was refused. The final plea of another ladykiller as he entered the gallows shed at Pentonville was granted, however. Neville Clevely Heath was asked, 'Do you have any final request? Is there anything you would like? A glass of whisky perhaps?' His reply surprised nobody, 'Yes, please, and while you're about it, sir, you might make that a double.' Pentonville officials duly obliged before Albert Pierrepoint sent one of the worst monsters to trawl the streets of 1940s Britain to Hell.

Handsome, debonair and a psychopath with a flair for living a Walter Mitty existence, Heath first pretended to Margery Gardner, aged thirty-two, an artist and sometime film extra, that he was a lieutenant colonel, his stories being sufficiently convincing to persuade her to wine and dine him before they repaired to a London hotel room in June 1946. There, he savagely murdered and abused her. When her body was found, descriptions of the dead woman given by friends, led detectives to quickly realise the killer was Heath. 'Wanted' posters showing his photograph went up in police stations throughout England.

Three weeks later, in Bournemouth, Doreen Margaret Marshall, aged twenty-two, met and went walking with fellow hotel guest Group Captain Rupert Brook. He took her to dinner and then walked her back to the hotel. Later, her severely mutilated body was discovered by a dog walker. 'Brook' was, of course, Neville Heath.

At his trial the criminal pleaded insanity, but unlike his victims, the jury saw through his deceit and convicted him of murder.

19

ACID-BATH VAMPIRE

HIS DEADLY APPOINTMENT with hangman William Marwood just hours away, Dr George Henry Lamson was desperate to send out a message he hoped would save others from his fate. It was: don't dabble with drugs. Well over a century since his execution, his warning remains more relevant and pressing than ever. It is one police and experts uphold, and yet the doctor, who should have known better, killed because he failed to heed it.

Just as Dr Crippen would do nearly thirty years later, Lamson used poison to kill his victim. Crippen killed because he wanted freedom; Lamson murdered a helpless brother-in-law to feed an addiction to morphine that had left him penniless. But while Crippen was meek and servile, Lamson was a hero who had won medals for his courage. Even so, his dependency upon the drug sent him spiralling into a pit of wickedness. From his condemned cell at Wandsworth Jail in late April 1882 the twenty-nine-year-old skilled surgeon wrote to a friend:

I have told you much and endeavoured to make clear to you my own impressions and ideas as to my mental and moral condition for a long-time previous to the act for which I am sentenced to death. The news of my brother-in-law's death roused me as from a species of cloud; then came my long period of imprisonment [while he waited for his trial]; and while there, necessarily the total deprivation of the drug I had so long been accustomed to. With great mental and physical suffering was the weaning accomplished, leaving, however, strongly perceptible results.

There was the fearful ordeal of the trial, the awful shock of the sentence, and then the sojourn in the condemned room here face to face with death cleared away all clouds from my mind, and now, getting back into the mists of the past, I believe I can truly and solemnly say, as only can be said under my present conditions, that in my right and normal state of mind the compassing and committing such a crime as that for which I now must die would have been utterly and absolutely impossible and altogether foreign to my whole nature and instincts. Subject to mental disturbances from slight causes from my earliest years, with a brain easily affected, the use or abuse of morphine and sedatives and narcotics made a ready physical, mental and moral victim of me. I earnestly pray Almighty God to pardon to yielding to such habits, and trust they may be an awful warning to others similarly tempted and assailed, seeing to what indescribably fearful consequences they have led in my case.

When a young medical student, American-born Lamson volunteered with distinction during strife in the Balkans and the Franco–Prussian War of 1870 to 1871, winning a number of awards for bravery. But he became addicted to the morphine with which he alleviated the suffering of his patients. He moved to England, qualifying as a GP and marrying Kate John on the Isle of Wight in late 1878, before moving with his bride to Bournemouth. His addiction strained not just his wife's love, although she remained loyal to him to the end. Morphine cost money, and even though many of his patients in the resort were wealthy and showed their appreciation of his obvious skill and care with generosity, his savings slipped away into the same blissful obscurity the drug brought him.

His creditors began making demands for payment. Beset by the unrelenting craving for morphine and desperate to break from the shackles of penury, he saw a way to end his problems. Kate's brother Percy, a nineteen-year-old boarding-school pupil, was severely disabled. Experts had diagnosed him as a hemiplegic because one side of his body was completely paralysed and there was no hope of recovery. Percy's parents had made a generous settlement on him to ensure he would always have enough funds to guarantee permanent nursing care. If he died, his two sisters, including Kate, would share the money. In December 1881 Lamson paid a call on Percy, taking the teenager a freshly baked Dundee cake and watching avidly as the youngster devoured a slice before offering Percy a pill that he said would ease his suffering. However, the pill contained a poison – aconite. Lamson had remembered a lecture during his student days in which a specialist had assured his listeners the drug was undetectable. In fact, medical advances had made that claim out-of-date, and when Percy died not long after the visit, a forensic expert quickly diagnosed the presence of aconite.

Lamson was arrested. In jail awaiting his trial for murder, he suffered nightmares from withdrawal symptoms but was helped and encouraged by friends and Kate. He was confident he would be cleared, his defence disputing the prosecution claim that aconite was found in the dead boy's body and arguing that even if it was, there was no proof it had come from Lamson. However, a chemist in business near his Bournemouth practice told of a visit by the doctor to buy the poison shortly before Percy's fatal 'illness'.

There were also hints of a further sinister secret. Percy had an older brother, Hubert William. He had been staying with Lamson and Kate when he died at their home in 1879 at the age of eighteen. There was thought to be nothing suspicious about his death, but his passing meant the removal of one more possible recipient of the money left to Percy.

In his condemned cell, Lamson admitted to prison officials

he had administered poison to Percy but emphatically denied implication in Hubert's death. His hanging was delayed for three weeks when friends in America, including the US President Chester Arthur, pleaded for time. They supplied documents suggesting there was a trace of madness in the Lamson family, but their evidence failed to persuade judges to overturn the death sentence.

On the afternoon before his execution, Lamson spent two and a half hours with Kate, who had stood by him throughout. Next morning, 28 April 1882, the bearded doctor, his black frock coat making his complexion appear even paler, had to be supported by warders on his way to the gallows. A reporter noted, 'He scarcely appeared to know or appreciate what was going on around him. When the words, "Blessed be the name of God" were uttered the convict appeared to make a slight bow, and the words, "In the midst of life, we are in death", uttered just before the cap was placed over his head, seemed to strike him with a deadly chill.'

Another who tried escaping the gallows by claiming insanity was John George Haigh, best known as the 'Acid Bath Murderer'. Haigh was hanged at Wandsworth in August 1949 after being convicted of murdering Mrs Olivia Durand-Deacon, a widow aged sixty-nine, and, like Lamson, he killed his victim because he was short of money. However, while the doctor protested he was not responsible for a second death, of which he was popularly suspected, the thirty-nine-year-old company director claimed, in one of the most astonishing confessions ever to be heard in a British courtroom, he had not just killed nine victims but had bled them to drink their blood.

Was his claim to being a mass-murdering psychopath a ruse to avoid hanging and instead be sent to Broadmoor, the high-security psychiatric hospital in Berkshire? During his opening speech at Haigh's trial at Lewes Assizes the Attorney General, Sir Hartley Shawcross, leading the prosecution, had no doubts. He told the jury, 'Haigh asked a police inspector, "Tell me frankly, what are the chances of anybody being released from Broadmoor?" There was certainly no sign then of reason tottering on its throne, but rather an indication of careful premeditation in the prisoner's mind about the line he would take.'

Haigh had denied murdering the well-off widow. But it was what he did with her body that left few in the court feeling he deserved mercy. Broke and in debt, Haigh had been staying at a hotel in South Kensington, London with Mrs Durand-Deacon. Creditors were chasing him for payment, and so was the hotel manager when in February 1949 Haigh interested Durand-Deacon in investing in a business of producing imitation fingernails. He persuaded her to join him looking over some of the items in a disused storeroom, and inside, he shot her through the head.

'The following day the defendant, using false names, was seeking to obtain money he needed by the sale of that poor woman's personal belongings,' said the prosecutor. 'I shall put this to you as a case attended by certain unpleasant, sordid, even nauseating features and in reality an exceedingly simple case of carefully premeditated murder for gain. Removing her fur coat and jewellery he pushed the body into a drum and filled it with sulphuric acid.' Four days later Haigh went back to the death scene. 'He emptied the contents of the drum over the earth in the yard, but he was a little too quick because when he poured the acid away not all traces of the body were finally destroyed.'

When Haigh was interviewed by the police he told a detective, 'If I tell you the truth, you would not believe it. It sounds too fantastic for belief. Mrs Durand-Deacon no longer exists. She has disappeared completely and no trace of her can ever be found. I have destroyed her with acid. How can you prove murder if there is no body?'

Sir Hartley said Haigh made a lengthy statement. 'The prisoner asserts that having killed this unfortunate woman he proceeded to drink some of her blood. That statement may, or may not, be true. It may or may not be relevant. You will remember that previously he had made the inquiry about the chances of being released from Broadmoor. When a man, apparently sane, is charged with a murder to which there is no possible answer on the facts, before he can look forward to getting out of Broadmoor, he has to consider whether and how he can get himself in.'

In the statement Haigh said, 'I shot her in the back of the head while she was examining paper for use as fingernails. Then I went out and fetched in a drinking glass and made an incision, I think with a penknife, in the side of her neck and collected a glass of blood which I then drank.' Then he made a fantastic claim that he had killed more victims: 'In 1944 I disposed of William Ronald McSwann in a similar manner, and of Donald McSwann and Amy McSwann in 1946. In 1948 Dr Archibald Henderson and his wife, Rosalie Henderson, also in a similar manner. I hit William McSwann on the head with a cosh, withdrew a glass of blood from his throat and drank it. I put him in a forty-gallon tank and disposed of him.'

He said he wrote letters to relatives of victims, posting them all over Britain to give the impression they were still alive. In each case he dumped the bodies in acid after drinking their blood. Victim number six was a woman aged thirty-five, whom he'd met in London. He killed her with a cosh and dumped her in the acid bath. Number seven was a young man in his mid-thirties and he was followed into acid by another young woman he knew only as Mary.

Was Haigh making this story up as part of a plan to feign madness? Police said they could find no evidence of other murders, but after the disappearance of Mrs Durand-Deacon, an examination of the storeroom revealed a gun, acid and a receipt from a firm of cleaners for her fur coat. Was he sane? His barrister Sir David Maxwell Fyfe told the court about a series of dreams Haigh had in which he was in a forest of crucifixes:

As the dreams developed the crucifixes became trees and men appeared to be collecting something from dripping trees. At first it appeared to be rain or dew, and then as the dream developed it appeared to be blood. You will hear that the dream is repeated six or seven times and the prisoner's account is that as the blood was taken he tried to get near the men, but could never get near enough and he felt an overwhelming desire for blood, and secondly that the controlling spirit of his was determined that he should have blood. When the opportunity came to do these dreadful deeds, he felt that he was carrying out not his own desires but the divinely appointed course which had been set for him in this way.

Haigh may have dreamed of crucifixes, strange men and of being sent to Broadmoor, from where doctors would eventually allow his release, but he was disappointed when, after a two-day trial, he was found guilty and executed at Wandsworth on 10 August 1949.

If it was possible for a crime to be even more gruesome than that of Haigh, then it was surely the case of salesman Patrick Herbert Mahon, aged thirty-nine, who was convicted in 1924 of murdering his girlfriend, Emily Beilby Kaye, in quaintly named Crumbles near Eastbourne, Sussex. Mahon, handsome and a married man, had a chequered past and a police record for fraud and robbery for which he had spent time in prison. He began an affair with the statuesque, fair-haired thirty-four-year-old secretary, and he would later claim she began pestering him to leave his wife, Mavourneen, and begin a new life with her abroad – something he was unwilling to do.

Emily had a very good reason for wanting their relationship to become permanent: she was two months pregnant. They rented a bungalow at Crumbles to have time to discuss their future, although he maintained he was intending to break off the relationship. They argued and the dispute turned violent; Mahon said his mistress hit him with an axe, and as they struggled she fell and hit her head on a coalscuttle. He later told police, 'The events of the next few seconds I cannot remember except as a nightmare of horror for I saw blood begin to issue from her head where she had struck the cauldron. I did my utmost to revive here. I simply could not at the time say whether I strangled her or whether she died of a fall, but from the moment she fell she did not move.'

He had left her body overnight in a bedroom while he travelled by train to his home in London to work out what to do. Next day, before returning, he bought a hatchet and knife and when she arrived, he set about the grisly job of getting rid of Miss Kaye. It was Good Friday and just as an act of bloody murder had caused horror nearly 2,000 years earlier, another would leave some in the courtroom unable to stomach the details when his statement was continued: 'When I got back I was still so upset and worried that I could not then carry out my intentions to then decapitate the body. I severed the legs from the hips, the head and left the arms on. I then put the various parts in a trunk and locked it. I left the trunk in the spare bedroom and locked the door.' A week later he opened the trunk. 'I burned the head in the sitting room grate. I next burned the feet and legs in the same grate.' A few days afterwards he returned to the task: 'I had to cut off the trunk. I also had to cut off the arms. I burned portions of them. The smell was appalling and I had to think of some other method of disposing of the portions. I then boiled some portions in a large pot, cut the portions up small, put them in a brown Gladstone bag and on a train journey pulled some out and threw them on to the tracks.' Some were still in the bag, and he left this in the cloakroom at Waterloo Station.

Her womanly instinct told Mavourneen that her husband, a serial philanderer, was up to something with another woman. But who was she? In between his exploits with Emily and cutting her up at the bungalow he was living with his wife, and one night she went through his pockets, discovering the Waterloo cloakroom ticket. She gave it to a policeman friend, who told his bosses. Officers used the ticket to collect the bag and after opening it and finding the bloody contents, they replaced it and waited for Mahon to turn up and claim it. When he did, he was arrested and told detectives about the death of Emily, saying it had been an accident after which he had panicked. He handed over the key to the bungalow.

Officers entered to a hellish scene. Among the ashes in the grates of each of the two sitting rooms were burned bones; there were more in the ashtrays; in the scullery two saucepans and a bath held boiled flesh and bones; on a bedroom carpet lay a bloodstained saw; in a trunk were dismembered human body parts; in a tin police found a human heart and intestines; while officers who opened a hatbox discovered boiled flesh wrapped in a sports coat and jumper.

There was an even more sickening aspect to the story. As the grisly remains of his pregnant mistress lay in the trunk, Mahon took another girlfriend to the bungalow. Ethel Primrose Duncan was thirty-two and unmarried when she began chatting to him as she sheltered from a rainstorm. He introduced himself as 'Pat Waller', an alias he used from time to time, and Ethel accepted his invitation to spend a few days with him at Crumbles. She saw the trunk in the spare bedroom but was told it was filled with books, and she returned to her London home oblivious to the carnage that had lain just a few feet from where she had made love. Despite his betrayal of her, his wife remained devoted to Mahon until his final date, this time with hangman Thomas Pierrepoint, under the Wandsworth gallows in early September.

20

THE FATAL DAB

MAHON'S ABUSE OF HIS victim's body disgusted the public. But at least he was caught. The identity of Jack the Ripper, the notorious murderer who severely mutilated women in the Whitechapel area of London between 1888 and 1891, remains a mystery. But one name put forward as a suspect continues to be that of George Chapman, a Polish-born publican also known as Seweryn Antonowicz Kłosowski. Because of the manner in which his victims were assaulted, Jack the Ripper appeared to have some medical knowledge, if not skill, and before coming to England, Chapman had worked as a doctor in Russia. However, Chapman killed not with a knife but with the lead-based poison tartar emetic, usually referred to as antimony and often confused with arsenic.

Despite having a wife in Poland, Chapman committed bigamy by marrying in England. He and his wife briefly lived in New York, but when they returned to England, they separated. Like Patrick Mahon, he was an obsessive womaniser who took a series of mistresses to live with him at his bar, the Crown in High Street, Southwark, London. When he tired of them, he poisoned them. When asked, he would convince local doctors their deaths were simply down to illness.

First to die was Mary Isabella Spink in December 1897. She was followed by Elizabeth Taylor in February 1901. However, the death of Maud Marsh in October 1902 aroused the suspicions of her mother, and when a post-mortem revealed traces of the poison, the others were exhumed and antimony found in their remains.

When police came to tell Chapman he was suspected of three murders, the publican insisted on going into his cellar. 'I want to make sure my beer is all right,' he told an astonished officer. He was formally charged with killing Maud Marsh, and at the police station, he said, 'She did not die suddenly. If she had been poisoned she would have done so.'

When his trial opened at the Old Bailey in 1903 the Solicitor General Sir Edward Carson told the jury, 'If you are to distinguish in degree between one murder case and another, I submit that no murder is more determined or malicious than that of poisoning such as is before you, no murder more demonstrative of the cruelty of the person who perpetrated it as he stood day by day at the bedside of the person he professed to love and saw his victim suffering and tortured and sinking from that which by his own hand he was administering under the pretence of curing an imaginary malady.'

Florence Rayner had a lucky escape. She had worked at the Crown as a barmaid and lived there but rebuffed Chapman's attempts to climb into her bed and, upset by his behaviour, left. Soon after, Maud moved in.

During the judge's summing-up, Chapman's composure and apparent indifference deserted him and he broke down. The jury took only twelve minutes to reach a guilty verdict, and when they announced it Chapman, sobbing bitterly, had to be held up in the dock by two warders. Among his possessions police had found bottles of medicine and packets of medicinal powders, and a copy of *My Experience as an Executioner* written by the hangman James Berry. However, Berry was retired by the time Chapman was helped to the scaffold at Wandsworth on 7 April 1903, and it was William Billington who sent him to his doom.

On the same gallows in 1905, brothers Alfred, twenty-two, and Albert Stratton, aged twenty, were executed for murdering an elderly couple while robbing their shop at Deptford, London. They went to their deaths never realising their story would go down in the history books. In 1901 Scotland Yard had formed the Fingerprinting Bureau and a year later had its first success when it identified and helped convict a burglar. The bureau was called in to the scene of the shop murder and found a greasy thumbprint on a cashbox. Witnesses told of seeing Alfred at the shop around the time of the killing and his thumbprint matched exactly that on the cashbox. As a result the case of the brothers became the very first in which a fingerprint convicted a murderer.

While they waited in prison for their trial, Albert called a jailer to his cell door and asked, 'How do you think I will get on?'

The turnkey, William Gittons, replied, 'I don't know.'

Pointing to Alfred's cell, Albert asked, 'Is he listening?' When he was told 'no', Albert continued, 'I reckon he will get strung up and I will get ten years. He led me into this. Don't say anything until I can see he has got no chance. I don't want to be strung up. He has never done any work in his life, only for about a week.' His prediction was only half correct. Both were found guilty of murder and executed together in May 1905.

One other unique case stands out among those that ended on the Wandsworth gallows. It is special for two reasons: for its notoriety as that of the only woman to have been executed there, and for its sheer horror. On 29 July 1879 Catherine 'Kate' Webster was hanged by William Marwood. Irish-born, she had stolen and cheated almost from the day she first learned to walk. She left an Irish jail to move to England, where her dishonesty and part-time prostitution brought her regular short stretches in jail, including one in Wandsworth, from where she was freed in 1877 to commit an act of horror on a par with that of Patrick Mahon.

After leaving jail, she found work in Richmond, Surrey, with rich widow Julia Martha Thomas, but within a month her employer was dead. Webster blamed others, but the night before she was executed, she made a dramatic confession in her condemned cell, admitting she alone murdered Mrs Thomas. Then she told, in her own words, what happened next:

On Sunday evening Mrs Thomas and I were alone in the house. We had some argument at which both she and myself were annoyed and she became very much agitated and left the house to go to church in that state, leaving me to remain at home. Upon her return from church before her usual hour she came in and went upstairs. I went up after her and we had an argument, which ripened into a quarrel, and in the height of my rage and anger, I threw her from the top of the stairs to the ground floor. She had a heavy fall. I felt that she was seriously injured and I became excited at what had occurred, lost all control over myself, and to prevent her screaming and getting me into trouble, I caught her by the throat and in the struggle she was choked and I threw her on the floor. I became entirely lost and without any control over myself, and looking at what had happened, and the fear of being discovered, I determined to do away with the body the best I could.

I chopped off the head from the body, assisted with the use of a razor, which I used to cut through the flesh afterwards. I also used the meat saw and carving knife to cut the body up. I prepared the copper with water to boil the body, to prevent identity; and as soon as I had succeeded in cutting it up, I placed it in the copper and boiled it down. I opened the stomach with the carving knife, and burned up as much of the parts as I could. During the whole of this time there was nobody in the house but myself. When I used to look upon the scene before me, and the blood around my feet, the horror and dread I felt was inconceivable. I was bewildered and acted as if I was mad, and I did everything I possibly could to conceal the occurrence and keep it quiet, and everything regular, fearing the neighbours might suspect that anything had happened.

I was greatly overcome both from the horrible sight before me and the smell, and I failed several times in strength and determination, but was helped on by the Devil in this vile purpose.

I remained in the house all night, endeavouring to clear up the place and clean away the traces after the murder. I burned part of the body after chopping it up and boiling the body, and I think one of the feet. I emptied the copper, and threw the water away, having washed and cleaned the outside. I then put the parts of the body into the little wooden box which was produced in court, tied it up with cord and resolved to deposit it in the Thames, which was afterwards done.

I put the head of Mrs Thomas into the black bag and being weary and afraid to remain in the house, carried it to Porter's house and had some tea there. I placed the black bag with the head in it under the tea table and afterwards took it away from the house and disposed of it. The disposition of this black bag gave me great uneasiness. The foot found in the dung heap was placed there by me for when I came to realise the true state of things and the great danger I stood in, I resolved to do everything in my power to keep everything secret and prevent being discovered. When I placed the box in the river and disposed of the head and the other parts of the body as best I could, and cleaned up the place so as that a person coming in might not suspect or see anything irregular, it was suggested to my mind to sell all that was in the house and go away.

The statement went on to tell how she sold furniture to the man named Porter, a friend whose home she had visited while carrying the dead woman's head in a black bag. But the alarm was raised when a neighbour spotted Porter's workmen carrying away furniture and called police. By then fishermen had found the box in the Thames and opened it. Webster was arrested in Ireland, while calling herself Mrs Thomas and wearing the murdered woman's clothes.

She added in her statement, 'I did not murder Mrs Thomas from any premeditation. I was annoyed and in a passion and I cannot now recollect why I did it. I am perfectly resigned to my fate and am fully of confidence in a happy eternity. If I had a choice I would almost sooner die than return to a life full of misery, deception and wickedness.' A few hours later she had her wish, and after her death was confirmed the astonishing confession was made public.

21

WOMEN ON THE SCAFFOLD

IN YEARS GONE BY – usually to avoid scandal or simply because they could not afford to raise them – mothers would hand over their babies, together with a few pounds, to women promising to find the children new homes. The practice, a form of unofficial adoption, was known as baby farming, and it led to some of the most monstrous crimes imaginable. Because instead of taking care of the little innocents until parents could be found, the farmers merely murdered those in their care and kept the money.

No one will ever know how many kiddies were killed in this appalling way. But occasionally these female murderers were detected. In 1889 Jessie King, aged twenty-seven, was hanged at Edinburgh after being convicted of murdering an infant boy and girl. 'Your days are numbered,' the judge said after her conviction. Britain's most prolific baby farmer is believed to be Amelia Elizabeth Dyer, who was held in Holloway after being sentenced to death for killing four-month-old Doris Marnon, daughter of a London barmaid, then dumping her body in the River Thames. Dyer, fifty-nine, was known as the 'Ogress of Reading', and the discovery of the corpses of other babies led to suspicions she had been responsible for dozens of deaths. Doris's unmarried mother, Evelina, said at the murder trial she had seen a newspaper advertisement offering to adopt a child and after replying met a 'Mrs Harding' – in reality, Dyer – who promised to care for 'dear little Doris' for £16. The next time Evelina saw her baby was at a mortuary. The night before her execution in June 1896 by James Billington, Dyer was secretly moved to Newgate Jail in London, where she was hanged.

But Holloway was by now being suggested as suitable for the execution of women. The first to die on the scaffold there would be two baby farmers. In 1902 Annie Walters and Amelia Sach were accused of involvement in the death of a four-day-old baby boy whose mother had paid them to take the infant for adoption. Walters, fifty-four, from Islington, London, was charged with murder, and thirty-six-year-old Sach, from East Finchley, who had a two-year-old child with her builder husband, with being an accomplice, both offences carrying the death sentence. However, the pair were later thought to have killed many other children, including that of a young mother who had been executed in 1900 for murdering her son.

The astonishing and ghastly story of the devilish baby farmers was told by eminent Treasury barrister Archibald Bodkin prosecuting when they appeared at Clerkenwell, London:

Mrs Sach, who described herself as a certified midwife and nurse, kept a house at East Finchley where women took up residence for the purpose of being confined, and paid a first amount of three guineas and afterwards a guinea a week. A Miss Pardoe put herself in communication with Mrs Sach, and in the course of a conversation Mrs Sach asked Miss Pardoe what she was going to do with the baby when it was born. Miss Pardoe replied that she intended to put it out to nurse. Mrs Sach said, 'I have fine ladies to adopt children, wealthy ladies and they will leave the children their money. They have no children of their own. These ladies like to have a present from the mother of the child they are going to adopt. Another thing the ladies like is that the mothers should not know where their children are in case they should come and claim them.'

Miss Pardoe agreed to the suggestion and it was arranged that £30 should be paid for the adoption of the child. While Miss Pardoe was at the house a Miss Galley was another inmate and to her Mrs Sach made the same suggestion regarding the child and the sum of £25 was mentioned. On 12 November Miss Pardoe was confined of a female child and the same evening Walters, who had taken lodgings at a constable's house, received a telegram from Sach and brought home a baby, which she said was a boy. There was no doubt the father of the child paid the money for the purpose of having the baby adopted. On 14 November Walters left the lodgings with a bundle and the child was never seen again.

Walters was seen with the bundle in Whitechapel, where she entered a refreshment place. Here, the wrap fell off and a waitress noticed the bundle contained something that looked like a doll. Walters, on being spoken to, told a most extraordinary story. She said the bundle contained a baby which was under chloroform, that it had been in hospital, that it was a boy about a week old, that it had just undergone an operation and that the chloroform effect would continue for three or four days. She added that she was going to take the child to Finchley. The waitress was of the opinion the child was dead and it would be shown the child was alive and healthy at nine that morning when she left the lodgings. She returned to her lodgings at eight that evening the worse for drink and told the landlady the baby had been taken to a wealthy lady who was to pay £100 for its adoption.

The prosecutor said that a day later Miss Galley had given birth to a baby and the father gave Sach £25 to have it adopted. Sach sent off a telegram to Walters. But her police constable landlord was suspicious following the disappearance of the earlier child, and told his son to follow Walters. She came home with another baby, saying it was a girl, but when she left the child briefly, the policeman and his wife examined it and found it was a boy who had died from asphyxia. The two women were arrested.

After the jury convicted them at their Old Bailey trial, the judge, Mr Justice Darling, said, 'It is plain that Sach received children from their mothers and obtained money on the pretext that they would be taken by people who would bring them up, and the children were handed over to Walters to be done to death.'

Because it was the first time the newly built gallows at Holloway was being used, hangman James Billington arrived early in the afternoon on 3 February 1903, the day before the women were to be executed. He wanted to thoroughly test the apparatus. Next morning, after both were dead, a statement from the prison said, 'The condemned women retired to rest at the normal hour. Neither had much sleep. Breakfast consisted of bread and butter. Both women displayed remarkable fortitude to the last, and Mrs Sach repeatedly expressed a desire to meet her fate as soon as possible and so put an end to her misery.'

It was twenty years before the gallows was used again, when Edith Jessie Thompson was put to death. Edith had told in letters to her lover of trying to kill her husband with poison and then feed him broken glass in his meals. The prosecution made much of a book, *Bella Donna*, found at her home. It told the story of a woman who had arranged to poison her husband so she could run off with a lover. The case aroused extraordinary interest. Because it continued into a second week, the jury had to remain together for the weekend and newspapers reported that on the Sunday, 'They went to divine service at St Paul's Cathedral and in the afternoon they were taken for a three-hour char-a-banc drive around London.'

While they were enjoying their sightseeing, crowds were already gathering outside the Old Bailey for the resumption of the trial on the Monday morning. Hopefuls were there from noon on Sunday, but not necessarily to listen to the proceedings, as reporters noticed: 'The crowd appeared to be composed mainly of unemployed who doubtless hearing of the high sums paid for stands sold their chances of admission when the doors of the court opened to the highest bidders. The two persons who headed the queue declared that they had each sold their place for £5. Others prices asked ranged from £3 to £1. Only three females were present in the queue, an elderly woman who gave up on seeing the slightness of her chance of getting admission to the court, a woman medical student and a frail looking woman of the unemployed class who said that her purpose was to sell her stand to get money for food for her invalid husband and children. In contrast with this poor woman were a number of fashionably dressed women in furs and sealskin coats who after viewing the extent of the crowd from a respectable distance departed.'

Another three decades passed before the Holloway gallows was needed, but then it would be required twice in just seven months before it became redundant. In the first case there was little, if any, sympathy for the victim, who was grey-haired, foreign, well into middle age and impetuous. In total contrast, the second to die was a glamorous blonde model whose hanging was so controversial that it turned her into a celebrity and signalled an end to women being executed.

Styllou Pantopiou Christofi survived one capital charge, but not a second. A Greek Cypriot, she had been cleared in Cyprus in 1925 of murdering her mother-in-law by pushing a lighted taper down her throat. In the early 1950s she decided to visit Britain to see her son, Stavros, his German-born wife, Hella, and her three grandchildren. She stayed with her son and daughter-in-law in London, but the two women did not see eye to eye, and Christofi went berserk when Hella ordered her to leave. She smashed the younger woman over the head with an ash pan before strangling her. Then, in a gruesome effort to hide the body, she set it alight. When police arrived she claimed she had been woken up by the sounds of Hella screaming and found her burning. But she had failed to wash away stains on the floor made by the dead woman's blood and was charged with murder.

Was she insane? A psychiatrist decided she was, but said

she was also fit enough to face a trial. The jury convicted her of murder and she was sentenced to death. Her pending meeting with hangman Albert Pierrepoint on 15 December 1954 elicited little public protest, and the only interest was in her plea for a Maltese Cross to be placed in the execution chamber. 'It will be the last thing I see before I die,' she said. And it was. She was fifty-four.

Ruth Ellis was everything Christofi was not. Born Ruth Neilson in Rhyl, Wales in 1926, she had a body stunning enough to earn her a living modelling nude in London. At the age of seventeen, she had a son to a Canadian soldier, became a prostitute, and married divorced dentist George Ellis in 1950. She even had a small part in the movies. While pregnant with her second child, a daughter, she played a beauty queen in the 1951 comedy movie *Lady Godiva Rides Again* – the cast included Joan Collins, Sid James and Diana Dors. Her marriage to Ellis had been stormy, and after they split up she became a nightclub hostess, a front for prostitution. One of her clients was former public schoolboy and racing driver David Blakely, who became her lover. They often argued. Once he punched her, causing her to miscarry his baby.

On 10 April 1955 she went looking for Blakely, and finding him leaving a public house, she shot him dead with a .38 Smith and Wesson revolver she had had in her handbag. At her trial she told the Old Bailey jury, 'It's obvious when I shot him I intended to kill him,' words that as good as pronounced her own death sentence. Officially that was done by the judge, Mr Justice Cecil Havers – grandfather of the actor Nigel Havers – after her conviction, but even he joined more than 50,000 people who pleaded for mercy for her. Their requests for a reprieve fell on deaf ears, and Ruth Ellis was hanged on 13 July 1954. She was just twenty-eight.

Was she unlucky? Many others had committed blatant murders but survived execution, and this inconsistency added to the argument against hanging. One of those lucky others was dressmaker Emma Byron. In November 1902, in broad daylight and in front of shocked passers-by she stabbed dead her married lover, stockbroker Arthur Reginald Baker, in central London following a violent row the previous night. She was first sentenced to death, but this was commuted to life imprisonment, then to ten years. Emma was freed after serving six years in Holloway.

Just over a year after Ruth Ellis placed her spectacles on the table in the condemned cell at Holloway, remarking, 'I won't be needing these any more,' her place was taken by Freda Rumbold, who had shot dead her sleeping husband with a shotgun, blaming the moon and his excessive sexual demands. She was told she would hang, but following the tragedy of Ruth, all death sentences were being commuted to life imprisonment. However, Freda had to wait in the condemned cell before a reprieve was announced.

Could any murder conviction have a more fortunate ending for the killer, though, than that of Olive Kathleen Wise, who was aged twenty-seven in 1931 and destined to become the luckiest women ever to be incarcerated in Holloway Jail? Hers is one of the most tragic stories to emerge from the prison. Wise was aged twenty-seven and already a mother of three boys when she gave birth to another boy named Reginald in March 1930. The father of the baby was firewood dealer Alfred John Wheatley, a widower, who did not want to marry her, and gave her only a few shillings a week.

Struggling to feed and clothe four children, she found herself deeper and deeper in debt. Towards the end of the year she owed eleven weeks' rent and told Wheatley, 'I hardly know what I am doing, if I have much more worry I will go mad.' At one stage she was so desperate she tried dumping Reginald on Wheatley, but he handed the baby back. She pleaded to be allowed to stay in the workhouse near her Walthamstow, London, home, but was turned away. On Christmas Eve 1930 she turned up at the home of a friend carrying a bundle containing Reginald's body 'I have done the baby in,' she said. 'I have gassed it.' Police inquiries revealed she had gassed the infant in her oven. 'I must have been made to do it,' she told officers. 'Can I see him?'

What had caused her desperation was her discovery that she was again pregnant and at her trial for murder at the Old Bailey in January 1931 a doctor said she would give birth within weeks. It was obvious there was massive support for her. Even the judge, Mr Justice Charles, told the jury, 'The case excites extreme sympathy because it is fraught with great sadness.' But he had to add, 'It would be improper for you to be influenced by the sadness of the case in coming to any other conclusion than that which the evidence warrants.'

Wise was found guilty of murder, the jury recommending she be shown mercy. But the drama did not end there. Immediately after the judge sentenced her to death, he ordered the doors of the courtroom to be shut and no one to be allowed to leave. Another jury was then sworn in. It was known as a 'Jury of Matrons' and it had to formally decide if the condemned woman was expecting a baby, because she could not be hanged while pregnant. To have done so would have meant the State taking the life of an unborn and innocent child. After a doctor said she would give birth within weeks, the jury confirmed she was pregnant, and at that, the judge ruled that her execution would be stayed until after the birth.

Within four days the Home Office announced Wise had been reprieved and instead of being hanged would serve a life sentence. Just over three weeks later she gave birth to twins, a boy, John Herbert, and a girl, Jean Barbara, in Holloway, while outside the prison a nationwide clamour for mercy gathered increasing strength. The twins were weaned in the Holloway Prison hospital but then mother and children were moved to a women's borstal, where security was much lighter, and in July 1932, a year and a half after being sentenced to death, Wise was released. As she was driven away by her father and sister she told reporters, 'I am so excited. I am overcome with joy and I am determined to live in the future for my children. Three of them do not know of my misfortune, and I hope they never will.' The following year she married John Wheatley.

22

DEATH AT THE TOWER

AS THE YOUNG MAN walked to his execution, the chaplain, clearly distressed and confused by the prospect of what was about to happen, took a wrong turn. 'Please, Father,' whispered the doomed man, gently taking the chaplain's arm and guiding him in the right direction. The previous night, exactly 309 years since the arrest of Guy Fawkes, the prisoner had written his final letters in his cell at the Tower of London. Fawkes and his fellow gunpowder plotters had been charged with treason. Now another man was to die for committing a similar offence, in his case spying for Germany. As he set off behind the chaplain to walk to his death, slightly built Carl Hans Lody turned to one of his captors. 'I don't suppose you want to shake hands with a German,' he said and was told, 'No, I won't shake hands a German, but I will with a brave man.'

It was 6 November 1914. Three months earlier, on 4 August, Britain had declared war and two days later Lody had turned up at the American Embassy in Hamburg to apply for a temporary passport allowing him to travel throughout Europe. He told embassy officials he was a US citizen and his name was Charles A. Inglis, that he worked for a German shipping line, had lived in New York and Nebraska, and had a wife in Omaha. Embassy staff had no reason to doubt the thirty-five-year-old, who spoke perfect English with an American accent. Almost immediately

Lody, an officer in the naval reserve, was off on his mission to spy on Allied shipping movements.

He travelled to Bergen, in Norway, arranging for a German agent there to receive his coded reports and forward them to spymasters in Berlin. Then he headed for Edinburgh, first booking into the North British Hotel and hiring a bicycle to pedal around the Firth of Forth, spying for signs of the Home Fleet. He visited London and Liverpool before returning to Edinburgh. But his days were already numbered. All letters sent abroad were opened and read by secret service censors, and one in particular from Charles A. Inglis had aroused suspicion. It read, 'Must cancel. Johnson very ill last four days. Shall leave shortly.' The reason for concern was that the Home Fleet was due to leave the Forth in four days.

Lody soon realised he was under surveillance and actually complained to the police in Edinburgh that he was being followed. Another intercepted letter gave details of the effects of Zeppelin bombs in London and Allied ships in the Mersey. Lody was arrested and interrogated. He was given the choice of giving the names of his masters and other contacts or being put on a trial that would certainly lead to execution, and chose the latter. He was held at Wandsworth for a time before being moved to the Tower, from where he wrote to a friend in America, telling him, 'I am prepared to make a clean breast of all this trouble, but I must protect my friends in the Fatherland and avoid as much as possible humiliation for those who have been near and dear to me.' And he wrote to his sister in Germany, 'May my life be judged worthy to be a humble sacrifice on the altar of the Fatherland.'

The chaplain led Lody to the miniature rifle range at the Tower of London, where he sat in a chair and waited for eight riflemen from the Grenadier Guards to shoot him. According to the *Daily Mail*, 'Lody maintained the calm imperturbability which characterized him throughout his three-day trial and when facing the firing party he refused to be blindfolded.'

Twenty years after his death, a memorial to Lody, a national hero, was unveiled at Lubeck, Germany. It depicted a knight in armour, his visor closed to reflect the secrecy of his work, his hands in chains to denote imprisonment and a hole in his armour to signify the manner of his execution.

Wandsworth would be the temporary home for others convicted of spying, some of them taking a short drive to the Tower of London the night before they met their end at dawn on the chair in the miniature rifle range. Seven months after Lody's death, he was followed by another fluent English speaker, Carl Frederick Muller, aged fifty-eight. As with Lody, Muller was detected when letters sent to a German agent in Belgium were examined and messages written in invisible ink were discovered between apparently innocent lines. A taxi taking Muller to the Tower broke down and he had to wait until one of his Army guards could flag down another cab.

The three-day trial of Lody had been an exception to the general rule that hearings were to be held in secret with usually only the name of the accused, the charge and sentence being released to the media. Haicke Petrus Marinus Janssen used his cover as a cigar salesman to telegraph a bogus supplier in Holland with information about Allied shipping. He was shot on 30 July 1915, and his blood was still dripping from the execution chair when his accomplice, Willem Johannes Roos, was led forward to take his place. Roos begged to be allowed a last request, to finish his cigarette, before he was blasted into eternity. A firing squad made up of Scots Guards executed forty-nine-year-old Swedish national Ernst Melin on 10 September 1915 and then, a week later, finished off Augusto Alfredo Roggen from Uruguay, who aroused suspicion by claiming he was off on a fishing holiday around Loch Lomond and Loch Long, both of which were restricted areas.

Fernando Buschman spent his last hours in the Tower playing his violin before the crash of gunfire from the Scots Guards brought the curtain down on his career as a spy and as a talented amateur musician on 19 October 1915. George Traugott Breeckow asked to be blindfolded with a woman's scarf as he sat in the fatal chair on 26 October 1915. Chicago-born Irving Guy Ries, aged fifty-five, was said to have shaken hands with the soldiers who executed him on 27 October 1915, while twenty-two-year-old Albert Meyer tried singing 'Tipperary' on his way to the miniature rifle range, where he struggled and cursed before being shot on 2 December 1915.

Meyer was said to be an ineffective spy who sent largely useless information to his masters. Ludovico Zender was simply incompetent. He was caught because he posed as a fish buyer who sent a coded message ordering a huge consignment of sardines to an address used by a German agent at Christiania, in Norway. Unfortunately for Zender, a native of Peru, sardines were out of season and experts soon worked out that the orders concealed details of Allied shipping movements. He was shot on 11 April 1916.

Lody, Muller, Janssen, Roos, Melin, Roggen, Buschman, Breeckow, Ries, Meyer and Zender were all given the traditional soldier's death by a bullet. Two other Great War spies perished on the scaffold at the end of a rope. Robert Rosenthal attracted little attention. He had been sent to Britain by the German Admiralty to gather information on the Allied fleet, which was based at Scapa Flow. It was 1915, and among a public constantly warned to watch out for nosey strangers, his questions caused curiosity. He was arrested and transferred to London, where, after being interrogated and convicted of espionage under the Treachery Act, he was held at Wandsworth Prison and hanged there on 15 July. However, the case of Sir Roger Casement was looked on as being considerably more significant, because it concerned a man who sought to satisfy his hatred of England's treatment of Ireland and the Irish by spying for Germany. What appalled so many was that just five years after being knighted for his services to King and Country, he was sitting in the condemned cell having brazenly betrayed both.

Born in the Republic of Ireland in 1864, Casement had a glittering career with the British Colonial Service as an overseas consul, exposing the abuse and appalling treatment of workers in the Congo and Amazon basin and earning his knighthood. Two years after bowing before the King, Casement retired on a generous £420-a-year government pension and concentrated on working for the cause of Irish nationalism. Long before being knighted he had told friends of his loathing for England, describing it as a 'poisonous compound' and the English as 'dirty cowards'. Now his passionate detestation of everything English began emerging into the open, as he forged links with organisations such as the Irish Republican Brotherhood. He sailed to America, where he encouraged Irish immigrants to give money to support an Irish revolution that would require Britain to divert valuable resources from her campaigns against Germany. He openly urged Irishmen to refuse to fight for the Allies and instead to join the Irish Volunteers, a group pledged to side with Germany.

From America he sailed to Germany, visiting a prisoner-of-war camp near Frankfurt holding captured Irish troops. James Gerard, former American Ambassador in Berlin, later wrote, 'There, efforts were made to induce them to join the German army. The men were well treated and were often visited by Sir Roger Casement who, working with the German authorities, tried to get those Irishmen to desert their flag and join the Germans. A few weaklings were persuaded by Sir Roger who finally discontinued his visits after obtaining about thirty recruits, because the remaining Irishmen chased him out of the camp.'

At Casement's trial in 1916 the Attorney-General, Sir Frederick Smith, provided even more detail of his activities at the camp: 'He was forming a brigade and incited all the Irish prisoners to join him. He pointed out repeatedly, and with emphasis that in his opinion everything was to be gained for Ireland by Germany winning the war, and now was the day for striking a blow for Ireland. He stated that those who joined the Irish Brigade would be sent to Berlin. They would become the guests of the German government and in the event of Germany winning a sea battle, he would land a brigade in Ireland and defend the country against the enemy, England. In the event of Germany losing the war, either he or the Imperial German government would give each man of the brigade a bonus of from £19 to £20 and a free passage to America. The vast majority of the Irish prisoners treated the rhetoric and persuasion of Casement with contempt. He was received with hisses and at least on one occasion booed out of camp. The Munster Volunteers were particularly prominent in their loyalty and in their resentment at the treacherous proposals made to them. One man actually struck Casement, who was saved from further violence by the intervention of an escort of the Prussian Guards assigned to give him this protection. The Irish prisoners who refused to receive the proposals were punished by a reduction of rations, which before this had not been in any way excessive. The few men who were seduced from their allegiance were rewarded by being given a green uniform, with a harp worked upon it; by being left at liberty and by exceptionally liberal rations both in quality and quantity.'

During visits to the Irish prisoners Casement handed out leaflets which read, 'Irishmen! Here is a chance for you to fight for Ireland. You have fought for England, your country's hereditary enemy. You have fought for Belgium, though it was no more to you than the Fiji Islands. Are you willing to fight for your own country with a view of securing the national freedom of Ireland? The object of the Irish Brigade shall be to fight solely for the cause of Ireland, and in no circumstances shall it be directed to the interests of Germany.' One of the Irishmen recruited by Casement was former Paddington railway porter Daniel Julian Bailey, who was taken to Berlin, where he was trained in acts of sabotage and in how to use explosives. Corporal John Robinson of the Royal Army Medical Corps refused to join the Irish Brigade after hearing Casement proclaim, 'Now is the time to fight for Ireland. Germany is going to free Ireland.'

Casement had pleaded with the German authorities for weapons to arm an uprising in Ireland against the English, planned by his Irish Volunteers. But when the Germans could not guarantee support, it was decided to put the rebellion on hold, and Casement, Bailey and Robert Monteith of the Irish Republican Brotherhood were taken by submarine to Tralee Bay, off the west coast, where they landed in a rubber boat in the early hours of Good Friday 1916, intending to make contact with leaders of the Volunteers and the IRB and pass on news of the postponement. By the time they reached the beach, Casement, who was suffering badly from tuberculosis, was too tired to continue. He decided to wait while the others went for help. But spies had tipped off the British authorities about their plans while their arrival had been seen by local farmers who noticed a flashing light out at sea and wondered if a ship was in difficulty and in danger of being wrecked. The light had in fact been from the German submarine, but gossip about goings-on offshore reached the police, who found the dinghy and Casement. He was captured and transported to the Tower of London. While he waited to be tried, Republicans refused suggestions they should attack the Tower and free him.

At the initial hearing in May 1916, he and Bailey were charged, 'That they did between the 1st day of November 1914 and on diverse other occasions thereafter and between that day and the 21st day of April, unlawfully, maliciously and traitorously commit high treason without the realm of England, in contempt of our Sovereign Lord the King and his laws, to the evil example of others in the like case, contrary to the duty and allegiance of the said defendants.' But before the start of Casement's trial the following month, the charge against Bailey was dropped.

Casement was found guilty and sentenced to death. He lost an appeal and was stripped of his knighthood. Pleas for mercy from Sherlock Holmes creator Sir Arthur Conan Doyle and Irish playwright George Bernard Shaw failed to save him, and on the morning of 3 August 1916, he was hanged at Pentonville by John Ellis, his body buried in quicklime within the prison. In 1965 it was exhumed and sent to Ireland, where he received a State funeral with full military honours and was buried in Dublin.

23

TRAPPED BY SAUSAGES

THE SCAFFOLDS AT Wandsworth and Pentonville would become considerably busier with the outbreak of World War II in 1939. The art of the spy had become even more effective with the development and use of new and more powerful wireless transmitters. But even the most sophisticated techniques remained at the mercy of human error. Men given many weeks and months of intensive training in avoiding discovery still made the most basic – and fatal – mistakes. And, unlike the government attitude during the Great War, now the authorities were more forthcoming about telling the population when spies were executed, the reasoning being that the greater awareness there was of the presence of enemy agents and of their activities, the more likely they were to be caught. In a number of cases it was a policy that paid dividends.

Fifteen months after Britain entered the conflict came the announcement that the first spies had been dealt with. A Home Office statement on 10 December revealed, 'Two enemy agents, acting on behalf of Germany, were executed at Pentonville prison today following their conviction under the Treachery Act 1940 at the Central Criminal Court on November 22. Their names are Jose Waldberg, a German born on 15 July 1915 at Mainz, and Karl Meier, a Dutch subject of German origin born at Coblenz on 19 October 1916. These agents were apprehended shortly after their

198

surreptitious arrival in this country. They were in possession of a wireless transmitting set, which they were to erect in the fields at night and of considerable sums of money in £1 notes. They had instructions to pose as refugees from enemy occupied territory and to move about amongst the population obtaining as much information of a military kind as possible. They had been made to believe that they would shortly be relieved by German invading forces.'

The statement was expanded by an officer specialising in anti-espionage, who said Waldberg and Meier had been told to concentrate on listening to conversations for talk about troop and naval movements, aerodromes, gun emplacements, ammunition dumps and, importantly, morale. 'In particular they were to mix among the civilian population in trains, buffets and public houses, listening carefully to all careless talk. We should make it an absolute rule never to discuss any subject likely to be of interest to the enemy in a public place such as the bus, the club or the train. In just a few hours an enemy agent might be sending the information back to the enemy causing inestimable damage and perhaps the loss of lives,' he warned.

The pair had planned to spend nights hiding in woods, quarries and abandoned buildings, surviving on large supplies of iron rations carried with them and using a miniature transmitter to send back their findings in Morse code to Germany. Waldberg and Meier had been picked up with two other agents, Charles Albert van den Kieboom, a Japanese-born Dutchman aged twenty-six, who had given up his work as a clerk to cash in on his excellent English by spying for Germany, and twenty-eight-year-old commercial traveller Sjoerd Pons.

Shortly before his execution, Waldberg claimed he had been tricked into pleading guilty and wasn't allowed to explain that he had undertaken the mission in the hope it would help his father, who had been arrested by the Gestapo. Kieboom had his own battery-powered transmitter, just eight inches by eight and weighing only a pound. He followed his fellow spies on the Pentonville scaffold a week after they had been hanged. Pons went free after convincing his interrogators that he had been caught smuggling by the Gestapo and only escaped being shot by agreeing to join the other three.

George Johnson Armstrong was a Geordie-born marine engineer, but even before war started, the British secret service held a file on him because he made no secret of his Nazi sympathies. When his work took him to New York in 1940 he mingled with Germans and offered to supply information about Allied merchant shipping to the Nazis. Clumsily he wrote to the German Consul in Boston, Massachusetts, offering help, even though he was aware his letter might be intercepted and read by the US authorities. In it he pledged, 'My intention is to make German contacts here in the US which may be beneficially used on my return to England. Naturally in the various capacities in which I was employed in England, I have information which would be very valuable in the proper sources. I feel that the information which I have and the value of someone so placed in England in these times would be greatly appreciated by yourself or those of who you would be in contact with me.'

Not surprisingly Armstrong, aged twenty-nine, was arrested when he landed back in Britain, and during his interrogation by the police and MI5, he claimed he was trying to discover the identities of German agents. He was convicted under the Treachery Act, the charge being: 'On or about 19 November 1940, being a British subject in the USA, with intent to help the enemy, did an act designed or likely to give assistance to the Naval, Military or Air operations of the enemy or to endanger life, to wit did write and endeavour to send a letter to Dr Herbert Scholz, German Consul at Boston, Massachusetts, USA, offering his services, information and assistance to the said Dr Herbert Scholz.' Armstrong lost an appeal against the judge's 'Guilty' finding and was hanged by Thomas Pierrepoint at Wandsworth on 10 July 1941.

The Englishman was described at his trial as a 'rank amateur', but it was a series of elementary bungles that trapped three professional agents within hours of their arriving on the northeast Scottish coast in late September 1939. And one of their mistakes was to bring with them German sausages. Karl Theodor Drucke, aged thirty-five; Werner Heinrich Waelti, twenty-five, also known as Robert Petter; and Vera Schalburg, a thirty-two-year-old native of Siberia, whose many aliases included that of Vera Eriksson, a young widow from Denmark, left Stavanger in Norway in a flying boat which landed them off Banffshire under cover of darkness. They climbed into a rubber boat together with their radio equipment and rations and three bicycles, the plan being for them to cycle more than 400 miles to London. However, in the choppy seas the bikes were washed overboard. Reaching the shore, Schalburg and Drucke went in one direction; Waelti in the other. The former found a railway station but their guttural accents immediately aroused suspicion. When Drucke pulled out a huge wad of money to buy their tickets, they were arrested. A search revealed they were carrying a wireless receiver and transmitter, lots of money, a loaded automatic pistol and a generous supply of food that included German sausage.

From the outset Schalburg, terrified for her life, told police details of their plans and said Waelti was making for Edinburgh, where he was arrested. As he was being seized he tried pulling out a loaded gun, but was soon handcuffed. All three were sent for interrogation to London and charged with treachery, but on the day their trial was due to begin it was revealed Schalburg would not be appearing after giving enough information to ensure her fellow spies would be convicted. Both were hanged at Wandsworth on 6 August 1941. Schalburg remained in England until the end of the war, when she was deported to Germany.

Just nine days after the executions, another German agent, Josef Jakobs, a forty-one-year-old native of Luxembourg, faced a firing squad at the Tower of London. Jakobs avoided hanging because as a serving non-commissioned officer in the German Army, he was tried by a general court martial, whereas the other spies were convicted by a civilian court. His story was yet another of a mixture of incompetence and bad luck. A Great War veteran, Jakobs was flown from Schiphol on 1 February 1941 and parachuted over Peterborough. However, as he was about to leap out, he smashed his foot against the side of the aircraft, breaking his ankle and injuring his right leg on landing. Lying helpless and unable to move, he summoned help by firing his automatic pistol. Members of the Home Guard found him still wearing his flying suit and steel helmet. A search of his knapsack uncovered the standard wireless transmitter and receiver, a spade with which to bury his parachute, £500 cash and a food supply that included brandy – and German sausage. The night before he was carried to the chair, where he would sit while he waited for the firing squad to take aim, he wrote a last letter to his wife and young family, telling them of his love and of his sadness at being unable to say his goodbyes. The letter was later forwarded to his widow.

Further positive proof that the public was taking note of the need to be on the alert came in May 1941 when Karel Richter, aged twenty-nine, a Sudetan German motor and marine engineer, parachuted into fields in Hertfordshire. He was a reluctant spy, having fled from Nazi Germany to Sweden, where he was arrested after police discovered some of his papers were fake. Deported to Germany, he found himself in a concentration camp where conditions were appalling, and it was hardly surprising that when Gestapo officers arrived and suggested a way out, he took it. His first mission was to trace another German agent in the London area, hand over American dollars and investigate whether this man was now working for the British. It was a simple task, but Richter bungled it. Instead of moving on immediately after he landed, he panicked and hid out in fields and woods for two days. Weak and hungry, he finally emerged from his hideout, and as he wandered along a lonely road, his hopes initially rose when a lorry stopped. Richter sensed he was about to be offered a lift to London, but his hopes were quickly dashed when the driver asked him for directions. Confused, Richter made an excuse and hurried off, but his foray into the world of spying was about to end.

The lorry driver next stopped a police constable, and during a casual conversation, he mentioned the odd behaviour of the unhelpful stranger. Suspicious, the officer chased after Richter and arrested him. At the local police station a search revealed he was wearing three pairs of woollen pants and two pairs of socks. In his pockets were a map of the eastern counties of England, a compass and hundreds of English pounds and US dollars.

Richter told police where he had been hiding, and there they uncovered a parachute and harness, German crash helmet carrying the swastika, trowel, flying suit, portable wireless transmitter, spare batteries, torch, loaded automatic pistol and food. During his interrogation he was joined by the spy he had meant to link up with, discovering too late that the man had been turned and was now working for the British secret service. After a trial, Richter was convicted under the Treachery Act and sentenced to death. He was determined not to sell his life cheaply. A strong man, he fought desperately with hangman Albert Pierrepoint and prison warders in the condemned cell at Wandsworth – even managing to snap one of the leather belts with which he was pinioned – before dying on 10 December 1941.

The following month, intelligence officers in Gibraltar, a key British naval base, became suspicious about the keen interest being shown in Allied shipping by thirty-four-year-old Jose Estella Key, and after weeks of surveillance, he was arrested and flown to London for interrogation by secret service specialists. Under intense questioning, Key admitted he had been using a transmitter to send reports back to Germany.

Alphons Louis Eugene Timmerman was a ship's steward who, on arriving in Britain in the autumn of 1941, sought sanctuary after telling immigration officials he was a Belgian who had escaped from his Nazi-occupied homeland. His documents aroused suspicion, and secret service officers had already been warned in an intercepted cipher to a German agent in Britain that a Belgian seaman was being sent to make detailed reports on Allied shipping. A search of his belongings proved fatal for the thirty-seven-year-old from Ostend. In an envelope were crystals which when added to water made invisible ink, and Timmerman admitted he was a spy. He and Key were hanged at Wandsworth on 7 July 1942 by Albert Pierrepoint.

It was almost inevitable that Duncan Alexander Croall Scott-Ford would go to sea. He was born in Plymouth, home to great mariners of the ilk of Sir John Hawkins and Sir Francis Drake, and his father had served in the Royal Navy. After joining the Merchant Navy, Scott-Ford plied regularly between Britain and Lisbon, where his infatuation with a prostitute and the need for money made him vulnerable. He was approached by a German agent, who promised him riches in exchange for information about Allied convoys and their escorts. His first payment was £18, but when his vessel next berthed at the Spanish port, Scott-Ford discovered he had fallen victim to blackmail, the agent telling him that unless he carried on supplying details of shipping, his deceit would be made known to the British authorities.

His contact with the German had been seen, however, and when he returned to Britain he was arrested and charged with treachery. After his conviction, the Home Office revealed that some of the information he had passed to his German handler had involved his own vessel. 'As a result he imperiled the lives of his own shipmates,' said a statement. 'Memoranda found in his possession gave details of convoy movements including the speed, course and distance travelled, a log of his final voyage, a description of the weather and information about the protection provided by aircraft.

'The moral to be drawn from this case is that British and Allied seamen, when visiting neutral ports, should be constantly on their guard against strangers who may frequently approach them for apparently innocent reasons. Such strangers are apt to be enemy agents who lure their unsuspecting victims into a course of conduct which may expose them to blackmailing attempts by the enemy and induce them to betray their country and the Allied cause.' Scott-Ford was just twenty-one when he was hanged at Wandsworth on 3 November 1942.

Johannes Marinus Dronkers told trawlermen who rescued him from a sinking yacht in the North Sea in May 1942 that he was a Dutchmen fleeing from the Nazis and wanted refuge in Britain. To show his joy at being saved, he danced on the deck and burst into song. It was true he was Dutch, but he was a member of the Nazi Party; the yacht had been provided by the German secret service and he had spent the months before his rescue training to be a spy. Interrogators soon suspected Dronkers, aged forty-six, of being an enemy agent. When confronted, he finally confessed he had been sent to Britain to collect information about American and Canadian troop numbers and movements and pass it back in letters written in invisible ink and posted to addresses in neutral countries. He was hanged at Wandsworth on 31 December 1942.

Franciscus Johannes Winter, aged forty, also posed as a refugee, the Dutchman claiming he had escaped from Belgium and made his way through France and into Spain, where he was held in a concentration camp. On his release he headed for Britain, but immigration officers did not believe his story. Large amounts of British, American, French, Spanish and Belgian banknotes were found on him, and he admitted he was a spy tasked with writing information about convoys in invisible ink in letters sent to Spain. Winter was hanged at Wandsworth on 26 January 1943.

Oswald John Job had also been given invisible-ink crystals. They were hidden in a set of keys. Job, born in London to German parents and public-school educated, had been interned in France after her fall. But other detainees noticed he was unusually friendly with the German guards. Months later he turned up in Spain, where his story of being a refugee was believed. It also fooled interrogators in England, but after he found lodgings in London, post office censors noticed an unusually high number of letters sent to former detainees at the internment camp. Investigators were about to accept the letters were innocent, until they noticed the oddly large keys, and a check revealed the ink crystals. At fifty-nine, he was the oldest spy to be executed when he was hanged at Pentonville on 15 March 1944.

Pierre Richard Charles Neukermans used the same route into Britain as Job. A Belgian, he was recruited by the German secret service, whose agents drove him to the Franco–Spanish border and left him with instructions on how to reach Lisbon. In London he was believed to be a genuine refugee, but once again postal officials became suspicious at the number of letters he sent overseas, and when he was questioned, he admitted being a spy. Aged twenty-eight, he met his end on the scaffold at Pentonville on 23 June 1944.

Belgian waiter Joseph Jan Van Hove had informed on French and Belgian workers at German airfields in France so successfully that, following the Normandy invasion, he was recruited to spy on Allied troops and shipping movements in England. He came to Britain via Sweden, but his previous activities were already known to anti-espionage officers, who arrested him. Van Hove, twenty-seven, was hanged at Pentonville on 12 July 1944.

Retribution against spies and traitors continued despite the end of the war. John Amery was the son of a Conservative government minister. He was already a committed fascist and a communist-hater by the time he went to live in France in the mid-1930s. He remained on the European mainland after the outbreak of war, and his views on the formation of a British Free Corps were admired by Adolf Hitler. Amery made radio broadcasts supporting fascism, and visited a prisoner-of-war camp trying to persuade captured troops to become British Free

Corps members. He was taken prisoner shortly before the end of the war, and at a brief trial in November 1945 he pleaded guilty to eight charges of treason, knowing his pleas meant certain death. Albert Pierrepoint, who hanged Amery at Wandsworth on 19 December 1945, described him as the bravest man he ever executed.

Just over two weeks later, the same gallows was used to hang Theodore John William Schurch, a private in the Royal Army Service Corps who, after being captured at Tobruk, turned traitor to spy for Italy. He had posed as a British Army captain, and had, according to the prosecution at his court martial, mingled with prisoners to get information from them. At least once he had sneaked over enemy lines to pass on what information he had found. Schurch, who objected to a Jewish officer sitting in judgement, claimed Italian agents had warned him that his parents, who lived in London, would be 'framed' as spies if he did not collaborate. After the capitulation of Italy, Schurch worked for the Germans and was sent to the Vatican to learn how it felt about countries occupied by Russia, but was arrested by American troops, convicted of treachery and desertion and hanged by Albert Pierrepoint on 4 January 1946.

The previous day the trapdoor of the scaffold at Wandsworth had opened and William Joyce, aged thirty-nine, an American-born Nazi propagandist, plunged to his doom. During the darkest days of the war, families had turned on their radios to hear Joyce's sneering voice tell them, 'Germany calling. Germany calling,' and begin a series of pro-Nazi rants. He was known as 'Lord Haw Haw' because many likened his voice to the braying of an ass.

London University-educated, Joyce had joined Sir Oswald Mosley's British Union of Fascists but, seduced by Hitler's fanaticism, he had fled to Germany in 1939. After working as a translator, he began broadcasting. As the war ended Joyce tried escaping to Denmark, but was shot by an American officer and taken to London on a stretcher, where he was found guilty of high treason and hanged at Wandsworth on 3 January 1946.

Joyce died for trying to destroy morale within Britain. A plot to cause mass disruption and chaos cost six other lives. Captured Germans and Italians schemed to make a mass simultaneous breakout from prisoner-of-war camps. The plan was discovered and the leaders separated and moved, some to Comrie Camp in Perthshire, Scotland. By mistake, Sergeant Major Wolfgang Rosterg, known for his anti-Nazi views, was also transferred to Comrie, where he was hauled before a mock trial and accused of tipping off the British authorities about the escape plan. Rosterg was found dead in December 1944. He had been severely beaten and hanged in one of the camp toilets.

Eight young German NCOs were charged with his murder. When they appeared before a British military court in London in July 1945, one German soldier witness told the hearing, 'I heard screaming and crying and then loud singing. Next morning I saw Rosterg in the hut with a rope around his neck.' It was held, he said, by Erich Koenig, one of the accused, aged twenty: 'Rosterg was bleeding from the eyes, nose and ears. Some of the men struck Rosterg at nods of the head from Koenig.' Later on he was told, 'Now the swine is hanging.' Koenig and four others – Joachim Palme-Goltz, twenty, Kurt Zuchisdorff, twenty, Heintz Brueling, twenty-two and Josep Mertins, twenty-one – were sentenced to death and hanged at Pentonville in October 1945. Rolf Herzig was jailed for life.

24

A MAN CALLED SNOW

JUST DAYS AFTER THE calamitous landing by parachute of Josef Jakobs, one of his masters in the Abwehr, the German military intelligence organisation, sent a coded message to an agent in England: 'Dropped man 31st 30 miles south Peterborough. Was badly hurt leaving plane. Perhaps dead. If you hear anything please let me know.' The agent was Welsh-born Arthur Graham Owens, and he is probably the most remarkable character ever to be held in first Wandsworth and then Dartmoor prisons. His story is nothing less than sensational.

Immediately he decoded the message, sent to a receiver supplied by the Germans, and made a telephone call. It was to a senior British espionage officer, a real life 'M', because the Welshman was a 'double', pretending to work for the Abwehr while actually confiding in the British. Or was he? Owens was allowed to head to the Peterborough area in search of information about the stricken spy. But he was not trusted. His British handler knew Jakobs had already been arrested, but deliberately withheld that information from the Welshman with the result that Owens arrived too late to make contact with the spy.

In official records held in the National Archives at Kew in Surrey, Owens is mainly referred to by his codename, 'Snow', an anagram of four of the letters of his surname. These records paint a fascinating picture of the life of a wartime spy.

Born in the little town of Pontardawe, South Wales in 1899, Owens served in the Royal Flying Corps during the Great War, after which he emigrated to Canada and started an electrical engineering business. When he returned to Britain in 1933, he was hired as a consultant by a firm specialising in producing batteries. His work took him to Germany, where the fact that his company had contracts supplying Royal Navy ships interested Abwehr spymasters eager to recruit foreigners who might be willing to pass on military secrets.

The official Snow file reports:

At his own request Snow was employed from January 1936 in the regular capacity of a British agent. In September 1936 however it was discovered that Snow was also in communication through a known cover address with the German Intelligence Service. He was therefore kept under observation with the result that in December 1936 he made what purported to be a full statement with regard to his relations with the German Intelligence Service. As a result of these disclosures Snow's employment as a British agent was terminated and it was made clear to him that anything which he did in the future would be done without the backing or consent of the British authorities. Nevertheless Snow continued his association with the German Intelligence Service and until the outbreak of war was active as a German agent. His services were evidently considered by the German authorities to be of increasing value to them.

Owens had been supplied with a German radio transmitter, given instructions how to use it and was told to begin transmissions with a secret code word that would demonstrate his messages were genuine. The radio transmitter would find itself in a highly bizarre setting.

Owens was married with two children, a boy who would be drawn into the intelligence web and end up in custody as a result, and a daughter, Patricia, who became a successful film actress, starring opposite Marlon Brando and James Mason. For much of Owens's career as a spy, his bedmate and companion was his mistress, Lily Bade. However, her continued presence by his side resulted in his wife denouncing him as a British agent to his German handler, a Major Ritter, who used the cover name Dr Rantzau. Fortunately for Owens, Ritter put his wife's allegations down to jealousy. But after the war, when Major Ritter was questioned by his Allied counterparts, he made a lengthy statement about Snow's activities and in a part of it he revealed the fine line that often existed between a spy's life and death.

During a meeting in Lisbon, Ritter had doubted whether Owens could be trusted: 'I then told him that I was not satisfied with his story, and that he must, in his own interests, be absolutely honest with me. I told Snow plainly that I should have to consider seriously if it would be safe for me to allow him to return to England, seeing how much he knew of my organisation and of me personally. I told him that he was wholly in my power and that I should have no difficulty in liquidating his case promptly in Lisbon. Snow was clearly very much frightened by this threat.'

Owens was hardly the popular picture of a spy. No tall, dark, handsome heartthrob he, no 007 looks or dashing, fearless ways. It was true that like the character Bond, Owens was a determined womaniser – one of his motives for agreeing to work for the Germans was the promise of a ready supply of available women. But he was no hero. Snow had been scared by Ritter's threat to kill him. Another fright was on the way. In August 1939 he went to Hamburg, taking with him his mistress and telling the Abwehr he had recruited yet another agent for them. The official file records that when he returned he 'disappeared completely' but in early September arranged to meet a Special Branch police inspector, who arrested him.

What happened next is unique in the annals of the history of the British prison service. Snow's official file states: 'Snow remained for a short while in Wandsworth Prison. It was then proposed that his wireless set should be used from the prison to re-establish contact with Germany under our direction. Snow readily accepted this proposal and the wireless set was installed in his cell. After some difficulty in making contact the following message was sent: "Must meet you Holland at once. Bring weather code. Radio town and hotel Wales ready." This message was explained by Snow in the following way. He had been instructed by Ritter that one of his principal duties in time of war would be the transmission of daily weather reports. He had also been told to discover the name and address of a reliable member of the Welsh Nationalist Party, and organisation which the Germans proposed to use if they could for the purpose of sabotage in South Wales.'

Owens was kept in Wandsworth for only a few days, but it was here that he experienced his second bout of fear. In the London prison he became the target for an unusually aggressive young man, and later an MI5 handler would report, 'I next asked Snow to describe to me the fellow-prisoner who had questioned him in Wandsworth Prison and of whom he had seemed very frightened at the time. He told me that he was a young man of twenty-three or twenty-four, whose name he did not learn and whom he had not seen before. He had spoken of Hamburg in a way which suggested to Snow that he was an agent of Rantzau.'

Who the unusually curious inmate was would remain a mystery, but happily for Owens, British spymasters were convinced the benefits from having a known German agent at liberty outweighed the risks. But at least the message from the prison-cell transmitter soon developed into a full-scale subterfuge. Once he was freed, Owens was allowed to make the rendezvous in Holland, meeting Ritter at Rotterdam. When he returned to England he reported on the meeting to MI5 and the outcome was a retired police inspector from Wales agreeing to play the role of a saboteur. Owens and the ex-policeman met Ritter, the German discussing a project for secretly shipping arms and explosives to South Wales by submarine. These were to be used for a major insurrection by the Welsh Nationalist Party. Before the outbreak of the war, Nazi planners, convinced that Germany would invade Britain, looked for ways to stretch Britain's military resources. Causing trouble in Ireland was one proposal, insurrection in Wales another, but once the war was under way and the invasion put on hold, enthusiasm for the plan waned.

Owens had been busy before, during and after his incarceration in Wandsworth, as his top-secret file reveals. The Abwehr was hard at work training batches of spies whose mission would be to infiltrate British military bases and try to worm out secrets from servicemen and -women and to mingle with members of the public to ascertain the level of morale.

In July 1940 Owens had given the Germans a ration book and identity card, both of which would be copied. The Abwehr now needed names and numbers for their forgers to insert in the fake books and cards, and in August he was asked to supply twenty specimen names and numbers of identity cards, which he sent. In November he was asked for three more numbers, one being for a single woman – Vera Schalburg. A few days later the Abwehr asked Owens to transmit the name of any London man whose house had been destroyed. His identity card initials and number were also transmitted. The details he sent were those of James Rymer of 33 Abbotsford Gardens, Woodford Green.

As he was answering the various requests, agents began arriving, some caught within hours or days. And those who were caught were discovered to have been given the identity details supplied by Owens. Among them were Gosta Caroli, who had the code name 'Summer', and his friend and fellow Nazi Wulf Schmidt, both of whom were arrested after Schmidt injured himself during their parachute landings in September 1940. The following month Kurt Karl Goose was arrested by a farmer soon after arriving by parachute and asking for directions. He too carried a forged identity card copied from that supplied by the Welshman. When Schalburg, Waelti and Drucke were searched after their disastrous exploits in Scotland, they were found to be holding identities taken from the Owens details. Dutchman Jan Willem Ter Braak, who had been born with the remarkable and unforgettable name of Engelbertus Fukken, lived in Cambridge after a successful parachute drop in Buckinghamshire. He survived on American dollars given to him before leaving, but when these ran out four months after his landing in November 1940, he shot himself in a Cambridge bus shelter. A search of the documents carried by Josef Jakobs revealed he had been given the identity of James Rymer of 33 Abbotsford Gardens, Woodford Green.

The findings confirmed to MI5 that the Germans were willing to accept information supplied by Owens, but his British spymasters clearly still distrusted him, as his file shows from a memorandum dated August 1943:

On 11.9.39 Snow was released at the request of MI5 and was thereafter employed by them on a number of missions both in this country and on the continent. These missions he discharged with success and his services proved to be of considerable value to MI5. In February 1941 however certain incidents occurred during a mission undertaken by Snow abroad, which made it impossible for MI5 to repose any further confidence in him himself, on whose account of the matter we are largely dependent, has never given any coherent or satisfactory account of the part played by him during this last mission. Two facts emerge, however, from his own statements; first, that he revealed to the German Intelligence Service matters which he had undertaken to keep secret; secondly that one of the results of his actions was to endanger the safety of another British agent. For these reasons Snow was arrested again on 23.4.41 and has since been detained.

His spying days over, Owens was locked up in Stafford Prison but then, as the result of an administrative mistake, he was transferred to Dartmoor, where he found he was the only British inmate. It was clear MI5 wanted to make sure nobody, particularly the Abwehr, discovered his whereabouts. He was kept under a rule known as Regulation 18B, which meant him being held 'under conditions of special secrecy'. A memo dated 23 December 1942 emphasised this: 'Snow is one of a small class of detainees whom MI5 particularly want to prevent from communicating information to anyone outside and whose whereabouts they want to keep as secret as possible.'

Owens was not a happy prisoner. His son had also been detained on grounds that he knew what his father had been up to and was held in a camp on the Isle of Man. The two wanted to be together, a development MI5 vehemently opposed. Owens believed he could be useful if he was set free, a view few in authority shared because MI5 was by now convinced the Abwehr would at least mistrust him, particularly following the demise or disappearance of agents who had been supplied with identities provided by him.

In Dartmoor, surrounded by hundreds of enemy sympathisers and suspected agents, he had begun informing on other inmates and often expressed worries over what might happen to him if his deceit was discovered. Meanwhile, as part of the determination by the British secret service to veil his existence and activities, he had been instructed never to use his name or codename in correspondence. A handwritten letter from him to his principal secret service contact, Scots-born Thomas Argyll Robertson – popularly known simply as 'Tar' – in late November 1942 summed up his feelings and rage:

I am writing this to you trusting it is in your power to do something for me. I have now been in prison nearly three years and as you know during this time have been unable to once see my son. I should very much like to be with him. I have never complained once although I am sure you were not aware of the conditions I went though at Stafford, being kept in solitary confinement nearly seven months and being forbidden a hair cut for ten months until my hair was down my shoulders and being made the laughing stocks of all the prisoners, these are only two instances. I am not worried about the loss of my liberty, but I am worried that I am unable to do and help this country in these difficult times. As you are aware I have done a considerable bit for this country and your dept, although perhaps not seeing eye to eye in our methods in arriving at a given point. I must frankly say I am consumed with rage to have to waste my time here when I can be doing useful work.

At desolate, remote Dartmoor, Owens tried to show MI5 he was a prolific source of information, but he had a motive for doing so. He argued that digging out secrets from his fellow prisoners put him in danger and that he should be moved away, preferably to the side of his son, before his secret was uncovered. The result was that senior intelligence officers wondered if he was simply too prolific – that he embellished some information.

In July 1943 his desperation to be set free had reduced him to shopping a Roman Catholic priest: 'I am sending you a report which to me is very distasteful as it concerns a Priest of the Roman Catholic Church,' he wrote to Robertson. 'However as I have taken a solemn vow to assist England, yourself and the Service I worked for from 39 to 41 I am in duty bound to report this and all other matters to you. The internee D . . . in previous agreement with the Priest who visits him here, has written a complete statement and account of his imprisonment, treatment, conditions and whereabouts. This document was handed by D . . . to the Priest during his last private visit, the document was eventually conveyed by the Priest from this prison to some destination unknown to me. As I am informed that this priest was warned by a member of your department and gave his word not to talk to D . . . regarding his internment or matters concerning it, I look on the matter as very serious, hence my rush to contact you.'

The case of the priest was investigated and found to be true, and certainly some of the material he came up with and passed on to Tar Robertson created deep interest. One subject on which he was able to supply details concerned secret experimental work by German scientists on rockets at Heligoland, the dual islands in the North Sea off the German coast. His information came through his questioning of a fellow agent at Dartmoor. In a detailed note to Robertson, Owens reported: 'Before firing, the Rocket resembles a large shell, after leaving the tube or gun this "shell" when it reaches a given distance or height discards a section of the base and at the same time flight vanes are released and exposed and the exhaust discharge rocket mechanism is automatically put in action. It will be seen that the weapon is virtually a large shell at the start of its journey but quickly develops into a Rocket to give it great range.'

Was Owens describing the forerunner of the V1 and V2 rockets that were to cause such terrible destruction – particularly in London – in the latter stages of the war? His letter caused a secret service agent to visit him at Dartmoor, The agent reported: 'He appeared to be in quite good form and did not, as I expect, ask to be let out but expressed a keen desire to be sent to the Isle of Man where he understands the leakage from the Internment Camps is very serious.' The report later went on to say that Owens had discussed 'rocket guns' with Dr Rantzau in 1939. 'He said that the Doctor had told him about a special gun which the Germans had which they proposed to mount on the French coast capable of firing 120 miles. He said that this was not a rocket gun but an ordinary type of gun.'

The fact was, though, that Owens did want away from Dartmoor, and by mid-1944 he was almost resorting to a form of blackmail to achieve a transfer. A report dated 27 July revealed: 'At an interview at Dartmoor on 23.7.44, SNOW after recounting a number of other incidents or allegations, finally alleged that he was certain that information was being illicitly got out of, and into, the detainees' wing in the prison. In response to questioning he said he did not know exactly how it was being done, but would find out in the course of the next few days.'

However, as the report indicated, there was a catch. 'Snow on more than one occasion stressed that if he got to the bottom of this alleged channel of leakage, he could not remain at Dartmoor, wherever else we might like to send him, particularly since it was known that he was responsible for informing us about D . . .'s attempted illicit communication through the RC chaplain.'

By this time MI5 officers were taking the view that Owens' work as a prison informer had all but run its course. A memorandum dated 10 August 1944 confirmed MI5 suspicions 'that S is striving his utmost to get transferred elsewhere, and is prepared to allow his imagination to give him all the assistance which it can to this end'.

While he continued to badger Robertson to leave Dartmoor, his son was also pestering the authorities to be allowed to join his father. Robertson had actually recommended that father and son be freed. 'Since his internment in Dartmoor Snow has been of considerable use to the Office in furnishing bits of information which he has picked up from his fellow internees about their past activities. He was also partly responsible for bringing to our notice the leakages of information which had occurred from camp WX in the Isle of Man . . . ' he said in a report which was destined for the Home Office, responsible for the final decision. The outcome was that within a few days father and son were freed.

Robertson, who had dealt with Owens throughout his career as a British agent, clearly felt sorry for the remarkable Welshman, who left Dartmoor with only a couple of pounds in his pocket. He arranged for accommodation for his one-time spy and pleaded for him to be given a helping hand.

At the beginning of 1945 Robertson told his superiors, 'I do not consider that Snow has made any very serious attempt to find himself a job and I am satisfied that so long as he feels, as he does, that we shall look after him he will be content to drift along without making any effort. In fairness to him I think that it ought to be said that, having regard to his age – he is nearly fifty – and to the fact that throughout the war he has had no proper employment, he may be for all practical purposes virtually unemployable, except in the one job of which he has any recent experience, namely as an agent and for this he is for a variety of reasons no longer suitable. I should like on parting with Snow to pay him a lump sum so that he is not cast on to the world without means.' Robertson asked for £500, and a cheque for that amount was duly handed to Owens on 6 March 1945. His signed receipt remains in his file. He had also signed the Official Secrets Act, binding him never to reveal details of his espionage work.

However, after going off to live in Canada, he told the British authorities that unless he was compensated for what he saw as his illicit jailing, he would publish his memoirs. A secret deal was reached. It enabled Owens to return to Europe and he set up home near Dublin. The life of the man who spied from inside the walls of two of the toughest jails in Britain ended with his death in Ireland in 1957.

25

SUFFRAGETTES

BRUTALITY AND CRUELTY are everyday features of life in any prison. They are formally detested, the instigators, whether inmates or warders, punished. And yet Holloway Jail was the scene of the most horrific officially sanctioned and condoned abuse of prisoners. The victims were women, their crimes relatively minor, and their overriding motive the right to vote. They were known as suffragettes. The torture many were forced to endure was known as forced feeding.

Suffragettes are mostly remembered through the tragic death in June 1913 of Emily Wilding Davison, aged forty, who suffered fatal injuries when she dashed in front of King George V's horse, Anmer, during the Epsom Derby, dying four days later of a fracture to the base of her skull. It is widely believed she planned her dramatic gesture as a way of drawing attention to the suffragette cause. But the movement really began in October 1903 when Emmeline Pankhurst and the eldest of her daughters, Christabel, formed the Women's Social and Political Union. As the number of their supporters mounted, so did a campaign of civil disturbance that included smashing the windows of government buildings, destroying letters in postboxes and throwing objects at leading politicians. Offenders were marched off to prison, many to Holloway. By the outbreak of the Great War up to 1,000 women had been arrested. To publicise their demands some began hunger strikes, and because the government would be legally responsible for the death of any prisoner, prison staff and doctors were ordered to force-feed the strikers.

This barbaric practice usually involved the inmate being strapped down, the mouth being kept open with a crude metal device and a long rubber tube forced into the stomach through the mouth or via the nostrils. Liquid was poured down the tube. As a consequence many of the victims suffered long-term mental or physical effects, including breakdowns and pneumonia. Women took advantage of a loophole in the law that meant those who became ill had to be freed. The government responded by introducing a law in 1913 that allowed them to be released on health grounds, but once they recovered they were rearrested and taken back to jail, and the process was repeated until they had served their sentence. It was informally known as the 'Cat and Mouse Act'.

In December 1911 Emily Wilding Davison was jailed for six months for setting fire to pillar boxes. She was taken to Holloway, where she knew what she would face once she refused to eat in prison. She had been force-fed many times, and once told a friend about a typical ordeal: 'The matron, two doctors, and five or six wardresses entered the cell. The doctor said, "I am going to feed you by force." The scene which followed will haunt me with its horror all my life, and is almost indescribable. While they held me flat, the elder doctor tried all round my mouth with a steel gag to find an opening. On the right side of my mouth two teeth are missing; this gap he found, pushed in the horrid instrument, and prised open my mouth to its widest extent. Then a wardress poured liquid down my throat out of a tin enamelled cup. The torture was barbaric.' Determined to sacrifice herself in the hope this would put a stop to the practice, she hurled herself down one of Holloway's metal staircases, causing terrible injuries to her head and spine and leaving her with a permanent pain that only ended when she was knocked into unconsciousness on the Derby course, an injury from which she never recovered.

Her suffering was typical of many. The Women's Social and Political Union produced its own newsletter entitled *The Suffragette*. In the issue of 11 April 1913, it reported:

News has reached the offices of the W.S.P.U. that Mrs Pankhurst, who has been hunger-striking ever since she entered Holloway on Thursday, April 3, is in a state of collapse. There has been no attempt to feed her by force. During the week four Suffragettes have been released from Holloway – Miss Olive Wharry, Miss Gibb, Mrs. Branson, and Miss Zelie Emerson – all on account of serious ill-health. Miss Wharry has been secretly hunger striking for 31 days, and is in a state of terrible emaciation and Miss Emerson, after five weeks' forcible feeding, was so dangerously ill that she was taken away from the prison in an ambulance. Rumours of a hunger strike that seems as if it were more or less general have leaked out from Holloway. Indignation and passionate protest are the order of the day inside prison as well as out.

Suffragettes knew what to expect when they were committed to Holloway. On arrival they were made to strip naked and given a cursory medical examination before being handed standard prison clothes that included a dark-green dress decorated with white arrows. They were locked in individual cells to prevent them talking to one another, their only break from the monotony of being on their own coming when they were allowed a brief visit to the prison chapel for daily service and a quick walk around the exercise yard before warders dogged their steps to ensure silence was maintained. They were given knitting and sewing tasks inside their cells. During their first month in Holloway, they were not allowed either visitors or letters.

The suffragettes looked on themselves as political prisoners, and for many, hunger striking was a way of protesting against insistence of the prison authorities and the government that they should be treated as common criminals. Annie Kenney, one of the very first suffragettes to be jailed and force-fed, described prison as, 'Too much discipline, too little companionship, too much gloom, too little laughter.'

Emmeline Pankhurst described being in Holloway as, 'civilised torture' and was appalled when she first entered the prison to hear the screams of women being force-fed. In her autobiography, *My Own Story*, written in 1914, she said, 'I shall never while I live forget the suffering I experienced during the days when those cries were ringing in my ears. Holloway became a place of horror and torment. Sickening scenes of violence took place almost every hour of the day, as the doctors went from cell to cell performing their hideous office.' Once she threatened to smash a clay jug on the heads of prison officers who tried entering her cell to drag her off to be force-fed.

Ada Flatman was aged thirty-two when she was arrested in 1908. She was not alone, however, for along with other members of a suffragette deputation were with her. They were taken in for demanding to see then Prime Minister Herbert Henry Asquith. Convicted of obstructing the police, she was given the option of paying a £1 fine or spending a month in Holloway, and chose the latter. Taken to the prison in a Black Maria, the slang term for a dark-painted police van, she later recalled being ordered to strip and bathe in a bath so dirty she refused, instead sticking in her toe. A set of prison clothes was thrown in to the bathroom and once dressed she joined other suffragettes who were shown a huge hamper filled with boots of all sizes. 'None of which fitted any of us,' she said. Ada said the sight of her fellow suffragettes wearing oversize boots, baggy prison clothing and large caps filled her with 'silent laughter'. Their smiles would not remain for long.

Each day Holloway officials had to compile a separate report on each suffragette. In an attempt to confuse the prison, police and magistrates, the artist Olive Wharry used aliases including Joyce Locke and Phyllis North. In December 1911 she was arrested as

Olive Wharry for smashing windows and spent two months in Holloway. While there she formally petitioned the government asking for a change in the conditions under which she was held: 'I am not a prisoner in Holloway because I have committed any crime, but because it was necessary to break the law for the purpose of making a political protest. I see no reason therefore why we suffragettes should not be treated as other political prisoners. Therefore I claim the right to see visitors every day, to write and receive letters, have daily newspapers and retain my watch.' Her plea was ignored.

She served another six months the following year in Winson Green Jail, Birmingham, for a similar offence. Shortly after her release she headed to Aberdeen, where she and others tried disrupting a political meeting. They were let off with just five days in jail. In early 1913 she and fellow suffragette Lilian Lenton set fire to a tea pavilion in Kew Gardens, London, wrongly believing it was Crown property. Unfortunately it was privately owned by two women who depended on it for their livelihood, and they had insured the building for just £500 while damage was estimated at almost double that figure. The suffragette pair said they had checked to make sure the pavilion was empty before burning it, but that brought them no sympathy and each was jailed for eighteen months, despite Wharry describing the hearing as 'a good joke'.

On this occasion Wharry had given her name as 'Joyce Locke' and even though the Holloway staff knew her real identity, her alias was used in the daily reports. Whoever had arranged the layouts of the reports knew what to expect from suffragettes. One column was headed 'If taking food voluntarily', another 'Attitude' and yet another, 'Effect, if any, of forcible feeding'. 'Joyce Locke' had clearly set out to be as troublesome as possible to her jailers. One daily report entry states: 'Has taken no food since entry. Smashed up everything in the cell she was first placed in. Removed to a special strong cell. Kept apart from all other prisoners and not allowed to communicate. All privileges suspended.' Another that she 'Refuses medical examination'. Under 'If taking food voluntarily', a warder had written, 'Cannot say at present as she has only just been received' while her attitude was described as 'general conduct bad, destructive and insolent'.

While others, including Emmeline Pankhurst, had openly refused food, crafty 'Joyce Locke' after an initial bout of force-feeding had pretended to eat normally, but when the backs of warders were turned, she handed her food to other prisoners. However, her subterfuge aroused suspicions, as a report on 28 March showed. Now listed as Olive Wharry, the section marked 'If taking food voluntarily' concluded, 'She may be taking a little, but how much it is impossible to say.' The truth, though, emerged in the same report: 'General conduct indifferent. She was weighed this morning and was 97lbs. It was then found she had an india rubber hot water bottle full of water under her clothes which weighed four and a half pounds so her actual weight is 92 and a half pounds, which is 14lbs less then on reception here 3 weeks ago. She is decidedly thin and probably a little weaker though there was no marked difference as compared with yesterday.' It was hardly surprising then that as *The Suffragette* revealed in its issue of April 11, when Wharry was freed on health grounds after serving less than a third of her sentence, she was emaciated. In fact, her weight had dropped to just over five and a half stones.

She was arrested regularly, never completing any sentence, and in mid-1913, she was back in Holloway, where prison doctors came to the conclusion that she was mad.

Her co-accused in the burning of the pavilion, Lilian Lenton, was just as obstructive. The daily report made just after her arrival at Holloway stated she 'has been in prison before but refuses to give any particulars'. It went on to describe her behaviour as 'general conduct: bad, very defiant. Refuses medical examination – Is rather spare.' And in a near copy of the remarks on Wharry, the report concluded, 'Recognised by officers as having been in prison before but name cannot be given. Has taken no food since reception. Smashed up everything in the cell she was first placed in. Removed to a special strong cell. Kept apart from all other prisoners & not allowed to communicate. All privileges suspended.'

The rigours of Holloway took their toll almost immediately on Lenton. On Tuesday, 25 February, just a few days after her arrival, she was gone, freed with the blessing of the Home Office, which, out of courtesy, ordered a senior civil servant to write to the magistrates who had jailed she and Wharry. The letter read:

I am directed by the Secretary of State to say that he thinks that he ought to inform the Justices of the circumstances in which Lilian Lenton alias Ida Inkley, who was charged at Richmond on the 20th instant with setting fire to a building and was remanded until the 27th instant, has been released from Prison. On her reception in H.M. Prison, Holloway, this woman refused to take food and by Sunday morning her condition was such that it became necessary to administer food artificially. After such examination as was possible this was done, but she did not retain most of the food, and her condition became so serious that in the opinion of the experienced Medical Officer of the Prison her life would have been in immediate danger if forcible feeding had been continued or if she had been allowed to remain longer without food.

On these facts being urgently represented to him by the Medical Officer, the Secretary of State felt he had no choice but to allow her to be discharged from prison. She was removed about 6 p.m. on the 23rd instant to 34 Harrington Square, Mornington Crescent to the care of her friends. Before being discharged she promised to attend the Police Court on remand, but as it is understood that her medical adviser believes that she is suffering from pneumonia, it is possible she may be unable to do so. I am to add that the other prisoner, Joyce Locke alias Olive Wharry, has also refused to take food, but it has been possible to feed her artificially without injury to her health.

Lenton, who spent most of the pre-war years under police surveillance, died in 1974, twenty-five years after Wharry.

The suffragettes had their own anthem, 'The March of the Women', composed by one of their number, Ethel Smyth, who was later created a dame for her services to music. One of her supporters was the conductor Sir Thomas Beecham, who told friends after visiting her in Holloway, 'Ethel was leaning out of her cell window and using a toothbrush to conduct her fellow suffragettes as they marched around the exercise yard singing, "The March of the Women."'

Sympathy for the suffragette cause grew, although public opinion waned as a result of some incidents such as the burning of the tea pavilion and the slashing in 1914 by Emily Wilding Davison's friend Mary Richardson of the 'Rokeby Venus', the painting by Diego Velázquez. Holloway and other prisons holding suffragettes were ordered to release them under a government amnesty in August 1914. In 1918 more than eight million women over the age of thirty were given the right to vote, and ten years later, this was extended to all women aged twenty-one and over.

26

INTERNEES

ON MONDAY, 15 JUNE 1215 on the banks of the River Thames at Runnymede, King John gave his seal to the Magna Carta, a bill of rights forced on him by leading barons. One clause stipulated: 'No Freeman shall be taken or imprisoned, or be disseised of his Freehold, or Liberties, or free Customs, or be outlawed, or exiled, or any other wise destroyed; nor will We not pass upon him, nor condemn him, but by lawful judgment of his Peers, or by the Law of the land'. In 1919 the British government introduced a variation. Known simply as Defence Regulation 18B, it suspended the right of every man and woman not to be jailed without a trial. It was one of the measures used to keep 'Snow' in custody. Now the highest in the land found themselves mingling in prison with the lowest – peers with prostitutes, rich with poor. What this hotchpotch of people had in common was that although they had done nothing wrong, they were officially distrusted. Usually their pro-Fascist views led to them to being locked up, but in other cases they were simply the wives or husbands of suspects. Many were held in Holloway.

Among these internees were Sir Oswald Mosley, founder of the British Union of Fascists, which later changed its name to simply the British Union; and his second wife, Diana; but among the many well-known figures held in Holloway the Mosleys attracted most interest.

Oswald Ernald Mosley was the 6th Baronet of Ancoats. He had been a Conservative Member of Parliament before switching to the Labour Party to hold the prominent post of Chancellor of the Duchy of Lancaster. However, his formation of the British Union with its thug Blackshirts minders who brought comparisons with Hitler's vicious Sturmabteilung – the SA – and friendship with Lord Haw Haw and Italy's Fascist leader Benito Mussolini made many wonder if his sympathies lay with Germany or his native England.

Following the death of his first wife, Cynthia, Mosley married his mistress, Diana Guinness, who had been born into the highly colourful Mitford family. At their wedding in the home of Minister of Public Enlightenment and Propaganda, Joseph Goebbels, in Berlin in 1936, Diana's sister, Unity, known in high society as 'Baba' and a fanatical supporter of Hitler, had introduced her sibling to the Führer, who was among the wedding guests along with his close confidant Joachim Von Ribbentrop. British secret service agents had been monitoring Diana for two years before her marriage, noting her regular visits to Germany to meet the Nazi hierarchy and secretly opening her mail and listening to telephone conversations. When her luggage was checked at Heathrow Airport in 1938, customs officers discovered an autographed photograph of Hitler. According to a Special Branch report, 'Lady Mosley is said to be far cleverer and more dangerous than her husband and will stick at nothing to achieve her ambitions – she is wildly ambitious.'

Oswald was the first to be interned in June 1940, two months after the birth of the couple's son, Max. Diana was still breastfeeding the infant two months later when, following pressure from members of her own family urging her to be taken into custody, police arrived at her home and told her to pack a bag. She was ordered to leave Max with relatives and taken off to Holloway Prison's F Wing, where female internees were held.

Conditions were appalling: food was short, and because German bombing attacks on London had severely damaged water mains, inmates could only bathe once a week at most.

Friends of Diana appealed to Prime Minister Winston Churchill, who instructed prison officials to let Diana have a daily bath, but this was rarely possible. She appealed unsuccessfully against her detention, but following another plea to the prime minister and another intervention by Churchill, instructions were given for the Mosleys to be reunited. Oswald was transferred to Holloway so he could be with his wife. At first they stayed in a special section of the prison reserved for married couples. However, as a result of pleas from influential friends, they were moved to a cottage in the prison grounds, where other inmates cooked and cleaned for them, and they read, played gramophone records and – when Nazi bombers were not darkening the skies above Holloway – lay in the sun.

However, being imprisoned, they had lost not only their freedom but their privacy too. They were monitored around the clock, and although visitors were allowed, records of all their callers were sent to Special Branch. Their incoming and outgoing mail was read and censored, and conversations with family members recorded. The Mosleys had, over the years, been used to the constant threats against their lives – as a result of their friendship with Hitler in particular. Even behind the high walls of Holloway, the authorities decided there was still a risk, not just of fanatics trying to break in to attack them, but of supporters seeking to help them escape, and as a result, four extra police officers were permanently stationed in and around Holloway for the duration of their internment.

Oswald and Diana remained in prison until 1943, when they were freed on grounds of his ill health and after it had been decided they could or even wanted to do little, if any, damage to the British war effort. However, more than 20,000 signed a petition protesting against the decision to let them go. Mosley recovered from his internment and lived until 1980, when he died in Paris aged eighty-four. Diana survived to the age of ninety-three, dying in 2003.

The Mosleys may have received special treatment because of their high profile and high-society contacts, but many others with links to the British Union were forced to endure the freezing, spartan and damp Holloway conditions. Heather Donovan was the drum major of the British Union Women's Corps and her husband, Bryan, the assistant director general of the union. Irish-born Fay Taylour had been a champion speedway rider and was thirty-five when war broke out. But her fate was sealed years earlier when she joined the British Union and became an active follower of Mosley. In 1940 plainclothes Special Branch detectives took her off to Holloway, promising her it would only be for 'a few weeks'. She was there until 1943.

Like Fay, Norah Elam was Irish born. But she had the unique distinction of being locked up in Holloway during both wars – in the first for minor lawbreaking as a suffragette, when she was known as Norah Dacre Fox, and in the second because of her prominent membership of the British Union. She had even been proposed as a potential candidate to become a Fascist MP. However, the election was suspended because of the war. Norah was detained in 1940 in Holloway under the notorious 18B, her husband, Dudley, being interned at the same time.

There were times when Holloway staff must have wondered if they were hosting a high-society ball. In addition to Sir Oswald and Lady Mosley, internees included Lady Alexandrina Domvile, wife of the distinguished and much honoured Royal Navy Admiral Sir Barry, and the mysterious Lady Howard of Effingham. Lord Domvile was a former head of naval intelligence whose work before the war had taken him to Germany, where he became fascinated by Fascism. He was a guest of Hitler's right-hand man, Heinrich Himmler, at the 1937 Nuremberg Rally and was shown around Dachau concentration camp. With Lady Alexandrina he founded 'The Link', whose the aim was to encourage closer relations between Britain and Germany. Lord Domvile had a mistress, Mrs Olive Baker, who was arrested in

June 1940 for distributing leaflets publicising German radio broadcasts. She was subsequently jailed for five years. A month later, the Domviles were arrested at their Hampshire home and interned, he to Brixton and Lady Alexandrina to Holloway, where one of her fellow inmates was Mrs Baker.

Domvile and Alexandrina insisted they should not be interned, and in interviews with MI5 officers, they argued in favour of being freed. But during the interviews it was pointed out that when he visited a home for ex-servicemen, Domvile was alleged to have said that Hitler would soon be in England, but that there was no need to worry: he would bring the Duke of Windsor from exile to be crowned as King. And in a letter to his wife, the admiral had written: 'The real enemies of the British Empire are the people of this country who have brought this catastrophe upon their ignorant countrymen.' Many saw this as evidence that he was plotting with other Fascists to bring down the British government.

Maria Malvina Gertler had been under surveillance by MI5 even before her marriage to Mowbray Henry Gordon Howard, the 6th Earl of Effingham, in 1938. She fled her native Hungary and came to England in 1935, but at the time of her wedding, MI5 agents reported she was being richly rewarded as the mistress of Edward Stanislas Weisblatt, a Polish Jew who became fabulously wealthy selling boats to the Republicans during the Spanish Civil War and was a gangster running guns into Spain and suspected of spying for Germany. A senior MI5 officer who met Lady Howard reported she was, 'a not unattractive Gypsy gamin type; highly sexed, I should say . . . an accent more foreign than it need be'.

The marriage was a bizarre affair. Files held in the National Archives reveal it was one made not of love but of convenience. His lordship needed money; Maria, British nationality so she could work on behalf of her lover. At their marriage she received a ring and her husband a cash handout supplied by Weisblatt.

At the start of the war the security services were worried about her friendships with people in high places, including the Eden family – particularly as Sir Anthony Eden was on the verge of becoming Winston Churchill's secretary of state for war. Was she a beautiful spy or a fantasist? MI5 was unwilling to take chances until senior staff could determine she was not a threat to British security. The result was that she was arrested in February 1941 and interned in Holloway, where she spent three uncomfortable months before being released. Her marriage ended in divorce in 1945 and she later went to live in Australia.

The Right Club was a pro-Fascist group that was closely monitored by MI5. Its secretary was Anna Wolkoff, a White Russian émigré, who stayed in London with her family after the Bolshevik Revolution had made it too dangerous for them to return. Wolkoff was close to the Duchess of Windsor, the former Wallis Simpson, who was friendly with Hitler and a number of his closest supporters. She wormed her way into the trust of a cipher clerk at the American Embassy in London and through him gained sensitive information, including details of confidential communications between Winston Churchill and US President Franklin Roosevelt, which were passed on to an Italian diplomat. The Italian was asked to make sure it reached William Joyce, Lord Haw Haw, so he could broadcast it. Yet again high society was embarrassed by one more of its circle being exposed as untrustworthy. Wolkoff was arrested and remanded to Holloway Prison to await her trial in November 1940, after which she was jailed for ten years. When she was eventually freed, her British citizenship was withdrawn.

Wolkoff's credentials as a spy were never in doubt. Mathilde Lucie Carre, alias Victoire, was on the other hand suspected of espionage, but while she was never formally charged she was interned for three years and sat in her cell at Holloway wondering whether she would be executed upon her release. After the outbreak of war she had been second-in-command of the Interallié, a French resistance network set up by Polish intelligence officers in Paris. It was always dangerous work. Capture inevitably meant torture at the hands of the Gestapo, and either immediate death by a firing squad or a lingering decline in a concentration camp. Most networks suffered losses, but by the end of 1941, the entire network comprising over one hundred agents had been taken by German intelligence. Carre somehow managed to get to Britain a few weeks later, in February 1942. She was suspected from the outset of having betrayed the Interallié and admitted she had passed information to the Germans with whom she had set up a new resistance organisation.

After pledging her loyalty back to the Allies, she was allowed to send bogus messages to her Nazi handlers and pleaded to be dropped back into France to continue the subterfuge. But it was clear she could not be trusted. MI5 had continued to investigate her activities, and after discovering she was responsible for the capture of resistance workers in her homeland, Victoire was interned until close to the end of the war, much of the time in Holloway. As the Allies closed in on victory, the grim surroundings of the prison must have seemed as paradise when compared with the ultimate fate she realised lay in store. Many loyal French men and women were dead as a result of her duplicity, and she was deported as a prisoner and held in jail until January 1949 when she was convicted of treason and sentenced to death. The sentence was commuted to twenty years' imprisonment, but she served just five years. After her release she continued to live in Paris, where she died in 1970, aged sixty-two.

27

THE FENIANS

IN 1865 AS THE American Civil War was coming to a bloody end, plans for another violent uprising were being uncovered and blocked. The scene would be Ireland. The plan was for up to 10,000 Irish Americans to land in the south and force an end to English rule. The conspirators were members of the Irish Republican Brotherhood and the Fenian Brotherhood, organisations determined to set up an independent Irish Republic. These rebels were known simply as Fenians. However, in 1865 a drunken courier left behind crucial documents at a railway station, and these included a letter written by James Stephens, leader of the Irish Republican Brotherhood and known as 'The Captain', in which he urged, 'There is no time to be lost. This year – and let there be no mistake about it – must be the year of action.' The documents were handed to police and led to mass arrests. Stephens was caught and remanded to prison to await his trial, but with the help of two warders who were Fenian supporters, he was able to escape and fled to France.

Meantime, the trials of the others before Special Commissions went ahead. In Dublin the main interest centred on the *Irish People*, a Fenian newspaper where most of the principal plotters worked, unaware that in their midst was a police informer, Pierce Nagle, whose betrayal and evidence resulted in a series of convictions.

English authorities were shocked by the ease with which

Stephens had been able to flee and, fearing more escapes, sent Robert Peel, son of Sir Robert Peel, the man credited with founding modern-day policing, to oversee security. Peel realised that prisons in Ireland could not be trusted to hold the conspirators, and he organised plans to ship those found guilty to the mainland to serve their sentences. The jail selected to house the Fenians once they reached England was Dartmoor, a choice that surprised many.

Largely due to Nagle's information, and the defiant attitude by some of the accused men, who made it clear they were not afraid to give their lives in the cause of Irish freedom from English rule, most of the Fenians were doomed. They faced a variety of charges including, 'High treason by compassing, devising and conspiring within the last three years with the members of a secret society called the Fenian Brotherhood in England, Ireland and America, of which society they are members to levy war against the Queen in Ireland, subvert her Royal authority therein and establish an independent republic,' and 'Conspiring and combining with members of the Fenian Brotherhood.'

As Christmas 1865 approached, the trial judges completed their work and left to go home under heavy guard, having received threats they would be attacked. The guilty men were held under the tightest security to await a ship to take them to south-west England. One of their leaders, Thomas Clarke Luby, had said defiantly from the dock as he was about to be told he would spend the next twenty years in prison, 'As long as there are men in any country prepared to expose themselves to every difficulty and danger in its service, prepared to brave captivity, even death itself if needs be, that country cannot be lost.' They were the sentiments of most of those for their grim judgement.

There had been a brief moment of humour during the hearings when the wife of accused man John O'Donovan was allowed to sit in front of the dock during his trial, the excuse being made by him that he needed her to pass messages to his legal advisers. She was not there for long because it was noticed that while passing papers to his lawyers, Mrs O'Donovan was also handing items to her husband, and when she was spotted handing him a bottle of whisky, she was ordered out.

At the end of his hearing, O'Donovan was sentenced to life imprisonment. The convicted men were gathered at Mountjoy Jail in Dublin, and on 30 December they were shipped off to Dartmoor. As well as O'Donovan and Luby, the party comprised John O'Leary (twenty years); Jeremiah O'Donovan Rossa (natural life); John Lynch (ten years); Charles Underwood O'Connell, who had been arrested after arriving by boat from America (ten years); Michael Moore, the group's armourer (ten years); father of seven John Haltigan (seven years); Patrick 'Pagan' O'Leary, who had fought in the Mexican War and at one time thought of becoming a priest (twenty years); and Thomas Duggan (ten years).

Dartmoor, in its desolate location, might have appeared the obvious spot to hold them. Although escape was relatively easy, the Irishmen were surrounded by an environment totally foreign to them, and without outside help, getting off the moor was nigh impossible. However, when it came to getting away, there was some safety in numbers. At the time the close-knit Irish group arrived at Dartmoor, the prison was continually under the threat of being overrun by mobs. In March 1862 the governor and deputy governor had been attacked by two convicts and were only saved from serious injury, or worse, by the intervention of warders. The attackers were each given thirty-six lashes from the cat o' nine tails. But with only 150 warders and troops guarding more than 1,200 convicts, fears grew about the ability of the staff to cope with a mass revolt, and senior officers pleaded for more troops to be stationed at the prison.

Yet even the arrival of extra help could not prevent escapes. In June 1863 reports emerged of just how lax security was. One of the inmates clambered over the prison wall with the use of a rope and sandbag. Although he was recaptured the next day ten miles away at Ashburton, the incident caused alarm because the escaper was one-handed, and authorities remained baffled as to how he made it over the wall. In November that year there was what newspapers described as 'another mutinous outbreak at Dartmoor' when dozens of convicts refused to return to their cells after Sunday service. According to the *Birmingham Daily Post*, 'The warders and the civil guard armed to the teeth advanced upon them and after a scene of outrageous confusion the convicts gave up and were locked up.'

Unrest continued and after the arrival of the Fenians, who were regarded as influential and persuasive and therefore potentially dangerous, it was decided they should be separated. Some, including Rossa and O'Donnell, were moved to the much tighter security of Pentonville. In 1870 the government announced an amnesty under which the Fenians were told they could leave prison provided they agreed not to return to Ireland until their sentences had expired. Some went to Europe, others to America – among them Rossa, who although elected an MP while held in Pentonville, his prison stretch made him ineligible to take his parliamentary seat. He had clearly missed the marital bed while in prison. Before being jailed he had married his third wife, by which time he already had five children. After his release he fathered a further thirteen.

Dartmoor would be the temporary home to other prominent Irishmen. Among them was another Fenian, Michael Davitt, whose family suffered appalling hardship during the Great Famine and fled to north-west England after being made homeless because they could not afford the rent for their home in County Mayo. Davitt was just eleven and working in a cotton mill when he lost his right arm in an accident. In 1865, at the time Fenians were being arrested in Ireland, Davitt joined the Irish Republican Brotherhood, campaigning in the north of England and Scotland and organising the smuggling of arms to Ireland. He was arrested in London in 1870, convicted of selling arms and sentenced to fifteen years' penal servitude. Eventually he found himself in Dartmoor, from where he wrote to a friend in 1872 complaining of horrendous treatment and abuse.

Davitt had been sent to Dartmoor from Millbank, in London. He hated the moor jail and was briefly transferred to Portsmouth Jail. But not long after arriving there, he was sent back to Dartmoor, where his fellow convicts included other Fenians, among them Corporal Thomas Chambers of the 61st Regiment of Foot. Davitt wrote:

Why I was brought here I do not know, unless it was because on the 12th of July I wrote a letter to my mother in which I told her that I liked Portsmouth better than I did this place. Three days after I wrote that letter I was brought back here. I had for my companion on my return journey a madman, or, as he would be called in prison slang, "a balmy bloke"; and here I am at my old work in my old quarters. You may suppose that my treatment has, after all, been such as the Government could not alter without subjecting itself to the charge of treating the political prisoners better than common malefactors; but if you look at the other side of the picture which my present life presents, you will see that it bears a striking resemblance to the side which I have already shown you.

A short time after my arrival here from Millbank I was ordered to empty a large tub which had been used by some sixty or seventy convicts for an unmentionable purpose during the day. I found that I was not able to do it, and so I told the officer whereupon I was reported and charged with 'disobedience of orders and refusing to empty the --- tub.' On being brought before the governor he told me he could make no distinction between prisoners, that he could not 'make fish of one and flesh of another.' I was kept one day in punishment cells, when the doctor inspected the tub and found it was too heavy for a man only with one arm to carry. [It was a coincidence that two one-armed convicts were held at Dartmoor.

Davitt was not the one-armed escaper mentioned earlier.] I was then liberated from the punishment cell. On another occasion I was charged by an officer with having a pencil and some paper in my possession. I was stripped and searched, and although nothing was found on me, taken to the punishment cells, kept there two days and two nights and then brought before the governor, who kindly gave me one day's bread and water and dark cells. Here is another instance of the partiality shown to the 'leniently treated Fenian prisoners.'

Corporal Chambers . . . was one of the gang of twenty men who were being searched on one occasion by some officer, when one of them found a newspaper outside the place in which they had been searching. Chambers got three days bread and water on the mere presumption that he was the man who had had the newspaper.

Davitt gave another example of what he alleged was bias shown against the Irishmen. 'Whilst employed in what is termed "cart labour", the rope with which I helped to draw the cart caught my right shoulder, where the arm had been amputated, and forced the bone through the skin. The doctor told me I should be careful, that serious consequences might ensue if I meet with another accident, but he did not remove me from cart labour. He said he would have something made that would prevent the bone from protruding through the skin. A week after this the prison shoemaker was sent to me who, on explaining what I wanted, said, "It was a job for the tailor." I am yet on the lookout for that gentleman. When six months ago Chambers fell off a building in course of erection and received a severe bruise in the leg, he was taken to the punishment cells, kept there all night and turned out to work in the morning. Had he been a Bill Sykes from Seven-dials, or a professional thief from Golden-lane, he would have been taken to the infirmary.'

The government ordered Davitt's release in December 1877. A month later, Chambers followed him to freedom. He had been caught with a group of other Fenians in a house in Dublin in February 1866 as they plotted a violent takeover of the city. Nine months earlier he had deserted and was convicted at a court martial of 'intended mutiny' but the original death sentence was commuted to life imprisonment. The harshness of his treatment in Dartmoor destroyed his health, and he ended up in an invalid prison at Woking. During his eleven years in prison, visitors had only been allowed to see him twice. Thomas Ahearn, another Fenian whose death sentence was reduced to life, had suffered at Dartmoor with Chambers.

Englishman Frank Digby Hardy was a notorious bigamist and forger who saw the inside of many jails during his remarkable life. In 1899 he was arrested and remanded to Holloway, from where he was taken off to Dartmoor to serve seven years. At the time, he did not know it, but Ireland would come to play an integral role in his story.

Following his release he travelled to Canada where he worked as a journalist and high-profile editor and was at one time wrongly accused of forgery. Later he would claim he had then moved into the United States and had been in San Francisco at the time of the 1906 earthquake, but he was unable to provide documentation to substantiate many of the stories of his travels. When he returned to England, he was again sent to Dartmoor to serve another seven years after fooling a gullible woman. Freed once more, he spent a short time in Ireland, and to his long list of victims he added the British Special Branch. Hardy convinced officers he knew where the IRA had hidden arms in Dublin and was hired to set up IRA director of intelligence Michael Collins for an assassination attempt. When he was unmasked, Hardy offered to turn the tables on his British spymasters, claiming he had been brutally treated during his spells in Dartmoor. But the Irish would have none of it and ordered him to leave Ireland forever.

Of the many Irishmen who were forced to see the inside of

Dartmoor, the best known was Eamon de Valera, who was arrested following the 1916 Easter Rising in Dublin, his original death sentence commuted to penal servitude for life. His time on the moor was short, however, because in June 1917 the government ordered his release and he returned to his homeland to a distinguished career in politics, the highlight of which was his being elected the third president of Ireland.

Thomas William Jones was another man who went on to achieve major success in politics despite having done porridge in Dartmoor. The Welshman was jailed during the Great War as a conscientious objector, beginning prison life at Wormwood Scrubs before being transferred to the moor. He became active in politics, and was elected as Labour Member of Parliament for Meirionnydd in Wales in 1951. In 1966 he was given a life peerage as Baron Maelor.

Another whose life took a different route after spending time in the damp, mildewed cells of Dartmoor was Richard 'Darkie' Hutton, who spent most of his young adulthood in prisons. Hutton was part of a gang that carried out thefts, burglaries and armed robberies at the behest of Charles Peace, an infamous criminal who ended his days on the gallows at Armley Jail, Leeds, in 1879. Hutton became a reformed character after meeting a Salvation Army Captain and spent the remainder of his life as an Army evangelist preaching in his prison clothes and chains.

Hutton developed a hatred for violence and, later, so would Jones. But that was an attitude in total contrast to that held by the vast majority of men who were committed to Dartmoor. Over the years the prison has held many of the worst killers in criminal history, but if it has a league table of sheer evil, two names vie for top place – those of John George Haigh and Donald Hume. Haigh, the 'Acid Bath Murderer', had done time at Dartmoor after being convicted of fraud offences before he embarked on his horrific career as a blood-drinking murderer. What he had in common with Hume was that both boasted about their crimes.

Known to have killed six times, Haigh, whose story is told in Chapter 19, claimed he had actually sent nine victims to their maker; Hume used a newspaper to brag that he literally had got away with murder.

Abandoned by his mother not long after his illegitimate birth, Hume had a miserable and frightening childhood in an orphanage, where one of the three women mistresses would terrify the youngsters by donning a green outfit and appearing as a stick-wielding gypsy. He grew up envious of those who had happiness and money and, desperate for wealth and status, he turned to petty crime, cashing worthless cheques and selling fake gin. Eventually he set up in business as an electrician, driving to assignments in a second-hand van bought from a flashy used-motor dealer who called himself Stanley Setty, and in his spare time learning to fly light aircraft – a hobby he used to smuggle drink, cigarettes and occasionally illegal immigrants.

Hume and Setty set up a lucrative racket, with the former stealing cars and the latter changing their appearance and selling them to unsuspecting buyers. But Setty sealed his own fate when he kicked his partner's dog after it brushed against a newly painted car. A meeting in Hume's flat turned violent and he fatally stabbed his rival then cut up the body, washing away bloodstains even while his wife fed their baby daughter. Hume cut up the body and dropped parts from his aircraft. He might have committed the perfect murder, but he greedily began cashing money issued to Setty by a bank just before his death. And instead of sinking, the dead man's torso washed ashore. Hume denied murder and went on trial for his life. He claimed the killers were three smugglers. The first jury could not agree and at a second trial he pleaded guilty to being an accessory after the fact to murder and was jailed for twelve years.

He was a model prisoner in Dartmoor and served only eight years, being released in February 1958. He emerged penniless, and in exchange for £2,000 – then a substantial cash payment

– confessed to a newspaper he had, in fact, murdered Setty.
Hume fled to Switzerland, but after running short of money, he
robbed banks in London and Zurich, each time shooting cashiers,
who survived. But as he fled the Zurich hold up, he shot dead
a taxi driver who had tried to stop him. A Swiss court jailed
him for life in 1959, and in 1976, at the age of fifty-seven, he was
returned to Britain, where he was declared insane and locked up
in Broadmoor, the high-security psychiatric hospital.

Dartmoor remains a scene of misery and mystery, and its walls
are steeped in brutality. Yet some inmates make the most of their
time on the moor. After he was jailed for five years and found
himself at Dartmoor, fraudster Arthur Cornish was taught by
other inmates how to box and emerged both a creditable amateur
and a reformed character. Others find little positive to remember
about the prison or the men it holds, as former police officer
turned armed robber Larry Shaw discovered when he was moved
to Princetown and had his jaw broken. 'Inmates view you as the
reason for why they are in prison, whether you dealt personally
with them in the past or not. You are perceived as the enemy,' he
said.

Scotsman Billy Ferris, twice convicted of murder, remembered
his arrival at Dartmoor in his biography *The Hate Factory*: 'I was
told, "We have tamed harder than you" then when I lashed out at
somebody hauled off to the punishment cell. I don't think it had
changed since the place was built. It was freezing, stank of urine
and damp, condensation ran down the walls and over the block
slate floor. The screws threw ice cold water over me and I heard
them laughing as they slammed the door and marched off. To me
Dartmoor felt as if it had been forgotten by time. I still think of it
as the wheelie bin of the prison system.'

28

DEAD AND ROTTEN

THE BEAUTIFUL CATHEDRAL city of Durham lies in historic tranquillity astride the meandering River Wear, its narrow streets filled with the sounds of the thousands of young people who study at its university. It is a city that embraces and survives on youth. And yet Durham Prison has held the worst of those whose names are synonymous with heinous atrocities against children and young adults. Ian Brady, Myra Hindley, Rose West, John Straffen and Mary Ann Cotton are some whose crimes will forever cause revulsion. While many others guilty of appalling acts of evil have passed through Durham's grim gates, who would deny a place in Hell for any member of this quintet?

Her apart, nobody really knows just how many victims there were of Mary Ann and her arsenic or, indeed, how many children she bore. But she is widely thought to be Britain's worst female serial killer. Although she was convicted of murdering her seven-year-old stepson, Charles Edward, by slipping arsenic into his soup the actual toll of her victims, mainly family members – who included her own mother – and a lover could have been twenty. Children in her native north-east of England would sing out, 'Mary Ann Cotton / She's dead and she's rotten / She lies in her bed / With her eyes open wide / Sing, sing, oh what can I sing / Mary Ann Cotton is tied up with string.' The string was the noose tied around her neck at Durham Prison on 24 March 1873.

The widow and one-time nurse and Sunday school teacher, who knew all about the poisonous effects of arsenic, went to her death protesting she had not killed Charles Edward. Many of her one-time neighbours in the Durham mining village of West Auckland were so shocked by what they believed she had done that they refused to sign a petition pleading for her death sentence to be overturned and replaced by life in prison.

The *Northern Echo* newspaper reported, 'The feeling with which Mrs Cotton is regarded by those among whom she went in and out while she was poisoning in rapid succession husband, child and lodger is one of deep sympathy, but of stern justice. They speak of her kindly, they write to her earnestly, filling their letters with the fervent outpouring of simple, sincere souls who are appalled at the sight of one they knew so well now standing upon the verge of another world.'

Yet most of the tears were for Mary Ann's companion in the condemned cell. While she awaited her trial, Mary Ann had given birth to a daughter, whom she named Margaret Edith Quick-Manning Cotton. The girl's father, an exciseman, was another of the poisoner's lovers and, as the newspaper declared, 'The keenest interest, however, has been excited by the little child, gaol-born of a murderess who, before two days are passed, will be orphaned by the hangman.'

More than 150 families, many from the wealthy farming set, had pleaded to be allowed to adopt little Margaret. But it was Mary Ann's next-door-but-one neighbours, the childless Edwards couple, who she begged to adopt the baby. The couple took a train to Durham and the newspaper described the moment in the condemned cell when Mary Ann held her daughter for the last time: 'The mother, up till then, had been nursing her child before the fire, sitting on a stool, sometimes giving it the breast, and sometimes laying it on her lap where it smiled and crowed in the cheerful firelight. She had given it milk for the last time now. Never again would the smiles of the little stranger enliven the gloom of the condemned cell. The mother was parting with her babe for ever! It was a solemn moment. Murderess though she was, she wept even when she was killing her children in the past, and the mother's feelings welled high in her breast as she took the last, long, lingering look at the unconscious little one, for whom no greater blessing can be craved than that it never may know its mother's name, nor learn its mother's doom.'

But did Mary Ann Cotton receive a fair trial? Probably not. She could not afford to pay for a barrister, and so a Leeds lawyer was appointed to represent her. Yet what leaves her case steeped in controversy was that the prosecution was allowed to introduce details of earlier deaths in her family when she had not been charged with murdering the victims, the intention being to paint her as a mass killer. She probably was, but nobody has ever proved it.

Two years after Cotton's execution, married woman Elizabeth Pearson, aged twenty-eight, from Darlington, went to the gallows for poisoning her seventy-four-year-old uncle, James Watson, by slipping mice powder containing strychnine into his food. Her motive? She wanted his furniture. Her defence pointed the finger of guilt at lodger George Smith, a razor grinder, who had vanished when the old man died. But the jury found her guilty.

How was Cotton able to literally get away with murder for so long? While infant and child mortality rates began to decline towards the end of the 1800s, families – especially those in the poorer communities – simply accepted and expected the loss of one or more children. Cold and hunger were the main culprits, plus diseases like tuberculosis and influenza were rife and fed on bodily weaknesses. The regularity of the child deaths in Mary Ann Cotton's family ultimately raised eyebrows, but until suspicion led to a proper inquiry, overworked doctors who often struggled to recoup their fees were largely content to record causes of death after a cursory examination and usually accepted word of the symptoms given by a parent. And generally the word of the family doctor was law and sacrosanct.

With a more capable defence team Cotton might have escaped execution by pleading insanity. That was certainly the excuse made on behalf of another child-killer, John Straffen, who was reprieved just five days before he was due to hang. But much to the relief of parents all over Britain, Straffen would never again taste freedom. He spent the next fifty-five years in jail, and was still a prison inmate when he died. His crimes were vile and motivated by a hatred for police officers, whom he blamed for the mental illness that dominated his life. His warped brain told him he had a mission to cause maximum trouble for the police. That mission would destroy many lives.

The son of a British Army soldier, it was clear that even as a youngster Straffen was a different child. His older sister had mental problems, and he was constantly reported for truancy. One probation officer recorded that his problem was that he could not differentiate between right and wrong. As a teenager Straffen strangled geese and chickens, but the real warning signs that something needed to be done about him came when he put his hand over the mouth of a thirteen-year-old girl and asked, 'What would you do if I killed you?' After spells of treatment for mental illness in prison and a hostel he was released back into the community and went to work as a market gardener.

Straffen was twenty-one when, on 8 July 1951 he read of the horrific killing of seven-year-old Christine Butcher. The youngster was excited because the legendary boxer Sugar Ray Robinson was training at her home town, Windsor, Berkshire, for a forthcoming world-title fight. She told friends she was off to his hotel to try to meet him, but she didn't make it. Her mutilated body was found in Home Park, Windsor. She had been abducted, raped, strangled and her dead body raped again. Her killer has never been found.

Criminologists think Straffen realised, from the widespread media coverage of Christine's murder, that such tragedies caused massive problems for police. His name has been linked to her death, but Windsor is almost 100 miles from Bath, where Straffen was based. A week later, though, he committed his own version of a child-killing when he spotted little Brenda Goddard, aged five, picking flowers near the Bath home of her foster parents. The child knew no better when he offered to help her and she went off with him. He lifted her into a nearby copse and strangled her, later claiming that she was already unconscious when she was strangled, having accidentally struck her head on a stone when she fell. With his victim's body still warm, Straffen continued to his original destination, a local cinema, where he watched *Shockproof*, the story of a female killer starring Cornel Wilde and Patricia Knight. Then he went home to bed.

Detectives began checking on the movements of suspects, Straffen among them, because of his past. But police action increased his desire to murder again. Wanting to trace his whereabouts and movements on the day of the killing led police to conduct a routine visit to his employer. This led to his past problems being revealed, and he was sacked. Less than a month later he met Cicely Batstone, aged nine, at the cinema and persuaded her to accompany him to another picture house. Then he took her to a meadow on the outskirts of Bath, where he strangled her. When the schoolgirl failed to return home, police began tracing her movements and found no shortage of witnesses, including the wife of one of their own officers, who confirmed seeing Straffen with the youngster. After Cicely's body was found, Straffen was arrested and admitted killing her and Brenda, offences for which he faced being hanged. However, a court decided he was insane and therefore unfit to plead, and instead of being executed he was sent to Broadmoor hospital, in Berkshire

The following year he fled from Broadmoor. He was at large for just a few hours, but in that time had met, abducted and strangled five-year-old Linda Bowyer after spotting her riding her bicycle. He was recaptured the same day, and when police came to interview him, before they could tell him the purpose for their visit, he said, 'I did not kill the little girl on the bicycle.' After a series of trials, Straffen was convicted of Linda's murder and told he would hang, but that sentence was commuted to one of life imprisonment. He was shuffled through a series of high-security prisons before, in May 1968, being transferred to Durham Prison, where, in E Wing, he found himself alongside Moors murderer Ian Brady.

Straffen continually demanded to know his release date, but he was so dangerous no Home Secretary would ever risk setting him free. His mental state qualified him to be hospitalised, but no institution could guarantee preventing another escape. A tall, friendless, gangling figure, he wandered around the perimeter of Durham Jail, occasionally banging his head on a fence. He was shunned by other inmates and lived in a virtually silent world of his own, only speaking when he asked for something. 'Probably the Devil alone would want to know what runs through his mind,' said a Durham Prison officer. 'He lives in his own personal Hell.' In the mid-1990s, newspapers reported that the Home Office had drawn up a list of men and women who would never leave jail. It included Brady; his accomplice Myra Hindley; former nurse Beverley Allitt, who was given thirteen life sentences for killing four children; Jeremy Bamber, who murdered his parents, his sister and her two children; Robert Black, who abducted and killed three little girls; Victor Miller, who sexually assaulted more than twenty boys then battered to death a fourteen-year-old newsboy; and Straffen.

He was moved from Durham Jail when its security level was downgraded. But after spells in Long Lartin and Full Sutton, he was sent back to north-east England and found himself in Frankland Jail, in County Durham. There he died of natural causes in November 2007, aged seventy-seven, having spent a record fifty-five years in British jails.

Myra Hindley and Ian Brady killed five times; Rosemary West murdered double that number, and her husband Fred even more.

Yet the revulsion felt towards the Moors pair is of a far greater intensity than that of the Wests, whose home at Cromwell Street, Gloucester became known as the House of Horrors. Perhaps it was the age of the youngsters Hindley and Brady tortured, abused and killed that made them so vilified. But the manner in which Rose and Fred West took the lives of most of their victims is just as horrific. Many were brutally tortured, raped, strangled and their bodies buried in the family home. After their arrests, Fred West lacked even the courage to face a trial and the imprisonment he knew would be accompanied by the inevitable abuse and violence he would expect from fellow inmates. He hanged himself while on remand in 1995. His wife was convicted of ten murders and will only leave prison in a coffin. Her victims were Charmaine West, her eight-year-old stepdaughter; Lynda Gough, aged nineteen; Carol Ann Cooper, fifteen; Lucy Katherine Partington, twenty-one; Therese Siegenthaler, twenty-four; Shirley Hubbard, fifteen; Juanita Marion Mott, eighteen; Shirley Ann Robinson, eighteen; Alison Chambers, fourteen; and West's own daughter, Heather Ann West, who was sixteen when she was killed and her body burned at Cromwell Street.

Now in her sixties, Rosemary West has denied being a killer. During her trial she was asked about the 1971 murder of Charmaine. Was it true she had 'secured the child's arms with a belt, tied her to a bed, beaten her, killed her and kept the body for Frederick West to dispose of when he was released from a prison term he was serving at the time?' She said 'no' to each allegation.

Yet this female epitome of evil has not appealed against the decision to refuse to allow her to ever apply for parole. How did others in Durham Jail see this matronly monster who slaughtered children and young woman as though they were pigs on a slaughterhouse gurney? 'She was very insignificant. Small and very quiet, like a little old lady,' according to a former prison officer. 'The sort of woman you might see in a supermarket queue.' Insignificant though she might have appeared, West was not short of suitors, of both sexes, but it was musician Dave Glover who seemed to succeed where others failed when she agreed to marry him in the prison chapel, only to call it off at the last minute.

Cotton, Hindley and Straffen are dead; Brady is in a secure hospital being fed through a tube; and West is still alive. Did they suffer during their time at Durham? A majority of the public believe prisons are too soft, convicts pampered, well fed, warm and given comfortable beds. Those who feel the guilty should be made to suffer and prison ought to be a punishment will gain satisfaction from the account of Sandra Gregory, jailed in Thailand for trying to smuggle heroin but allowed to serve the last three years of her sentence in England before being pardoned by the King of Thailand. After being originally held in Holloway, Gregory was moved to Durham, where she found herself alongside Hindley and West. 'Durham was so much harder to endure than Bangkok. There were times when I felt I was on the verge of collapsing with insanity,' she said.

In examining a handful of the high-profile criminals who have seen the inside of Durham, it is worth remembering that in addition to the likes of celebrity gangsters including the Kray twins, John McVicar, Frankie Fraser, the Richardson brothers and others convicted of atrocities during the Northern Ireland Troubles – among them Judith Ward, Martina Anderson and Ella O'Dwyer – Durham was selected to hold three of the most prolific spies to betray Britain. Civil servant William John Christopher Vassall passed secrets to the Soviet Union after being tricked by the KGB into getting drunk at a party and posing for compromising photographs with other men. He was jailed for eighteen years in 1962, and after his release he changed his name and worked for a firm of London solicitors. He died from a heart attack during a bus journey in 1996, aged seventy-two. Harry Houghton passed secrets of Britain's submarine fleet to Poland and the USSR with the help of his mistress, Ethel Gee.

Both were jailed for fifteen years in 1961 and married when they were released. He died, aged seventy-nine, in 1985. Frank Clifton Bossard's lavish spending brought him to the notice of MI5, and an investigation revealed he had been passing secret documents to the Soviet Union. He was sent to Durham after being jailed for twenty-one years in 1965, serving ten years before being free to change his name and work for a firm of lawyers in Hull, where he died of natural causes in 2001, aged eighty-eight.

Durham was chosen to cage the spies because there were concerns that jails in London and the south of England lent themselves more easily to well-organised escapes, a fact borne out by the disappearance in 1966 of George Blake from Wormwood Scrubs. However, the reputation of Durham was sorely dented when John McVicar and his companions legged it over the walls two years later. The prison's age and city-centre location became worries for prison security experts, and would lead to the building and opening in 1980 of Frankland, County Durham, which took over the task of holding those with the highest security risk ratings – 'A' and 'AA' men.

29

CELEBRITY CON

FEW PEOPLE HAVE HEARD of George Hall – who he was, what he did or what made him so special. Yet a huge crowd of more than 20,000 packed New Street railway station in Birmingham on the night of Wednesday, 5 March 1884 to greet him on his arrival there. Who was he? A killer. What had he done? Murdered his wife. What made George Hall so special was that in making such a fuss over him, that enormous throng created the first celebrity to spend time in Pentonville Jail.

Many more who are modern-day household names would go on to do porridge in the same landings that George wandered – so many that Pentonville is known as England's Personality Prison, the nick where the famous do time. But George, a mild young workman who found the equivalent of hell and stardom because he fell in love, was the very first of them.

Remarkably, his astonishing tale began on the happiest day of his life when, on Christmas Day 1863, at the age of just twenty, the jewellery stamper wed his sweetheart, Sarah Ann. But a few hours after the marriage ceremony, as he looked forward to his wedding night, his bride pleaded she had a headache and walked out on him, leaving him to wait in expectation for her to return, only to find himself spending his honeymoon night alone. Next day he set off to look for his wife and found her in bed with Martin Toy, an old flame, although she claimed she had spent the first night of the marriage in her mother's home. The following day she returned to her husband, but a week later walked out again, and this time Hall discovered her cuddling in a theatre with Toy. Racked with frustration and jealousy, Hall brooded over his lost bride. He turned up at her work, demanding she give him back the wedding ring. She agreed to take a walk with him to discuss their future, and as they strolled through the Birmingham streets, he shot her through the head.

At Warwick Assizes in March 1864 a jury found him guilty of murder but asked for mercy because of the provocation he had suffered. Reports of the hearing revealed:

> The prisoner then made a long and affecting statement of his wrongs, which moved the whole court to tears. He said, 'I may be allowed to say a few last words before I am condemned to die. I have kept company with her for about three and a half years and during that time there is no man on earth that loved a girl better, and during that time she has loved another. I married her, for she said she had no home to dwell in. I says, "Sarah, I have a good home and will you share it?" She says, "George, if you will give me one chair and a stool I will dwell with you till the day I die." I married her on the Christmas Day and on the Saturday night she was in bed with another. But when I leave this earth and go before the bar of Jesus Christ, he will know what was done, and will judge me righteously. Martin Toy has been the ruination of my life, that might have been comfortable and happy.'
>
> The poor wretch fell into the arms of two warders who were near. His Lordship then assumed the black cap and with great emotion passed sentence of death, stating that while he would forward the jury's recommendation to the proper quarter, he could not hold out any hope. The prisoner was carried helpless from the court.

While Hall sat in the condemned cell, local businessmen and politicians pleaded on his behalf; a petition containing 50,000 signatures was sent to the Home Secretary begging for a reprieve, and as a result of these efforts, on the night before he was due to hang, Hall was told he was being spared but would serve a life sentence. Astonishingly, the sympathy for him lasted more than twenty years. He spent the early part of his sentence in a hulk ship, where he was taught how to make boots, before enduring the next fourteen years in Dartmoor. After that time, he was transferred to Pentonville, from where he was released to start his train journey home. Newspapers reported he was 'met by thousands of people who exhibited intense excitement and accorded him a tumultuous welcome. A detachment of police had to be called in to preserve order, and when Hall alighted from the train, vociferous cheers were raised and continued until he drove off in a cab with his friends.'

In interviews, Hall said of his time in Dartmoor, 'I don't agree with one that says it's a jolly life there. It's like being dead. You're starved and cut to pieces with the wind and you talk to nobody except a mate when you walk in pairs on Sunday afternoon. I was a good conduct man for the best part of the time. I wore blue breeches and a drab coat and they let me walk as far as the outer walls, else I should have died.

'The rest of the time I spent in Pentonville. There it's worse still. You mustn't talk to anyone from year's end to year's end. If you try to talk to the warder he reports you for insubordination. The chaplain is the only good sort in the prison; he's the only chap you can speak to but he doesn't have time. There ought to be ten chaplains and fewer warders. I don't consider my sentence was just. I ought to have had six months. I little thought I should ever come to such a thing. I thought she was a good girl, and maybe she was to start with. But she was tempted by a villain, and the pair of them together made me a drunkard and a murderer all in a month. If I had shot the man I should have got off easy, but I shot her and I'm a murderer. I reckon I am beginning my life at the age of forty-one.'

Two weeks after Hall had been told he would not hang, the Grim Reaper was claiming a life in Pentonville Jail, and this time the victim was a young man who had already made newspaper headlines.

Valentine Bambrick held a unique distinction among all the tens of thousands who served time in the prison. He was the holder of the Victoria Cross, the highest award for bravery a member of the British and Commonwealth armed services can win. Born in 1837, Bambrick was aged twenty-one and a private with the 1st Battalion, 60th Rifles when he was posted to Asia to help quell the Indian Mutiny. While clearing rebels from the narrow stinking streets and houses of Bareilly, in the north of India, in May 1858, he became trapped in a cluster of buildings and found himself confronted by three attackers. Bambrick had often been in trouble with officers for ill discipline, but his commanders knew he was a man who would never let his comrades down. The three rebels were about to discover that to their cost. He killed one, and despite being wounded twice, he chased the others off. He was awarded the VC. The citation in the *London Gazette* in December that year read: 'For conspicuous bravery at Bareilly, on the 6th May 1858, when in a Serai, he was attacked by three Ghazees, one of who he cut down. He was wounded twice in this occasion.'

With the medal came an annual pension of £10, enough to live on, but he stayed on in the Army until mid-November 1863 when a moment of drink-fuelled madness changed his life forever.

Bambrick and a woman friend, Charlotte Johnstone, got themselves involved in a brawl with lance corporal Henry Milner Russell. During this fight, they ripped four medals from Russell's chest before running away. Both were caught soon after and the next day Bambrick was discharged from the Army. At his trial in December, he and Johnson denied violently assaulting Russell and stealing his medals, worth 30 shillings. The *Hampshire Advertiser* reported: 'Prisoner in his defence said he was possessed of the VC and its accompanying annuity which was an incentive to avoid a crime such as this and which the commission of would involve the forfeiture of. He would if he were starving, scorned to have stolen medals. The judge said it was a matter of grief to him to see a man in such a position. Prisoner – I do not care now if I am imprisoned for fifty years. I am the victim of perjury and I will have my revenge on Russell.'

Bambrick VC was sentenced to three years' penal servitude and Charlotte Johnstone to twelve months' imprisonment. He was sent first to Winchester Gaol, where he was a model prisoner, and then to Pentonville. The governors at both were convinced Bambrick had been wrongly convicted, and steps were taken to have him released. He did not know this, because on 1 April 1864, two weeks before his twenty-seventh birthday, he tied his handkerchief around his neck and hanged himself from a ventilator grille in his cell. On the slate used by inmates to pen messages he had written, 'Becoming quite tired of my truly unbearable existence, I am about to rush into the presence of my Maker uncalled and unasked.' He had added this postscript, 'Before I die, I protest solemnly my entire innocence of the charge for which I was punished.' An inquest jury returned a verdict of 'suicide while of unsound mind'. To ensure the name and heroism of Valentine Bambrick are never forgotten, in 2002 a memorial plaque to him was unveiled at St Pancras and Islington Cemetery, where he is buried.

Charles Peace was another who became the subject of considerable attention, but for very different reasons. A prolific thief whose crimes took him into private homes throughout England for nearly thirty years, he spent time in Pentonville before being executed for murder in 1879. Oddly, he was also a gifted musician who played the violin in local concert halls and could easily have had a successful career as an entertainer. Peace's musical abilities earned him the nickname of the Ethiopian

Paganini, and while he awaited his meeting with the hangman, crowds packed into an auction room in Sheffield to bid for three of his violins and a pianoforte. One violin went for twenty and a half guineas (£21.55), a huge sum at the time, while the pianoforte fetched twenty-four and a half guineas.

Peace's exploits fascinated writers of the calibre of Sir Arthur Conan Doyle, who referred to him by name in a Sherlock Holmes story, 'The Adventure of the Illustrious Client'. Two films told his story, *The Life of Charles Peace*, made in 1905, and *The Case of Charles Peace*, starring Michael Martin Harvey in the title role and co-starring Valentine Dyall, released in 1949. It is still occasionally shown on British television. In the 1960s the popular comic *Buster* ran a series entitled 'The Astounding Adventures of Charles Peace'.

Peace was probably the first celebrity musician to hear the dull notes of the clang of cell doors being shut in Pentonville. Hugh Cornwell, frontman of the highly successful pop group The Stranglers, was aged thirty-one when he was locked up there in 1980. He was arrested returning to London from a concert in Cardiff, and jailed for two months for drug possession. He was a model prisoner and his good behaviour earned him maximum remission. As a result, he was allowed home after just five weeks. On his release he wrote an account of his time behind bars, called *Inside Information*. Cornwell left The Stranglers ten years later, and could look back with pride on his time with the band, notching up a remarkable forty hit albums and singles. He has since written a novel, *Window on the World*.

Pete Doherty fronted the band The Libertines, but his well-documented problems with drug addiction continually caused problems with the group. He was arrested in 2003, and weeks later, had his sentence of six months reduced to two. Two years later he was remanded to Pentonville after police were called to investigate a row with a filmmaker who was compiling a record about Doherty's life and the difficulties caused by his drug taking. Initially unable to raise bail, Doherty had to spend four days in Pentonville before the money could be guaranteed, but later the charge was dropped for lack of evidence. His involvement with the jail did not end there, however. Doherty, a talented poet and actor, wrote a song he called 'Pentonville' for the group Babyshambles, which he joined after splitting with The Libertines. He was back inside the prison walls in 2011 for six weeks after being arrested for cocaine possession.

As singer and songwriter with the group Culture Club, George Alan O'Dowd, popularly known as Boy George, had massive hits with 'Karma Chameleon' and 'Do You Really Want To Hurt Me?' Despite misgivings that he would be attacked, he discovered he was a hit with other lags when he was confined in Pentonville in December 2008. During a sensational trial, O'Dowd was accused of assault and false imprisonment. The victim, Norwegian Audun Carlsen, aged twenty-nine, claimed he met the entertainer through a gay dating website and agreed to pose for photographs in exchange for £400. But he said O'Dowd, then forty-seven, had pinned him to a bedroom floor, handcuffed him to a hook beside the bed and hit him on the head with a metal chain as he attempted to escape. 'I don't understand why anyone could be so evil,' Carlsen said when he gave evidence. 'I would never have consented to that. I would never have been chained up.'

O'Dowd denied the allegations but was convicted, jailed for fifteen months and taken to Pentonville to start his sentence. Hardened cons claimed he was terrified when he arrived, fearing attacks because he was suspected of being gay. He was given a job in Pentonville Prison, dishing out meals to other inmates, but many were upset that what was regarded as a prized perk should have been given to a newcomer. He was secretly photographed sitting in his cell signing autographs for his fellow prisoners, but gained credit for not asking to be housed in a wing specially set aside for inmates seeking protection from the rest of the prison population. He was eventually moved to another gaol where conditions were said to be more relaxed and freed in May 2009 after serving just four months.

O'Dowd was one of several showbusiness celebrities who wrote to singer Georgios Panayioto – one-time Wham star George Michael – trying to cheer him up after he was jailed in 2010 for eight weeks. Others who put pen to paper included Sir Elton John. The singer found himself in trouble when routine police tests on him following a crash in his Range Rover revealed he had been using cocaine – the second time this had happened to him. In court, he admitted driving while unfit through drugs and possessing two cannabis cigarettes.

He was held in Pentonville while he debated whether to ask for bail pending an appeal, but after deciding to serve out his sentence, he was moved, after a few days, to another jail where security was light. After his release, Panayioto said, 'I didn't feel sorry for myself. I thought, "Oh my God, this place is absolutely filthy," because it was Pentonville. I just thought I would get my head down.'

The writer Ciarán Henry Dunphy spent six months in Pentonville. In 1916, the Dubliner was arrested for trespassing. He had tried to get into a Wales internment camp that was holding leaders of the Easter Rising in Ireland. The experience confirmed him as staunchly anti-English.

When the Hungarian writer Arthur Koestler arrived in Britain from the war-torn European mainland without papers, having fled from Nazi oppression, he was interned in Pentonville, during which his best-selling novel, *Darkness at Noon* – inspired by a spell in a French jail as a suspected Nazi sympathiser – was published in London. Once he had satisfied the authorities he was a genuine refugee and not an alien, he was freed. But unlike the legacy of bitterness prison left on Dunphy, Koestler's six-week spell in Pentonville had a totally different effect. He encouraged others in prisons and psychiatric hospitals to express their writing and artistic skills by setting up a series of awards. These began in 1962, and the annual Koestler Awards have encouraged many thousands of men and women to take part and challenge for prizes worth up to £30,000.

30

THE NAUGHTY VICAR

VICARS ARE FREQUENTLY the subject of innuendo and smutty jokes, but the sensational case of the Reverend Henry John Hatch, chaplain at Wandsworth Prison, was no laughing matter. It shocked staid, moralistic Victorian Britain, left the clergyman languishing in a prison cell for something he did not do, caused a huge outcry and sent a schoolgirl heiress to jail. Hatch had been First Chaplain at Wandsworth for eight years, ministering to the religious needs of the inmates there, helping resolve family problems and generally encouraging them to see the errors of their ways, when he and his wife, Essie, made a decision they would regret for the remainder of their lives.

The couple had no children of their own but had adopted an orphan named Lucy. Despite being short of money, they appointed a governess; then in 1859 they advertised in *The Times*, offering tuition and accommodation to other youngsters. The outcome was that wealthy Thomas and Caroline Plummer from Wiltshire took their daughters Mary Eugenia and seven-year-old Stephana Augusta to the vicar and his wife. Mary Eugenia was a spoilt child who had been allowed by her mother to do what she wanted, even drinking beer. She was the heir to a huge fortune of almost £20,000 which would have made her a millionairess nowadays. And even though she was only eleven years of age, she was already betrothed to the Plummers' doctor, John Hay.

However, the arrangement did not last long because Caroline Plummer enjoyed a drink and had bizarre beliefs: when a thunderstorm broke she was convinced it was a message warning her she should not have left her daughters with the Hatch family, and took them home.

A few weeks later the Rev. Hatch opened a letter from his bishop, saying the Plummers were alleging he had indecently assaulted their daughters. The vicar would later admit to being 'stupefied' at the claim. Distraught at the shame the accusation would bring on his wife and Lucy, he resigned from his job at Wandsworth Jail, following a discussion with the prison governor over what to do, and fled the vicarage, moving into lodgings. The Plummer letter went to the police and a warrant was issued for his arrest. He handed himself in and was locked up to await trial on two charges of indecently assaulting the Plummer children. Normally he would have found himself among the convicts he had helped in Wandsworth, but friends and colleagues persuaded the authorities to remand him to Newgate, another of the London jails. While he was there, the Plummers contacted Hatch and his thirty-six-year-old wife. They promised to drop the charges if he would admit his guilt, but he refused, determined to publicly prove his innocence.

In the spring of 1860 Hatch went on trial at the Old Bailey. The witnesses included Mrs Plummer and her daughters and Dr Hay, who fainted as he was being cross-examined. At one stage Caroline turned up in court drunk and had to be carried out. Hatch's solicitors bungled the defence, not calling him, his wife or witnesses.

The case attracted massive interest. Crowds queued every day hoping to get a seat in the public gallery, but after a week-long trial and a summing-up by the judge (which lasted almost eight hours), the Rev. Hatch was convicted of both charges and sentenced to a total of four years with hard labour. At the age of forty-two he went off to prison.

Newspapers, friends and even hundreds of people who had never met him were appalled by what most saw as a terrible miscarriage of justice caused by his incompetent defence team. A public fund raised enough to hire new lawyers, who gathered enough evidence to suggest Mary Eugenia had lied. While the days and weeks dragged by for Hatch in his prison cell, the youngster, now aged twelve, went on trial herself, charged with perjury. She was found guilty, and even though the jury pleaded for her to be shown mercy, she was ordered to be sent to Holloway Prison for three weeks and after that to spend two years in a reform school.

Public opinion had been totally behind Hatch and against Mary Eugenia. The *Manchester Times* reported, 'No doubt it is an awful thing that a child so young should perjure herself but Eugenia Plummer appears to be a premature woman. Her education has been a singular one. She has been a petted, spoiled child apparently indulged beyond all reasonable limits both by her father and mother and treated as a companion by a mother who acknowledges her devotion to sherry and brandy and water. It is most terrible to contemplate the depravity of this child.'

Hatch was granted a Royal pardon and released after spending more than six months in jail. After a fortnight in Holloway, Mary Eugenia too was freed. Her wedding to Dr Hay did not go ahead and she did not marry until 1886. Hatch sued his original solicitors for negligence, and after a jury found in his favour, he was awarded £40 damages. He never again worked as a prison chaplain, but was at least restored to being a respected clergyman, finally dying as rector of Little Stambridge in Essex in 1895 at the age of seventy-seven.

Just as Dartmoor would become an unwelcome home to rebels, Durham to sex beasts and Pentonville the famous, so Wandsworth would be linked to the clergy. The Rev. Hatch had been a model of integrity and devotion during his years there as chaplain, but others, either genuinely or apparently of the cloth, ended up in

Wandsworth for breaches of the eighth commandment – Thou Shall Not Steal.

The Rev. Mr Thomas Wycherley had the unique distinction of joining his female accomplice in Wandsworth Prison after the pair took cruel advantage of an elderly widow. As Baptist minister of a chapel at Clapham, London, one of his flock was wealthy Mrs Sophia Levy, widow of a British Army officer, and her servant, Mary Ann Newton, was missing her soldier husband, James, serving in India. Mrs Levy, infatuated with the fifty-two-year-old minister, invited him to her home to preach and would later tell friends his prayers were 'beautiful'. His reward for his efforts was to be given tea.

Unknown to Mrs Levy, the Rev. Wycherley wasn't only calling to join her in the living room on his knees in supplication. He was slyly playing court to the youthful Mary Ann, who took elaborate steps to make sure that her boss remained unaware of many of his visits. Annoyed by what she saw as Mrs Levy's meanness towards the penniless minister, who sometimes secretly slept on the kitchen floor when he could not afford lodgings, the servant took matters into her own hands, stealing shirts that had belonged to the dead Mr Levy and taking £50 in notes from an escritoire. She gave half the money to her clerical lover.

Newton went on the run shortly after Mrs Levy discovered the money was missing and issued a warrant for her arrest. Wycherley persuaded her to give herself up and took her to a police station, where she confessed to stealing, was jailed for eighteen months and locked up in Wandsworth. In prison she admitted giving the shirts and money to the minister, who was also arrested and charged with theft. Accounts of his trial at the Old Bailey in June 1863 reported that he regularly visited Mrs Levy's home in Stockwell, London, 'in a secret manner and that, upon some of the family going down into the kitchen he was, on one occasion, concealed in the beer cellar; upon another in the broom cellar and once when he and Mrs Newton were suddenly disturbed, the Reverend gentleman was placed under the kitchen table and an ironing blanket thrown over it to conceal him.' The jury took just fifteen minutes to convict Wycherley, who said, 'I solemnly swear before God that I am innocent.' He was jailed for six years and taken off to Wandsworth.

The *London Standard* asked, 'What shall we say to this singular revelation of the scenes occurring in the middle-class life of England? We pass by the mistress who invites a clergyman to give her a specimen of his beautiful praying, rewards him with a tea and then has to appear in a police court to complain that he was drinking her port and sherry without her leave, sleeping in her kitchen without her knowledge and helping her servant to commit a serious act of robbery.'

At least Wycherley had been a genuine minister. That could not be said of Thomas Freeman, a career fraudster, who may well have come up with the idea of posing as a clergyman as a result of talking to other convicts while he was serving a lengthy stretch in Wandsworth for obtaining money by false pretences. 'He has for years past managed by a most artful and extensive system of swindling to obtain a very good livelihood,' said the prosecution when Freeman appeared in court in London, charged with swindling unsuspecting businessman out of money, property and, in one case, a piece of land.

Like most conmen, prison did not deter him. In 1862 he had gone to a businessman in Bromley, Kent, pretending to be the Rev. Thomas A. Freeman, who had qualified to be a doctor of divinity at the non-existent University of Oberlin in America. He begged the businessman for land on which to build a congregational chapel. The businessman was taken in by his story and gave his caller a plot – on which Freeman put a notice pleading for money. Local clergymen and well-to-do families chipped in generously, particularly after reading a list of other men of the cloth who, according to the notice, had agreed to back the building of the chapel. The names of Mr Samuel Morley, M.P.; Rev. Dr Oxley;

the Rev. Dr Edmonds; Rev. Dr. Hewlett; Rev. W. Woodhouse; Rev. W. Miall; and Baron Rothschild were listed as subscribers. All were genuine, but they knew nothing about the project. Well-meaning local people handed the American clergyman money; someone gave him an organ worth an impressive £200; a widow gave him a gold watch and loaned the 'Rev. Freeman' £30, money she never saw again; while a number of tailors made him clerical outfits, but their bills were never paid.

Almost as soon as Freeman emerged from Wandsworth, he was back at his old tricks, this time almost within the shadows of the prison walls. At one time, posing as the Rev. Thomas Mitchell from St Mary's Barnsbury, he began collecting subscriptions for a new congregational chapel he promised he was building at Lavender Hill, Wandsworth. Arrested yet again and tried, the prosecution said, 'For this purpose he had some circulars issued, pointing out the urgent need for such a church to which was attached a regular form of bequest. In this instance a large sum of money was obtained. The pseudo reverend has also victimised many householders where he has taken up his abode and at one time had a large portrait of himself in full canonicals.' Freeman did not stop at his chapel-building racket. When he was arrested in November 1870 he had convinced a builder to sell him two houses and as police pounced the clerical imposter was about to buy a pub. He was forced to swap his minister's robes for drab prison uniform when he was sentenced to hard labour in Wandsworth once again.

A different form of promise landed Ernest Smith, alias Samuel Marshall, aged twenty-five, in Wandsworth Jail. He was no stranger to the surroundings, having spent twelve months there in 1866 for theft. But now, in January 1875, he was jailed for five years. A jury had convicted Smith of robbery, but also of a much worse crime in the eyes of Victorian society – he had jilted a girl at the altar after taking advantage of her body and her meagre bank balance. And to make matters even worse, he was a married man.

Smith met up with Emily Prescott when he was labouring near the house in Chancery Lane where she worked as a below-stairs domestic servant. Emily told the jury at Middlesex Sessions, 'He represented himself as a single man and proposed marriage. He always stated that he was a single man and during the whole course of our courtship he never varied in that statement or did he ever say anything to induce me to believe that he was a married man.' Emily gave her fiancé most of her £15 savings to buy items for the home he promised she would have when they were wed. And she said he even took her along to meet a clergyman, paying two shillings to have the banns called for their wedding on 13 September 1875 at Holloway. It was an unlucky choice because Smith called off the marriage on the eve of the wedding, claiming there had been a muddle with the paperwork. He wanted Emily to go to Liverpool with him, but she refused and went to the police instead and the callous Casanova was arrested. A few days later she bumped into his wife Maggie, who had turned up at a police station with food for her wayward husband. Three more young women came forward to tell how he had seduced them, taken their money and dumped them. Smith was convicted of breach of promise and robbery, the judge telling him, 'A more abominable offence than the one you have committed it would be impossible to conceive.'

Was Wandsworth Jail a nursery for fake clergymen? It certainly seemed that way when yet another clerical imposter was arrested in 1886. And this astonishing case would have a remarkable sting in the tale. In Dublin, Theodore Oswald Keatinge went on trial, charged with obtaining money from two priests and the Dublin Priests Protection Society, 'by representing that he was a clergyman in holy orders'. The case was the subject of massive interest in the city, where many refused to believe the 'Rev T. O. Keatinge' who often lectured to the public was not a genuine priest. Keatinge had complained that the prosecution was 'actuated by envy and malice', and the authorities were careful to make sure that the jury consisted of six Protestants and six Roman Catholics.

His wife had announced she was standing by him. Newspapers reported that, 'She states that she was married to Dr Keatinge twenty-five years ago. Notwithstanding her husband's conduct, she continues to be shown a great deal of sympathy, and very many of his admirers have exhibited a determination to aid him in his trouble.' In fact, the devoted woman was in for a terrible shock after her husband was found guilty and jailed for eighteen months.

In a letter to the *Dublin Express*, it was revealed that some years earlier an English priest, on a goodwill visit to a relative in London, had been asked to call on a man down on his luck. He was penniless and living in a filthy attic in the city. The tramp turned out to be Keatinge. He had just been released from Wandsworth Prison, where he had spent a year locked up for tricking an MP and a businessman into giving him money by posing as a priest, the Rev. Dr Morton. In Wandsworth Keatinge had dreamed up a vocation in the priesthood and spent every spare moment studying the Bible. He emerged from jail renamed as the Rev. Dr Keatinge, broke but so convincing that the priest helped get him a post at an independent church in south London. However, his sermons were so appalling that he was quickly fired.

According to the letter, Keatinge headed to Bradford in Yorkshire, where he charmed his way into the bed of a boardhouse owner and widow with three children. He married her, then went about begging for help for the family. But, tired of being poor, he dumped his new flock and went back to London, writing to his deserted wife and saying he could 'do nothing more for her and that she had better look out for another husband as soon as she could'. He had then briefly gone to Dublin. There, he wormed money from the two priest victims and the Society before returning to London, where he was arrested.

Yet the story did not end there. After he went off to prison in Dublin, it emerged the Rev. Dr Keatinge had been living a lie for a very long time. His real name was Joseph Crouch, son of an English farm worker who, as a youngster in a London workhouse (he'd gone there after his father deserted the family) had a fascination with popular sermons. He spent most of his time copying these out and learning them by heart. The fact that he lived in a fantasy world did not stop him continuing to wear clerical robes or calling himself the Rev. Keatinge when he was released in September 1887. Within a month he had taken to the stage to give a lecture in Dublin on 'Why does evil exist?' *Freeman's Journal and Daily Commercial Advertiser* reported, 'The hall was fairly well filled, many of these present being ladies.' But after his talk he faded into obscurity.

Many well-known names have appeared in the records of those who have spent time in Wandsworth. Jimmy 'The Dip' Kensit, whose daughter Patsy is the *Emmerdale* and *Holby City* actress, was an associate of the Richardson brothers, whose torture gang terrorised London and rivalled the Kray twins. Kensit started a five-year sentence in Wandsworth in the late 1960s after being jailed for breaking into a warehouse.

Around that same time, Wandsworth opened its gates to admit James Earl Ray, subject of a worldwide hunt following the fatal shooting of civil rights activist Dr Martin Luther King, Jr, at a hotel in Memphis, Tennessee in 1968. Ray was on the run from an American prison and was caught at Heathrow Airport using a fake passport. He was held in Wandsworth until his extradition to America, where he was jailed for ninety-nine years for assassinating Dr King.

31

A THIEVING QUEEN

TALL, FULL-BOSOMED and fashionably dressed, the prisoner in the dock smiled briefly as the wardress from Wormwood Scrubs Prison read out extracts from her recent history. It already included two stretches in the Scrubs. Now she was heading back there again, after a jury found her and a male accomplice guilty of a series of robberies at well-known hotels in London's posh West End.

The packed courtroom at County of London Sessions at Clerkenwell in August 1900 listened intently as the curiously named judge, Mr Loveland-Loveland, read out their sentences. He sent the woman, artists' model Mary Crane, to Wormwood Scrubs for twenty months and told her lover, frock-coated, smart-looking Martin Harvey, aged twenty-four, he would serve five years' penal servitude and on his release a further three under police supervision.

It may have seemed odd that what appeared to be a fairly routine case should have provoked such interest. Harvey was suave and handsome and came from a good home. But it was his married mistress the crowd had come to see. Mary Crane was just one of many names she used. She was no ordinary petty thief but a master criminal who had recruited some of her women cohorts from Wormwood Scrubs. She was a ruthless desperado who for years had led London's police in a merry dance, blackmailing politicians and wealthy old men, stealing from the rich and using her sex appeal to encourage pretty young men to help her. Under the heading 'Remarkable Story', the now defunct *Lloyd's Weekly Newspaper* reported the following day:

[I]n Mary Crane, the good-looking thief, the law has once again placed in durance vile [a long prison sentence] one of the most dangerous women in the metropolis. She is none other than the notorious Polly Carr, who, as the head of a gang of female depredators [plunderers], was known as 'Queen of the Forty Thieves' and who caused such a sensational in London a few years ago.

Despite her assertion that she was only 'twenty-nine' the fact remains that she is some seven years older for she was born in Smith-street, Westminster in 1864. Her first appearance in the dock was in 1876, when, just twelve years of age, she faced the magistrate at Westminster on a charge of petty theft, escaping, however, with a caution. We next hear of her as a flower-girl in the Strand, where she soon became noted for her good looks and engaging manners. Possessing unusual tact and ability, she managed to get round her a gang of young women who gave her complete obedience as their leader. This was the notorious 'Forty', whose criminal operations were of the most varied character. Blackmail, however, was their favourite game and a very paying one. The younger members of the gang, girls in their teens, were sent to approach well-to-do-looking old gentlemen, and under pretence of seeking an address get them to walk with them. At a convenient spot two or three others of the gang would appear, a charge of assault would be made, and more often than not the victim would hand over any valuables he possessed rather than face the police on such a charge.

If one more sturdy than the others said, 'Call the police,' his watch and chain would be snatched and the gang would disappear. In one such case, however, Polly met her match. She snatched, under the usual circumstances, the watch and chain, valued at 25 guineas, of an elderly gentleman in Soho and made off. An alarm was raised and pursuit given, Polly being run to earth in a greengrocer's shop where she was found doubled up under the counter.

This episode resulted in her being sentenced to four months' hard labour in 1890.

She was undeterred by the threat of further unpleasant spells in Wormwood Scrubs, because the newspaper went on to report, 'On her release from prison she started a new form of blackmail. A clever mimic and actress she would get herself up like a very young girl, with her hair down her back and lure gentlemen to a house in Pimlico, kept by a supposed "aunt". Here a charge of assault would be preferred in such a way that the victim felt he was compromised. So blackmail was freely levied and paid, several Members of Parliament being amongst the sufferers, one well-known legislator paying no less than £400 in order to preserve his previously spotless reputation.'

She used her body in other ways, posing for distinguished artists including Sir Frederic Leighton and going under the name of Jenny Lesley. 'That she made a fine model there can be no doubt, for she is the possessor of an exceptionally fine figure and carries her head in a stately manner that gained for her amongst her associates in those days the nickname of "Swanneck",' reported *Lloyd's Weekly News*.

The same newspaper told how, in 1896, Polly went back to Wormwood Scrubs for a bizarre crime. The previous year a five-year-old gypsy boy had been stolen from his family on Epsom Downs. Eleven months later, the youngster was found at her Blackfriars, London, home, but she refused to say how he got there. Reporters were gushing in their accounts of how she appeared in court charged with child stealing: 'She was dressed magnificently. She wore a rich, black velvet mantle, heavily

274

trimmed with fur over a splendid silk dress while on her head was a broad Rembrandt hat trimmed with five large ostrich feathers. On her fingers glittered diamond rings valued by an expert in court at £300.'

When Polly was ordered to serve three years' penal servitude she merely smiled at the recorder, said, 'Thank you,' and went off to the Scrubs Jail.

Her evidently gentle acceptance of the prison sentence hid a vicious determination to get even with those whose evidence resulted in her arrest. In Wormwood Scrubs her tentacles reached out to a network of criminal friends, who were ordered in particular to track down Michael Parker, a police informer. He was discovered lodging in London, and after Polly had completed her sentence she made sure his secret work as a 'copper's nark' was made known in the underworld. The result was a terrible attack on Parker in his lodgings. He was set on by his landlady and two men with a bludgeon, broom, fire shovel, broken jug, kettles of hot water, broken bricks and lamp glasses before managing to escape through his bedroom window with severe head and face injuries. His three attackers were fined.

In between modelling assignments, Polly, meanwhile, was back to her old routine of stealing. She was suspected of involvement in a host of crimes, including bank thefts and funding the defence for gang members and associates when they were arrested and charged. She teamed up with Harvey, and the pair targeted the rooms of wealthy hotel guests. At the Walsingham House Hotel in Piccadilly, their victims were two American women. They robbed them of gold, silver and pearl jewellery. Police told Mr Loveland-Loveland that guests at almost every hotel in the West End had been victims at some stage. This time Polly said nothing as she went off to begin her twenty months. 'Altogether in Mary Crane or Carr the police have had to deal with one of the most astute criminals of our time,' said *Lloyd's Weekly News*.

It was a statement that might have been applied to so many who followed her into the cells of Wormwood Scrubs in the future. No one, for example, could deny that the men who carried out the Great Train Robbery almost seventy years later were not astute. Planning and carrying out what was, at the time, the biggest robbery in British criminal history required not just daring but imagination, and an ability to uncover and stick to incredible detail. From the moment the overnight mail train left Glasgow, its departure was watched and reported. In the south of England it was briefly stopped by an awaiting gang, who tampered with the signals. The driver, Jack Mills, was brutally beaten and forced to drive the train a further half a mile. When it came to a halt in Buckinghamshire, the gang made directly for a coach carrying high-value packages and smashed the windows. Within minutes, 120 mailbags containing more than £2,630,000 – equivalent to more than £40 million nowadays – had been unloaded and driven off. In the coming weeks, most of the robbers were arrested, having been caught because of carelessness. They'd failed to stick to the plan of wearing gloves throughout their time at the hideout where they'd shared out the loot. Those considered the ringleaders were given long sentences – in some cases thirty years – then they were dispersed to prisons all over England.

However, Wormwood Scrubs would, from time to time, become home to some of the team. Bruce Reynolds, widely regarded as the mastermind behind the plot, had done time in the Scrubs for petty crime – it was there he met Ronnie Biggs – before setting in motion the Great Train heist. He would see the inside of its walls again. While his fellow crewmembers were being picked off by police, Reynolds went on the run, moving to and sometimes settling in London, Belgium, Mexico, Canada and France, before being caught in Torquay five years later. He was sentenced to twenty-five years, some of which he served in Wormwood Scrubs, and during which time he missed the formative years of his devoted son, Nick. After he was freed on parole in 1979 he admitted, 'I look back on my past life and sometimes it seems as if I am watching an old film about this character who did this. That's not to say I remove myself from it, though – I know what I did.' He died in 2013, aged eighty-one.

Hairdresser Gordon Goody, who was given thirty years, put his time in the Scrubs to good use by learning Spanish. He reasoned that when he was eventually set free, if he stayed in England he would be too tempted to drift back into criminal ways, so he might as well go somewhere else. In fact, when he was released he went to live quietly in Spain. Fellow Scrubs inmates sometimes referred to him as the 'Birdman' after he asked to be allowed to work in the prison aviary, but this was refused.

Nightclub owner Ronald Christopher 'Buster' Edwards also vanished following the hold-up of the train, taking his family to live in the relative safety of Mexico. But they missed their native London and he agreed to return to England in 1966 for a fifteen-year sentence. He spent a total of nine years behind bars, some of the time in Wormwood Scrubs, and when he was freed he opened a florist stall in London. He was aged sixty-three when he was found hanged in a lock-up garage in London in 1994.

John Donald Merrett was more than simply astute – he was cunning and conniving, attributes that would make him into a dangerous psychopath. As a teenager and the apple of his mother Bertha's eye, he blotted his copybook after being found in bed with a young woman at a public school in England. Determined to keep an eye on her son, Bertha moved with him to Edinburgh in the mid-1920s so he could study at the city university. However, he would sneak out from the house where they lodged to attend a dancing hall, funding a high life by forging cheques stolen from Bertha. In 1926 she was shot while having breakfast. He claimed she accidentally killed herself, but the following year he was charged with her murder. Remarkably, Merrett escaped the hangman's noose after the jury in Edinburgh returned the unique Scottish verdict of 'Not Proven', one meaning they believed he was guilty but felt there was insufficient evidence to prove it. He was given a short prison sentence for forgery and served this in Wormwood Scrubs, where, in the company of hardened, devious crooks, he was schooled in the ways of career criminals. Merrett emerged to become an astute, sophisticated liar.

Despite the suspicions that remained over his role in his mother's death, there were some who believed him innocent, among them an old friend of the dead woman, Lady Mary Menzies, who invited him to live at her London home. Merrett moved in, changed his name to Ronald Chesney and married Lady Menzie's daughter Vera. The pair went on a wild spending spree throughout Europe after he came into a huge inheritance.

During World War II, Chesney, by now estranged from Vera, became a minor hero as skipper of a torpedo boat – this before he was dismissed for stealing and turned to smuggling. When his money ran out in February 1954 he demanded cash from Vera, who refused him. She was murdered in her bath and her mother battered to death. Days later, Chesney was found shot in a forest in Germany, but questions remain as to whether he killed himself or was murdered by members of the German underworld.

Another who lived a double life was former high-flying politician John Stonehouse. The father of three was Postmaster General in the late 1960s in Labour prime minister Harold Wilson's government. But Stonehouse was also a long-time spy for Czechoslovakia. Worried about his long-term political future after the fall of the Labour government, Stonehouse set up a series of companies, but these hit money troubles and he found himself falling in love with his secretary, Sheila Buckley. Desperate to start a new life, he faked his own death by leaving his clothes on a Miami beach in 1974. It was believed he had gone swimming only to be attacked and killed by a shark. Instead he was already on his way with Buckley to Australia, where he opened bank accounts in false names.

He was arrested when a bank clerk discovered 'Clive Mildoon' and 'Joseph Markham' were the same person. For a short time police even believed he was really runaway peer Lord Lucan, wanted for questioning about the murder of his children's nanny in London around the time of the Miami clothes incident. After a lengthy trial in 1976, Stonehouse was convicted of fraud, deception and theft and jailed for seven years.

However, he was not the first politician to spend time in a Scrubs cell; in 1954 MP Peter Baker was sent there after being jailed for seven years for forgery. Still, Stonehouse's affair with attractive Miss Buckley made him a minor celebrity. Moors murderer Ian Brady later claimed he played chess with Stonehouse, who was said to have moaned at the constant pop music played in the prison workshops. In 1979 he was freed early after a series of heart attacks, and two years later he married Buckley. He died in 1988, aged sixty-two, after another heart attack.

Colleagues of civil servant Dennis Nilsen described him as 'astute and intellectual' but failed to add 'extremely dangerous'. The former soldier and police officer from Fraserburgh, in the north of Scotland, made a hobby of picking up young men from gay clubs and pubs in London, taking them home then killing and dismembering them. Nilsen was caught and jailed for the rest of his life in 1983 when workmen, called to clear blocked drains outside his flat, found traces of human remains. In Wormwood Scrubs he came up against another Scot, who won secret plaudits from the families of many of Nilsen's victims for what happened next. Albert Moffat told a court Nilsen made gay advances on him, and when these were rejected he arrived in an exercise yard carrying a knife, a silly move because he ended up slashed across the face and chest. 'The man was a murderer and I didn't want to give him a second chance,' said Albert, who was cleared of attacking Nilsen.

Jeremy Bamber believed himself astute, but his efforts at cunning earned him only a natural-life prison sentence. His crime remains one of the most cruel and vile to come before a British court, because it involved the killing of his adoptive parents,

Nevill and June, sister Sheila 'Bambi' Caffell and her six-year-old twin sons, Nicholas and Daniel, in his parents' home at White House Farm, Essex in August 1985. All had been shot. Trying to place the blame on Sheila, Bamber had put the murder weapon in her hand before calling the police.

Bamber's spell in Wormwood Scrubs was one of many he has spent in England's high-security jails for long-term prisoners. Inmates like him are occasionally ordered to join the 'Cooler Circuit' – also known informally as the 'Ghost Train' and 'National Draft' – which involves spending about a month in different prisons before being moved on, to avoid establishing relationships with other convicts.

32

RED-BLOODED BLUE BLOOD

LOVE AND HATE ARE two of the most common reasons why men and now also women have found themselves behind the bars of Holloway Prison. Love born of admiration and respect followed by hate spawned out of betrayal cost the Scots-born Shakespearean actress Isabella Glyn months of freedom. Hers is a case so astonishing that it could well have been mistaken for a plot by the bard of Avon himself. Yet Isabella, a brilliant performer, a star on the stage in a hundred theatres on both sides of the Atlantic, was not a criminal. Indeed had her wayward husband, E.S. Dallas, not himself performed in the beds of other young women, Isabella would never have seen the inside of Holloway.

Her first marriage had been happy but was cut sadly short when her husband, Edward Wills, died suddenly. She then met and fell in love with the well-known journalist and occasional philosopher Eneas Sweetland Dallas. When he popped the question, she agreed. It would be a decision she would bitterly regret. They wed in Glasgow in 1853 and then repeated their vows at St George's Church in Hanover Square, London, two years later. But it soon became clear to her that the marriage was a mistake. They drifted apart, then separated, although it was not until May 1874 that the union ended in divorce on her petition for his desertion and adultery.

Just how bitter Isabella felt was reflected in her response to his legal request two years later for her to return some of his furniture and letters. She ignored a court order compelling her to swear an affidavit detailing what property of his she had, and to the shock and fury of her multitude of friends and fans, she was hauled off to Holloway. Some among her supporters argued Isabella had simply been too busy and had forgotten to comply. But as the days in Holloway passed and public demands for her release grew, she dug in her heels and refused to give the information her ex-husband and the courts wanted. Newspapers raged at her treatment. The *Penny Illustrated Paper and Illustrated News* summed up the feelings of most when it trumpeted in July 1876: 'The case of Miss Glyn, the great actress, is one of the most deplorable that has come under our notice for some time. This distinguished lady has actually suffered the indignity of imprisonment in Holloway gaol for ten days – seemingly from a misunderstanding.'

Most believed Isabella would be freed quickly. However, her stubbornness was matched by that of the courts. She languished in prison for ten months before her release in April 1877. Almost immediately she resumed her career with great success. Dallas, however, survived only two more years before his death at the age of fifty-one in 1879. Isabella outlived him by ten years.

Love cost John Francis Stanley Russell, second Earl Russell, his liberty in 1901, and not even the peer's distinguished family background or the fact that as a barrister he was an expert in matters of law could save him from doing porridge in Holloway among thieves and fraudsters. Born in 1865, the Earl was the grandson of the former prime minister John Russell, the first Earl. His younger brother was the philosopher Bertrand Russell. He was a man whose blue blood mingled with lots of red, and he had a reputation as a collector of both wives and mistresses.

Divorce at this time was still frowned upon in high society, although Russell was no respecter of propriety. His first marriage to variety-hall singer Mary Edith Scott in 1890 was soon on the rocks. Almost as soon as the honeymoon was over she discovered he was breaking his vow to be faithful, and a year later she tried to divorce him. Her efforts to be free failed when he objected. In a tit-for-tat move, when he separated from her and sought a divorce, she successfully fought it. Soon after, his mother-in-law decided to get in on the act, and her comments about her son-in-law resulted in her being convicted of libel.

By now Russell had pledged his love to twice-divorced Marion Somerville, daughter of an Irish cobbler, and he was convinced he had discovered a solution to the problem of how to end his marriage to Mary Edith. He travelled to Nevada, in the USA, was granted a divorce there and married Marion. Furious, Mary complained that British law did not accept the divorce in Nevada as being valid and claimed that he was still wed to her. As a result, his lordship was accused of bigamy. He appeared amidst the pomp and grandeur of the Royal Gallery at Westminster in July 1901 to be tried by his peers, arguing he had been assured by the best legal brains in America that he was breaking no laws. Despite much sympathy for him – including from the Lord Chancellor, who told him Mary was a 'harridan who had poisoned the whole atmosphere in which he lived' – Russell was packed off to Holloway for three months.

While he was in prison, Mary finally agreed to a divorce, freeing him to legitimately marry Marion. However, she divorced him in 1915. Within a few months he had married again, this time to Elizabeth, widow of Count Henning August von Arnim-Schlagenthin, at St Martin in the Fields, Trafalgar Square, London. Once again the relationship soon broke down and they separated but never divorced.

His spell in Holloway did not prevent Russell from distinguishing himself as a politician. He was an enthusiastic motorist who became a Labour peer, and as Parliamentary Secretary to the Minister of Transport, he introduced the Highway Code and abolished speed limits before his death in 1931.

His troubles stemmed from a wife who cared too little. Sarah

Cooper, on the other hand, cared too much for her own good. Her love made her vulnerable and gullible, traits of which publican William Bloomfield was all too ready to take advantage, and in an extraordinary manner. In 1867 Sarah's railway traffic manager husband Arthur was sentenced to a month's hard labour in Holloway after admitting to indecently assaulting domestic servant Jane Carter in one of his company's second-class carriages. At court Sarah had vowed to stand by her husband, even though the conviction meant losing his job. She had even scoured the neighbourhood around their lodgings in Clerkenwell, London, trying to find him work when he was freed.

Then, just halfway through his sentence, thirty-two-year-old Bloomfield turned up at her home with a most incredible offer. He claimed he was a scripture reader and schoolmaster at Holloway Prison who had been helping Arthur, and said that if she handed over £5 he could get her husband released. Astonishingly, she fell for the story, particularly after Bloomfield told her, 'I have good news from your husband. If you can get me £5 tonight or early tomorrow morning, I can get your husband out and prevent his having his hair and whiskers shaved off. He told me you had plenty of things upon which you could raise the money.' Promising to find the £5, Sarah went off in search of help, but it was late at night and she came back empty-handed.

Bloomfield realised she was the equivalent of putty in his hands. When he told her he did not want to spend the night in a hostel and had to be up at five the next morning in time to get to Holloway to say prayers for Arthur and the other convicts, she gave him her bed. She told the bogus schoolmaster's trial that when she woke him up a few hours later, 'He said he had passed a wretched night, and had not closed his eyes thinking of my husband. He said my husband's shirt was dirty, and my husband had asked him to ask me for some clean linen. I gave him drawers, vest and shirt.' She also went off and raised the £5 by pawning Arthur's prized watch and chain. Her suspicions

284

were only aroused when Bloomfield vanished with the money and was later spotted wearing Arthur's cufflinks, which had disappeared from her bedroom.

During his trial, Bloomfield claimed Sarah had offered to get money from a local bookmaker so she could run off to Paris with him, and had even slept with him. It emerged he had pulled similar cruel confidence tricks on the families of other prisoners. The judge told him, 'After what we hear of your former career, it is startling that such a man should have the assurance to attack the character of a respectable married woman to whom, in the absence of her husband, you have acted as a great scoundrel.' Then he sentenced him to five years' hard labour – starting in Holloway.

Naturally, there was little sympathy for a cad of the ilk of Bloomfield. Yet courts could occasionally be the scene of sympathy and surprising generosity. The case of Walter James Midwinter was an example. *The Daily News* in its edition of 10 June 1874 reported that at the Old Bailey Midwinter, 'a gentlemanly-looking young man was indicted for misdemeanour, in having knowingly and wilfully made a false declaration with intent to procure the solemnisation of a marriage between him and one Laura Tomline.'

It was a case where a sour note had crept into love's old sweet song – and that tone of discord was played by Laura's stepmother, Emma. The background was that when Laura's father, William, a rich lighterman – skipper of a Thames barge – died in 1866, leaving a considerable fortune, it was decided to make the then eight-year-old girl a ward of court, effectively handing judges and the trustees of William's substantial estate the sort of responsibilities normally left to parents. Walter Midwinter was a friend of the Tomline family. He was seven years older than Laura, but during his calls at her Bow, London, home, friendship blossomed into love. The rest of her family realised this, and had no objection because they knew it could go no further as long as Laura remained a ward of court. In any case, her stepmother believed the couple were too young to marry.

The lovers had other ideas. Walter was granted a certificate to marry by special licence after telling the registrar Emma had agreed to the marriage. One day in July 1873, when her stepmother was out and seventeen-year-old Laura was on holiday from school, she crept out of the house and married Midwinter. It was two months before their secret leaked out. The bridegroom was immediately arrested, accused of contempt by marrying a ward of court without first getting formal permission, and locked up in Holloway, where he stayed for almost a year before his trial.

The *Daily News* reported how Midwinter's lawyer told the jury it was, 'abundantly clear, from all the facts, that the defendant had no sinister motive for his conduct, but that he was actuated solely by love and a desire to make the young lady happy.' The jurors agreed. They found him not guilty 'and when the verdict was announced the court erupted into applause and cheering as he was told he was free to rejoin his young wife.'

Another jury showed sympathy, but in very different circumstances, in the case of George Thompson, aged twenty-nine. He was a butler to a general when he appeared on trial at Middlesex Sessions in June 1887, charged with obtaining money by false pretences with intent to defraud. The victim – in legal terms of the day the prosecutrix – was domestic maid Annie Moden, aged twenty-two. Under the heading 'A Heartless Scoundrel', *Lloyd's Weekly Newspaper* reported that Thompson, 'a well dressed young man', had met Annie and began courting her: 'He made love to her, proposed marriage to her, and, under that promise, succeeded in seducing her. He pretended great affection for her, and, under the representation that he had become the proprietor of a public house in High Street, St Albans, he induced her to give him the whole of her savings. His love then cooled and it was ultimately ascertained that there was no such public house in St Albans.' Thompson was arrested and held in Holloway until the trial. The jury found him guilty and he was sentenced to five years' hard labour.

But the plight of poor Annie, who had lost all her money and was described in court as penniless, brought tears to many of those in court. What followed was a bizarre scene in which police, magistrates, a judge, lawyers, spectators and even the jury held a whip-round for her. The all-male jury dug into their pockets and came up with 30 shillings (£1.50) while contributions from others lifted the total to £9 4s (£9.20) – about a third of the amount she gave the rascally butler. 'The unfortunate girl most gratefully accepted the money,' said the newspaper.

Eighty years later the case of Valerie Kim Newell – another whose story of love and hate would lead her through the grim gates of Holloway – was one in which nobody in the court during her trial from jurors to judge displayed the slightest sympathy. Newell, a blonde nurse in her early twenties, had a desire for sex that made her irresistible to many men, among them draughtsman Raymond Sidney Cook, aged thirty-two, and forty-five-year-old plant manager Eric Jones. She bedded one, then the other, then both. The case, which became widely sensationalised as the 'Red Mini Murder', began with the discovery of a slightly damaged red Mini car against a roadside tree near Peppard, in Oxfordshire. An ambulance took the injured occupants off to hospital. One was the fatally hurt driver, schoolteacher June Cook, and the other her slightly injured husband, Raymond, who said his wife had been blinded by the oncoming headlights of another vehicle.

Police immediately suspected something was wrong. It seemed odd that the injuries which led to June's death could have resulted from what was a very slight impact, while spots of blood fifty yards off matched those of the now dead woman. It was obvious she had been badly battered and her injuries made to look as if they had resulted from the crash. Investigations led detectives to Eric Jones, known for carrying out illegal abortions. In his car boot was the murder weapon – a tyre lever. He pleaded guilty to murder and gave crucial evidence against the others, admitting he had performed a number of abortions on Newell, who then blackmailed him into killing June so she and Raymond could live together and profit from the dead woman's will. The jury found Newell and Cook guilty after the judge told them, 'This is a very human story, as old as the hills. The eternal triangle – in this case one man and two women. You are not dealing with things in the imagination, a detective story. You are dealing with real people, actual things which actually happened.'

As all three began life sentences, Newell was rushed to the mother and baby unit in Holloway because she was seven months pregnant with Cook's child. She gave birth to a son, but many believed her truly evil, a modern-day Lady Macbeth who plotted the murder of a lover's wife. After spending years in Holloway, she was moved to a jail near York, where security was less strict. She was freed in 1979 and died of cancer in 1990, aged forty-seven.

Of the tens of thousands of men and women who have been imprisoned in Holloway few, if any, have been the subject of greater bitterness and hatred than Maxine Ann Carr. Indeed, such has been the extent of threats against her that the authorities have created for her a new identity, and the law has ruled that for her own protection and that of her family, she can never, ever be identified. Carr was the mistress of Ian Huntley, caretaker of a school at Soham, in Cambridgeshire. In August 2002 when two local ten-year-olds, Holly Marie Wells and Jessica Aimee Chapman, were murdered, Huntley was questioned by the police but initially eliminated as a suspect after Carr provided him with an alibi that later proved false. Her lies caused huge problems for investigators before Huntley was arrested and then told he would spend the rest of his life in prison. Carr was jailed for three and a half years for perverting the course of justice. She was held in Holloway for the majority of the twenty-one months she actually served of the sentence, but in the all-women jail she was constantly the subject of threats from other inmates, and was at one stage placed on suicide watch, meaning her cell was checked by guards every fifteen minutes. Even though she is now free and has a new identity, former inmates at Holloway say that like her evil lover, Carr is also serving a life sentence because she will spend the remainder of her days looking over her shoulder and fearing discovery and savage retribution.

33

DEADLY DRINK

IN ONE OF THE MANY hilarious episodes of the *Porridge* TV series, Fletch and Godber (Ronnie Barker and Richard Beckinsale) cook up an illicit and extremely potent home brew – hooch. The surreptitious making and selling of hooch – brewed with yeast stolen from prison kitchens, and mixed with ingredients that may vary from potatoes to shoe polish before being hidden and allowed to ferment – is an activity that has long been a feature of life behind bars. Generally, the consequences are no more than a sore head, but in 1967 a boozing session in Wormwood Scrubs ended in tragedy. Three prisoners were rushed to hospital seriously ill; one of them died, another went blind and more than a dozen others became violently ill.

The lethal concoction was distilled largely from copying fluid taken from the prison tailor shop. It was later found to include a third industrial methylated spirits and a third industrial alcohol. A pint sold for half an ounce of tobacco.

After church on a Sunday morning prisoners got together for a sly boozing party, mixing the hooch with orange juice. It was not long before the drinkers began feeling the effects. Inmate George Thomas Pickering fell flat on his face and was put on a couch, where he promptly went to sleep before lapsing into unconsciousness. Warders discovered another prisoner lying unconscious over a table in the recreation area. Queues began forming outside toilets. Ambulances were called. Pickering, who was serving life for killing a prostitute in her Soho, London flat; Patrick Joseph Willis, aged forty-seven, doing a five-year stretch for conspiracy; and thirty-five-year-old lifer Alfred Edward Osborne, who had been convicted of murder, were rushed to hospital. Despite frantic efforts by doctors and nurses to save him, Pickering died. Experts were called in to try to save the sight of Willis, who had gone blind, while Osborne was able to recover.

Following a police investigation, Henry Howard Mitchell, thirty-three; Alan Frederick Potter, thirty; and Gerrard Francis Creed, twenty-two, were remanded to the Old Bailey. They were accused of unlawfully killing Pickering, but after a brief trial they were acquitted. Defence barrister Michael Havers QC, son of the previously mentioned Mr Justice Cecil Havers and father of actor Nigel, said: 'We are dealing with perhaps the most curious case of its kind to come before the courts for many years in that among the witnesses are seven murderers.'

Like drugs and tobacco, PlayStations and now satellite television and drink, no matter how appalling the taste, provide a distraction from the boredom facing men and women locked away for year after year. While the popular image of prison life – one all too often portrayed by television series and sitcoms – is of regular meals and Sky television, films, plays and books, media's representation tends to overlook the loss of liberty and the freedom to go where and when. Convicts adapt in many different ways to cope with the routine and regimentation, the waiting for time to pass.

George Bidwell simply waited, waited and waited in perhaps the most bizarre antic of anyone to be imprisoned within the British system. Bidwell was one of four Americans who pulled off an audacious swindle that hit the Bank of England, the Old Lady of Threadneedle Street. He was thirty-three when he arrived in London with his twenty-five-year-old brother, Austin, in April 1872. The pair had committed a number of small swindles against banks in America but saw the Bank of England, with its boasts of impregnability, as the ultimate challenge. To help them they recruited expert forger George Macdonnell, aged twenty-six, and petty crook Edwin Noyes Hills, twenty-nine. Then they set about passing forged but authentic-seeming Bills of Exchange. In only three months they pocketed just under £100,000 – a fortune – before the swindle was uncovered. The gang was eventually traced, and after a trial at the Old Bailey all were sentenced to penal servitude for life.

George Bidwell was sent to Dartmoor, but when he was told to join a working party in the prison quarry he refused. 'I will not work there or anywhere else,' he said. He was transferred to other jails but for the next fourteen years he stayed in his cell, spending the entire time in solitary confinement in bed. This led to a deterioration of his health: his weight dropped, and when it was decided to release him on the grounds that he appeared to be dying, he had to leave prison on crutches. But even that was a confidence trick. He went back to America, regained fitness and began another career – this time as a lecturer, touring halls talking about his experiences in and out of jail. He also wrote an autobiography. To Bidwell, alone and friendless, the days must have crawled by.

34

LUM UP

JOHN 'BOYCIE' BOYCE, on the other hand, discovered that porridge went down more quickly and easily when liberally flavoured with humour sometimes aimed at prison staff, in the same way that *Porridge*'s Fletch made Mr Mackay a butt of jokes. Boyce has served time in several British jails, including Wormwood Scrubs, Wandsworth, Pentonville and Durham. In an exclusive interview with me for this book, he revealed all.

Porridge was a never-ending war between us, the inmates, and them, the screws. To win you had to be constantly on your toes and no matter how tough things might get, never let them get the impression they were winning because once that happened they'd turn the screw and make sure you knew you weren't going to get up.

When I was in my late teens at the Scrubs the governors had decided to brighten the place up by installing tanks filled with posh fish. I saw an opportunity to make some money, and one by one started lifting the fish out, hiding them in milk churns and having them smuggled out. There was a big inquiry but nobody realised I was the fisherman.

As a newcomer I was put in a cell on a landing right at the top of one of the wings. I had to wear a tie all the time, have my collar tidy, be freshly shaved each morning and wasn't allowed to grow sideburns; instead my hair had to be cut level with the top of my ears. Not realising this, on my first day I came downstairs for breakfast but a screw was standing at the foot of the staircase looking me up and down. He told me, 'Your tie isn't straight, go back and put it right,' so I ran back upstairs, looked in the mirror, straightened the tie, came back down and the same prick was still there. Now he told me, 'You haven't shaved properly, go back and do it again,' and off I went. By the time I'd f**ked up and down the stairs getting it right there was nothing left for breakfast and the c*** put me on report for not eating.

When you did make it to breakfast, you'd have coffee, which consisted of about a quarter of a pint tipped into your mug from a ladle. The c***s serving it were inmates and most of the time you'd get short measure because they were always looking after themselves, which was fair enough, we all did that. I hadn't been there long when one day I said to the guy dishing it out, 'Stick another ladleful in,' and he started, 'Hey man, don't monkey with me,' and I eyeballed him and said, 'For fuck sake just stick another one in.' By now he was bawling and shouting, so I picked up the whole fucking lot and threw it over the fucker. The Visiting Committee of magistrates sentenced me to 'Nine days' bread and water'. I hadn't a clue what that meant so I asked, 'What the fuck's this bread and water?' They repeated, 'Nine days,' then asked, 'You understand what this means?' I said, 'I haven't got a clue,' and they said, 'It means you're on bread and water for three days, then three days off, then three days on, three days off and then another three days on till you've done the nine days.'

The screws took me down the segregation block and on that first day came along, all very sophisticated, with a set of scales to weigh off six ounces of bread. One c*** weighed it in front of me and I was then ordered to check it said six ounces on the scales and say, 'Yes that's six ounces.' Then he told me, 'It's not too bad, you can have as much water as you want.' This went on for three days. Nothing but this wee cut of bread to eat and all the water

I wanted. After three days my stomach had shrunk. I went back to the hall to join the others, who said, 'Oh, you're back on food,' and one of them thought he was doing me a good turn by filling my plate. Only after a few bites I couldn't eat any more because my stomach had shrunk. By the time it was back to near normal and I was starting to enjoy normal food again, the bastards came back and took me off for another three days on bread and water.

When I finished the third set of three days everybody was going, 'Poor c***, bread and water, you must be starving,' and were giving me hunks of meat and double everything, but I ended up in agony because my stomach was so knotted and shrunk. Screws knew what the effects of being on bread and water would be but said nothing, just laughed when they saw a guy in pain.

The cell windows were of really thick glass and come the summer it was stifling hot. Everybody was complaining, saying, 'Fuck it, let's get some air in,' and using their shoes to break one of the panes. Of course when it came to November and December, it was pretty chilly. I went down to one of the governors and said, 'Excuse me, these windows, it's fucking Baltic in here, the wind's blowing straight in.' He asked, 'What do you think has caused that?' I told him, 'Well, there are so many broken windows.' He said, 'OK, I've got the solution for you.' I said, 'That's great,' thinking he was going to send workmen in to replace the broken panes. Instead he said, 'You can have an extra bar on your window.'

When it came to your release, it didn't matter if you'd done thirty days, thirty months or thirty years, you were given a discharge grant, the equivalent to one week's dole money. I got about four and a half quid and a pat on the back to start a new life. Most people getting out of jail thought, 'Fuck it, I need a blow,' and spent the lot their first day out. I did a couple of stints in borstal at Wormwood Scrubs and when you were released from there, they'd measure you up for a suit, or you could choose a jacket and pair of pants. You always knew what the jacket and pants were like because every screw in the place wore them, they were getting them for nothing. The fashion at the time was for Italian stripes, but the stripes on the discharge suits were about four inches apart, they looked like the blazers cricketers wore, but everybody knew that if they saw a guy in one of these striped suits near the Scrubs then he must have just got out. So you either signed up for the jacket and pants and looked like a screw, or the suit. Either way, everybody knew where you'd come from. They might as well have put a notice on your back – 'Wormwood Scrubs'.

No matter which jail I was in, my aim was always to pick the easiest job going. Most screws sussed me out and went, 'Give that c*** the job he wants. That'll keep him quiet and we'll have an easier life.' Sometimes they took advantage of that. Once in Pentonville, approaching Christmas, they put me in the Officers' Mess. Now the good thing about the Officers' Mess was that it was about three pence for a sausage, a penny for a rasher of bacon, two pence for an egg and so on. They were all miserable bastards and never bought a full breakfast, just a few items because it was cheaper that way.

Now a few of us decided to have our own Christmas party. We'd nick a few cigarettes, cigars, get a couple of bottles of wine smuggled in but then decided to make it even better by brewing our own hooch. Above the door into the Mess was a shelf holding big empty ten-gallon pots and we decided to use one of them to make the hooch. We poured in the yeast, sugar, potatoes, you name it – fuck me, Smirnoff didn't have a look in – and put it back to ferment. Now you should always let a bit of air in to help with the fermentation, but some c*** shut the lid and, fuck me, two days before Christmas we were at the Mess about six in the morning with the screws gagging for their breakfast when the pot exploded and the fucking place was showered in hooch. They knew what had happened, but couldn't pin the blame on any of us.

Every prison has its own bookmaker and Pentonville was no exception. Bets were in the prison currency, tobacco. During one of my stays there, a smartarse handed over a shag packet of baccy, claiming there was an ounce inside, but he thought he was clever by filling up the middle with pressed dough. It was a big bet, an accumulator, and, fuck us, it all came up. Next day, Sunday, the punter turned up to collect and the bookie handed him a loaf. 'What the fuck is this?' asked the punter and was told, 'You stinking c***, you stuck a slice of bread in the packet. It wasn't tobacco so here's a loaf back. That's your winnings.'

Now and then they'd put me on the Ghost Train. Eventually I ended up at Wandsworth and was set to sewing mail bags. You weren't allowed to talk and there had to be so many stitches to the inch. A screw would come around with a tape measure checking each inch and counting stitches and if there were too many or too few you were made to unpick the whole thing. Because the level of your wages depended on you finishing a set number of mailbags, it meant you lost out moneywise.

The first day I was doing this, after a couple of hours, one of the screws shouted, 'Right, lum up.' At that every cunt pulled out their roll-ups and lit up. But because we were new boys we didn't know about this. So we had to get our baccy tins out and make a roll-up then find a match and by the time we were ready to start a smoke the screw was shouting, 'Right, silent labour,' and we had to put our smokes away. Unless you knew the score and had your roll-ups ready made, no matter how much you were gasping for a smoke you wouldn't even get a drag by the time 'lum up' was over.

The Home Office ruled that prisons had to contribute towards the cost of running them and so we started doing more types of contract work. One was making furniture, wardrobes, dressers and so forth. I was told to operate a big machine that glued furniture together. Everybody was shouting, 'Helloooo, all this fucking glue, you can get as high as a kite.' Then guys were sitting down with bits of paper and writing on them things like, 'Hello missus, this was made in such and such a prison for nothing, and you've just been humped for two hundred quid by buying it because it was made for buttons and, by the way, it's made by a paedophile.' So somebody would go along to the shops, buy a beautiful new wardrobe, take it home, give it a clean and discover the note from some child abuser.

Now and again you'd be allowed a bath. So you opened the taps but before you got in a screw came along carrying a piece of wood six inches long. He'd stick it in the bath and if the water level came over the top he'd pull the plug and drain out a couple of inches so you had to bathe in four inches of water.

When you're in the jail, before you even say you're sick, you've got to have the equivalent of terminal cancer before anybody shows interest. The rule is that even though you're sick, you are not allowed to lie on your bed but have to sit in a chair even in the prison hospital. Six o'clock in the morning, you've to make your bed and then sit in a chair next to it. You might have a stroke but they'll still tell you, 'You can't lie in your bed, sit in the chair. You can't get back into bed till seven o'clock tonight.' This was a general rule. You might be told you could rest in your cell – but you still couldn't go to your bed. And if you were in your bed and they caught you they'd take the bed out of the cell and you'd be left with just the chair.

They could be so fucking petty. At one time the rule was one letter a week in and one out. I come from a big family but I was hardly getting any mail and I thought everybody had deserted me. I'd done two years eight months, and when the day came when I was being released I went to reception and they gave me a mailbag with all the extra letters in it that they'd held on to once I'd had my one for the week. I walked out like Father Christmas.

The food could be really crap and one day I followed the proper procedure by writing a letter of complaint – they called it a petition – to the Home Secretary. Now the rule was that a prison could not interfere with a petition. Obviously if somebody sent off a petition, the prison governors would be potty with curiosity wondering what was being written about them. I said the chips were so hard they broke your teeth and to show what they were like stuck a few in my letter. A couple of hours later I was amazed when I was handed a letter and inside was my petition complete with the chips. I was raging and complained confidential mail to the Home Secretary had been illegally opened. The screws came back and said they couldn't forward my petition because the sharp edges of the chips had cut open my letter.

In every jail, cons used to pull a string of thread from their blanket, tie it to the handle of your mug and then swing it out of the window to guys close by or on landings below. You'd stick a note inside saying, 'Send me a match' or 'I need a pencil' and so on. One night I'd put the mug out and was lowering it downstairs where there were lads who were unconvicted. I was serving a sentence, which meant I wasn't allowed to have tobacco brought in, but these guys were because they were technically still innocent and so I'd arranged for them to get a visit from pals who left some tobacco which was for me. I was shouting out, 'Hello, I'm sending the mug down for that baccy,' and heard a voice saying, 'Down a bit, down a bit more, keep it coming down.' I thought I was running out of thread when I heard, 'Right, your stuff's there, pull it up.' I did and at the end of my thread was a plastic mug and it was on fucking fire. Two screws downstairs had put a cloth in it, set it on fire and sent it back up to me. Next morning they decided to do an inspection and asked, 'Where's your mug?' Of course they had mine, so I got done for damaging prison property, a mug.

Sometimes it seemed it was just for devilment that they'd give you a full body search. You went up three steps, stood on a kind of pedestal, stripped off all your gear and then you were put in a kind of cage and had to bend over in front of everybody with your bum cheeks spread. It was their way of winding you up, but we had plenty of ways of getting our own back.

Once, I was taken in front of the Governor at Wandsworth and shown a report sheet which said I was charged with 'dumb insolence'. I said to him, 'I don't really understand how it can be dumb insolence, because you cannot judge my attitude, can't guess what I'm thinking, because if I'm dumb I can't say anything. I might be standing here thinking, 'You're the biggest prick in the prison system.' That would be an example of dumb insolence, but I wouldn't call you that to your face.' Before I could get another word out he said, 'That'll do me. Fourteen days' solitary.'

You never knew when the Ghost Train was coming for you. Five o'clock in the morning a screw would open your door, shout, 'Pick your gear up,' and you'd be in a bus heading through the gates. They never told you where you were going, even when you tried looking out of the window for road signs. Your mail never caught up with you and you couldn't correspond with your family because by the time they wrote back you'd be somewhere else. It was just one of the mind games they played with inmates.

I was a cook in various prisons, absolutely fuck all to do with being able to cook or being a Gordon Ramsay; but I was a trustee, allowed to get knives and sharpen them and even hatchets if somebody said they needed one. I used to be the night cook, which meant brewing what seemed like about 300 gallons of tea to go around the wings and I'd dish it out from a trolley. The tea they used was cheap and came in big wooden chests. I was allowed two scoops into a fucking pillowcase – they didn't bother much about health and safety then. I suppose it was a sort of ancient form of the teabag. Then the screw would come along and put two shovels of sugar in, because sugar was a prison commodity, you could use it to get other things; sugar was a form of currency. So they kept it locked up to stop us nicking it. He would also put the fucking bromide in. There was a market for the sugar, but there was absolutely fuck-all market for the bromide. The trouble was that once it was in the teabag you couldn't get it out, or the sugar for that matter. Then I'd tie the top of the pillowcase and drop it into a huge vat of boiling water and shuffle it around with a huge wooden spoon until the water turned brown.

The bromide was totally at the discretion of the screws and was to lower men's sex drive. It was fuck all to do with me, but every c*** was running about with limp dicks shouting, 'Fuck sake, what are you putting in that fucking tea?' I'd have to shout back, 'Don't fucking blame me if your cock can't stand to attention.'

In one jail during the day I worked in the butcher department. Screws would sneak in with a hard-luck story like, 'Oh, I've done a long shift and I'm hungry. Any chance of a wee steak? There's a wee ounce of baccy in it for you.' There were so many after their wee steaks that sometimes the place resembled a branch of Frankie and Benny's. Or they'd be sidling up saying, 'Hello, there's a half ounce of baccy. Any chance of a wee bit of steak and a couple of chops for the house?' It was dreadful. By the time I'd sliced off a couple of steaks for my mates and hidden them under the potatoes that had been cut ready for the next day, there'd be hardly anything left for the prisoners. They'd be lucky if they got a spoonful of mince.

Just as bromide in the tea was a fixture of prison life, so was white Windsor soap. Ask anybody who ever did time what soap they had in jail and they'll tell you it was white Windsor. It had its uses, not necessarily for washing with, but for making a chib, a weapon, or for cutting a single match into four. A lot of guys had a chib. During my early years in prisons, for shaving you were issued with a double sided, double-edged Gillette razor blade. When it was finished, you were supposed to throw it into a bucket while the screw watched and he'd then give you a new one. But if you were quick and careful, you could pretend to throw it in and palm it or even pull another one out of the bucket. In the cell you'd get a spare toothbrush, a couple of blades, use white Windsor to weld the whole lot together and if somebody was threatening you, then you'd drag the chib down their face with the result that there would be a big enough gap between the two blades. Because the cuts were wide apart, doctors couldn't stitch up the wound and it left a permanent scar.

I thought things had improved when I was held briefly in Durham Prison on my way south from Peterhead jail in Scotland to the Old Bailey for a trial. When I arrived I found that because I was being treated as a sort of lodger, I was sent off to a cell at the very top of one of the wings. There were no televisions or even a radio then and all they'd given me to read was a Bible. So I was sitting on my own on a Saturday afternoon when a screw popped his head round the cell door and asked if I wanted to see a movie. 'Whoa, I'm up for that,' I told him and he said, 'OK, take your chair.' The chairs were solid oak and weighed well over a stone and I had to hump mine from the far end of the landing to the stairs, then down three flights, out the door, over the exercise yard and every second the chair was feeling heavier. Then it was into the net shed where you sat and sewed nets for fishermen. By the time we got there I was absolutely knackered and as soon as I put the chair down and sat on it I fell asleep. I missed the film, an old Hammer horror movie, and as it was finished they were shouting for me to hump this fucking bastard chair all the way back out of the shed, across the exercise yard, back into the wing and then up all the stairs and right to the end of the landing.

From Durham I went to the Old Bailey and when the case ended I was back on the National Draft all the way up to Scotland, stopping again at Durham and back to the cell in the heavens. On the Saturday afternoon the screw came along and asked, 'Well would you like to see a film?' and I thought of humping that bloody chair all the way to the net shed and told him, 'You can stick your film up your arse.' So they stuck me in solitary for insubordination.

During another stint in Durham, after I blew up a pub in Newcastle-upon-Tyne, I got to know one of the bosses and put in for a weekend leave. He had to approve it. We'd often argued about football. All his family were notorious Glasgow Rangers fans while I supported Hibernian, the Catholic side in Edinburgh. A condition of the leave was that you went to your hometown and stayed there and I'd said I'd be staying in Newcastle. Now it happened that that weekend Celtic were playing Rangers in Glasgow. I went along to get my leave form signed by the officer, but he told me, 'I'm not signing this.' I asked, 'What you mean?' and he said, 'You need to stand on the table and say, "Rangers are the greatest team in the world." You can't go till you do that.' I told him, 'Go fuck yourself.' He said, 'I'm not signing it.' So I got put to the back of the queue and thought, 'This bastard's not kidding.'

When I got up to him again I told him, 'OK' and stood on the table and said, 'Rangers, the greatest fucking team in the fucking world.' He said, 'On you go, but remember to stay at your home address.' Next day I'm in Glasgow, full of drink watching Celtic hump Rangers. I rang Durham nick, got through to the officer and shouted, 'Orange b******, we screwed you,' then hung up. Back in Durham Prison on the Monday he said, 'I want a word with you. Where did you phone me from?' 'Newcastle, I was in the pub,' I lied. 'I never heard so many hairy-arsed Jocks in Newcastle in my entire life,' was the reply. 'You're a slippery bastard.'

I met a lot of guys over the years. In Wandsworth I got to know Frankie Fraser, who was, and still is, a real gem. Because I was from Scotland, it was too far for my family to travel to visit me and I told this to Frankie when he asked how things were. 'Don't worry, I'll sort that,' he said and, good as his word, he did. From that moment I got visits from guys I'd never met in my life but they always left me a can of beer or a bottle of wine. He introduced me to lots of his friends and I was with some of them in a Glasgow pub one night when a lorry came in through the window. A guy got out, looked around and apologised, saying 'We've got the wrong place,' and they drove off.

Not everybody was on my Christmas card list. Prisons aren't run by a governor; the man who makes the decisions, who has his finger on everything and knows what's going on, is the chief prison officer. In Wandsworth, the CPO came to see me, mentioned the name of another inmate and asked if I knew him. I told him 'yes' and he asked, 'If you and him bump into each other, what will happen?' I said, 'I will take one of your metal trays and decapitate him. I'll take his fucking head right off his shoulders.' So it was decided for *my* care and protection to put me in solitary. There was only one other person there on care and protection. It was Frankie Fraser.

Guys like Frankie taught me that if you could keep your sense of humour then you'd survive prison. It is a lesson everybody thinking of committing a crime should learn. One December in Pentonville it was approaching Christmas. Somehow I'd been lucky and issued with a feather pillow instead of the usual horsehair lump. I decided to create my own version of a White Christmas and emptied the pillow out of the window. Feathers snowed down into the yard below and were everywhere, but one of the screws had spotted they came from my window and I was dragged off to solitary. Next day I was fined twenty pence for damaging a pillowcase and told I had to clean the yard up until all the feathers had been gathered. They give me a hurdle to collect them on and at the slightest breath of wind the feathers were back all over the yard. It took me until the summer to pick them all up. Through all my time in prison I might have lost my freedom, but I made sure I kept my sense of humour.

'Boycie' Boyce is now a successful businessman and believes the many lessons he learned during several prison sentences fitted him well to face the often difficult manoeuvring of negotiating contracts and dealing with the general public. He remains on good terms with many of his old fellow prisoners and knows he can call on them for help should the need ever arise. He is also a staunch campaigner for prisoners' rights, asserting that with a few exceptions men and woman sent to jail may have lost their liberty but are entitled to retain their dignity. He says, 'No matter how many times I was banged up, I always came out wearing the same smile I had when I went inside. The lesson I learned from old times was that you may not be able to fight your way through the system, but you can certainly laugh all the way along it.'

EPILOGUE

SADLY THOMAS PITMAN, ordered to be incarcerated on the other side of the world for being hungry, never made it back to his home. Nor did many thousands sent to America and Australia for the crime of being poor and in need. But did those long-wigged judges who adjourned for their pheasant and port after condemning starving, half-naked wretches to the unknown in fact indirectly help create two of the most thriving nations in today's world? The foundations of the success of America and Australia were laid by criminals and those forced to flee oppression. In both countries, prosperous twenty-first-century families can trace their roots to men and women who were shipped off rather than banged up.

Hard work and imagination were behind their success. They blossomed beneath clean air and sunshine while others dragged into the so-called model prisons emerged to the same dreary grime and uncertainty of industrial Britain, to a not-so-merry-go-round of poverty and want almost inevitably leading back inside prison walls.

Their journey has been our journey. We have looked inside the worst that society can create, of rogues and robbers, killers and cutthroats, but we have learned too of courage and dignity: the determination of the great actress Isabella Glyn; the bravery of a German spy; the ingenuity of the gang that took on an Old Lady in

Threadneedle Street; the Queen of Forty Thieves; of a one-armed escaper; a deadly doctor; the horse-and-cart getaway vehicle; a vicar wronged by a spoiled child and her drunken mother; and even of a prison officer and his six-inch ruler.

Over the decades many hundreds of thousands of men and women have supped their porridge and dry bread and water in our six prisons, in Dartmoor, Durham, Holloway, Pentonville, Wandsworth and Wormwood Scrubs, and each one has his or her own account to tell. But there are more than 120 other prisons in Britain behind whose walls and barbed wire have been and are inmates so countless that it would take a library of books to recount even a fraction of their tales.

Some use the protection of weapons or even a minder to survive prison. Too many others need drugs to relieve the tedium of life inside. In these days when cannabis, cocaine and heroin have replaced tobacco as prisoners' currency, remarkable ingenuity is needed to smuggle in packets of powder that have the equivalent worth of gold dust – one inmate not currently inside had his permitted musical instrument sent out for twice yearly maintenance and was fortunate at not being asked to play it immediately on its return.

The weapon used by John Boyce was humour. He is the only lag to have been evicted from a jail after being told he was a disruptive influence at HM Prison Wolds in East Yorkshire.

From being banged up, Boyce was banged out. But that's another story . . .